WHEN
ASIA WAS
THE
WORLD

WHEN ASIA WAS THE WORLD

STEWART GORDON

DA CAPO PRESS
A Member of the Perseus Books Group

Library of Congress Cataloging-in-Publication Data

Gordon, Stewart, 1945–
  When Asia was the world / Stewart Gordon.
      p.   cm.
  Includes bibliographical references and index.
  ISBN-13: 978-0-306-81556-0 (hardcover : alk. paper)
  ISBN-10: 0-306-81556-7 (hardcover : alk. paper) 1. Asia—Description
and travel 2. Travelers—Asia—History. 3. Asia—Civilization. I. Title.
DS5.95.G67 2007
915.04—dc22   2007035608

Maps by Patti Issacs

Text design by Trish Wilkinson
Set in 12 point Adobe Caslon

Published by Da Capo Press
A Member of the Perseus Books Group
http://www.dacapopress.com

Da Capo Press books are available at special discounts for bulk
purchases in the U.S. by corporations, institutions, and other organizations.
For more information, please contact the Special Markets Department at the
Perseus Books Group, 2300 Chestnut Street, Suite 200, Philadelphia, PA 19103,
or call (800) 255-1514, or email special.markets@perseusbooks.com

1 2 3 4 5 6 7 8 9

Contents

INTRODUCTION

I n the thousand years from 500 to 1500, Asia was an astonishing, connected, and creative place. It had the five largest cities
in the world, all at the heart of great empires. A few, such as
Delhi, Beijing, and Istanbul, remain major cities today. Others,
such as Vijayanagara in southern India, exist only as ruins. It was
in Asia that mathematicians invented zero and algebra. Astrono-
mers there tracked the stars more accurately than ever before and
invented the astrolabe for navigation. Poets and writers produced
literature that still touches the heart. Philosophers generated systems of thinking and justice that influence us today. These works,
as well as translations of Greek and Roman knowledge, formed
the core of vast libraries.

Buddhism and Islam arose and spread along Asia's far-flung
trade routes. So did luxury goods, such as silk, pearls, spices, medicines, glass, and simple things like rice and sugar. Asia produced
money and credit that traders knew and accepted from the Middle
East to China, and art that fills museums around the world today.
The elegance and complexity of its architecture amazes travelers in
our modern world.

Each chapter of this book is based on the actual memoir of a man
who lived, worked, and traveled in this great Asian world between
500 and 1500 CE. At the beginning of each chapter are the dates of
travel. These intrepid adventurers navigated oceans, traversed great
deserts, and crossed the passes of the highest mountains in the

world. They knew how to operate in languages they didn't understand, among an extraordinary variety of peoples, from the Bulgars in southern Russia to the Bugis in Southeast Asia.

How did they manage to survive and prosper? Some had families and friendships that sprawled across much of Asia. Others were supported in their travels by chains of monasteries and rest houses. Many discovered that royal courts across Asia shared similar customs, forms of address, and codes of honor. Learning these customs eased their way in. Along the way, these travelers found people eager for the knowledge they brought, whether the subject was tropical plants, ideas of justice, inventions, or architecture. Their memoirs allow us to go along on the caravans and ships, experience the cold and fatigue, live the hopes and fears, and know the luxury and wonder of this great medieval Asian world.[1]

1

MONASTERIES AND MONARCHS

Xuanzang, 618–632 CE

Into the lush fields along the Yellow River fled two young brothers, Buddhist monks. Abandoning their monastery, they set out from Luoyang, the eastern imperial capital, for Chang'an, 200 miles upstream. There, according to rumor, a prince and an army maintained order. China in 618 CE was no place for peaceful Buddhist monks.* Around them, the brothers witnessed the final collapse of the Sui dynasty. Decades later, one of the brothers, Xuanzang, described this time to his biographer: "The magistrates were destroyed and . . . [monks] either perished or took to flight. The streets were filled with bleached bones and the burnt ruins of buildings. . . . At this time the books of Confucius and the sacred pages of Buddha were forgotten, everyone was occupied with the arts of war."[1]

The wearying, dangerous journey to Chang'an proved fruitless. The brothers found no prince and no army. Like other monks,

---

*By the time Xuanzang fled his monastery, three successive dynasties had been involved in wars of conquest more or less continuously for fifty years. Invasion of the south of China was successful, however, and north and south China were unified for the first time in three centuries. The Tang dynasty emerged while Xuanzang was away.

1

Xuanzang and his brother walked another 300 miles south to Chengdu, located in the current-day province of Sichuan. There, they finally found respite and a surviving Buddhist community. Xuanzang's brother said later, "There was abundance and peace. Hundreds of men assembled under the pulpit of the Preaching Hall."[2] Xuanzang and his brother stayed on to study Buddhist texts and practices at the monastery.

Who was this young monk, Xuanzang? By birth and training he belonged to a class of elite public officials who served emperors. His grandfather had been head of the Imperial University at Beijing; the reigning emperor at the time endowed the family with the revenues of a medium-sized town. In normal times, sons of this sort of family could expect to serve and prosper in the imperial bureaucracy. The times, however, were far from normal. For three centuries before the Sui, no dynasty had united China. Powerful families established competing, short-lived dynasties. Huns—nomads from the eastern steppe—overran and ruled the northern half of China where Xuanzang's family lived. Xuanzang's father chose to retire from this chaos far from the capital:

> Anticipating the decay of the Sui dynasty, he buried himself in the study of his books. Many offers of provincial and district offices were pressed on him, which he persistently refused; he declined all magisterial duties on the plea of ill-health. . . .[3]

Xuanzang grew up reading classical texts under the guidance of his father. His older brother became a Buddhist monk, and when he noticed Xuanzang was "deeply given to the study of religious doctrine," he took him to his monastery at the imperial capital of Luoyang and taught him the basics of Buddhism. Xuanzang entered this monastery at age thirteen. He studied, listened, and meditated until forced to flee seven years later.[4]

Buddhism was already 1,000 years old at the time of Xuanzang. The historical Buddha had lived in India, in the eastern Ganges Valley and nearby foothills of the Himalayas, in the sixth and fifth centuries BCE. He meditated on life as he saw it around him and concluded that people wanted what they did not get and got what they did not want. All were subject to disease, aging, and death. People mistakenly believed they possessed some unchanging core, some soul, but were surprised at how they changed over time or in different circumstances. The Buddha saw as the human condition people's lingering desires, lack of any continuity of self, and inevitable death. This analysis is the earliest assertion of a common universal human religious experience, regardless of language, beliefs, occupation, or ethnicity.

The Buddha found no existing belief system and no supernatural being that could help this condition. He personally experimented with the path of pleasure and the path of extreme austerities to overcome this condition and found both wanting. Finally, meditating under a tree at Bodh Gaya in the valley of the Ganges river, he arrived at his answer. The cause of personal suffering was desire, mainly the doomed desire to stop inevitable changes in oneself, as well as in other people, relationships, and even things.

The Buddha offered more than just an analysis of a universal human problem. He laid out a path of deliverance that required neither hedonistic pleasures nor extreme austerities. He termed it the Middle Path and, though difficult, it was available to every person regardless of gender, language, region, occupation, or position in society. The Middle Path nevertheless required a sharp break with the normal flow of life. To begin the Middle Path, a person renounced all possessions, left family and friends, and retained only a simple robe and a begging bowl. It was essential that the new follower, whether man or woman, join a group of fellow Buddhists, known as the *sangha*, for training and support. Monastic vows of poverty and chastity were designed to help the initiate become free from desire. Buddhism put the renunciation of possessions and residence in monasteries as absolutely central to spiritual progress. Traveling in search of learning and insight was an intrinsic part of the Middle Path. Although anyone could follow the Middle Path, it was monks and nuns, not lay people, who pursued insight and deliverance. Lay people gained merit by supporting the monastic institutions.[5] Almost certainly, ideas of deliverance from the suffering of the human condition were at the core of the regular discussions and lectures at Chang'an, attended by Xuanzang, his brother, and many other monks and laity.

In 623 CE, five years after the weary pair arrived at Chengdu, the new Tang dynasty established minimal order in many areas of China. Now fully ordained as a Buddhist monk, Xuanzang defied his older brother, left the monastery, and resumed traveling to hear oral teachings. Xuanzang sailed down the Yangtze River [Jinsha Jiang] to a famous monastery, stayed a season, traveled north through his home province of Henan, attended lectures, preached, and gained some fame.[6]

In Buddhism, the individual monk was responsible for his own progress toward enlightenment. It was up to him to seek knowledge, study, and find the correct path. In Xuanzang's time, the institutional structure for this search was the chain of monasteries across much of China. Heads of Chinese monasteries were strong individuals, and monasteries differed in style, meditation practices, and interpretation of Buddhist doctrine. When a traveling monk visited a monastery, he had to engage in formal discussion and debate before the resident monks and laity on subjects posed by the head of the monastery. To be successful, a monk needed to know his texts, be able to form a good argument, and draw points from an apt story.

After the death of the Buddha, a millennium before Xuanzang, Buddhism spread steadily within India and out from India
along both land and maritime trade routes. By the first centuries
of the Common Era, Buddhism was the predominant religion in
the sprawling Kushan Empire that stretched from Central Asia
through Pakistan and Afghanistan to the plains of India. Monasteries were an important part of every oasis town on the caravan
routes from Afghanistan to China. Some monasteries were built
in isolated places to accommodate caravans whose traders, in
turn, donated money for their upkeep. Along water routes, Buddhism spread from India to Sri Lanka, into Southeast Asia, and
eventually reached coastal China. Early in the second century CE,
the poet and naturalist Zhang Heng noticed foreign Buddhist
monks in China. During its long period of expansion, Buddhism
divided into several competing systems that emphasized different
texts.[7] Nevertheless, all monasteries followed the core beliefs,
looked to India as the Buddhist heartland, and entertained Buddhist traveling monks of all persuasions. Many Buddhist writers
were aware of prior travelers and equally aware of the outer limits
of the network of Buddhist monasteries.

A spectacular recent archaeological find reflects the variety of
Buddhist images and practices at the time of Xuanzang. In 1996,
in the city of Qingzhou, about 300 miles east of Xuanzang's monastery, earthmoving machinery cut into a vault that contained a
horde of more than 400 Buddhist stone sculptures.[8] Most of the
pieces date from just a few decades before Xuanzang. The pieces
are breathtaking for their preservation of original color. Equally
striking is the variety of styles. Nomad invaders who formed dynasties seemed to favor styles common in Afghanistan and oasis
towns on the caravan routes to China. Other patrons seemed to
favor statues similar to those made in Southeast Asia at the time.
Some statues wear traditional Indian robes; others wear Chinese

robes of the period. All these sculptures once belonged to shrines and temples throughout the region. Because they had become worn or damaged, they were apparently ceremonially buried together sometime in the twelfth century.[9]

By age twenty-six, Xuanzang had become dissatisfied. "Having visited and learned from all the teachers," he "found that each followed implicitly the teaching of his own school; but on verifying their doctrines he saw that the holy books differed much, so that he knew not which to follow."[10] For a young man, this was a remarkably astute summary of Buddhism in China.

Xuanzang "made up his mind to travel to the West in order to clear his doubts" and bring back crucial books from India, the center of Buddhism. It says much about the continuity of monastic tradition in his day that Xuanzang knew he was not the first to make such a quest and opted to follow the path of Fa Xien and Zhi Yan, who had ventured to India in similar searches two centuries earlier. Several other monks in later centuries would make the same trip.

The beginning of the journey was difficult. Because of banditry and disruption outside the core areas of China, the Tang government forbade commoners to travel to the West. At the first sign of government opposition to the illegal trip, Xuanzang's two companions lost their nerve, turned tail, and left for Chang'an. Xuanzang avoided capture and pushed on alone, traveling by night, often with the covert aid of Buddhist monks and laymen. He hired a guide who had traveled to the West many times, who described the troubles ahead:

> The Western roads are difficult and bad; sand streams stretch far and wide; evil spirits and hot winds, when they come, cannot be avoided; numbers of men traveling together, although so many, are misled and lost; how much rather you, sir, going alone.[11]

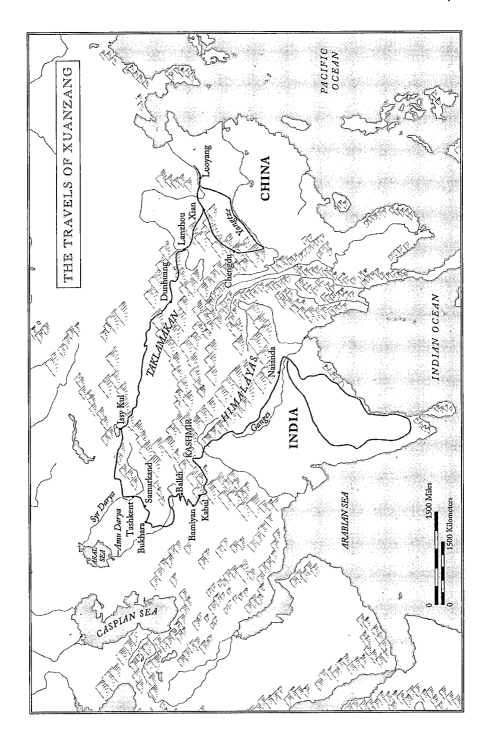

THE TRAVELS OF XUANZANG

PACIFIC OCEAN

CHINA

Luoyang

Lanzhou
Xian

Yangtze

Dunhuang

Chengdu

TAKLAMAKAN

INDIAN OCEAN

Nalanda

HIMALAYAS

KASHMIR

Issy Kul

Ganges

INDIA

Samarkand

Balkh

Syr Darya

Tashkent

Amu Darya

Bamiyan

Kabul

Bukhara

ARAL SEA

ARABIAN SEA

CASPIAN SEA

1500 Miles

1500 Kilometers

0

0

The immediate obstacles were seven fortified government outposts, about thirty miles apart, on the road to the West.* Xuanzang knew that the Tang government had circulated a warrant
for his arrest and return to China, but he was determined to proceed. He and his guide successfully circled around the first four
outposts, but the guide then abandoned him and Xuanzang lost
his way in the desert. After three days' wandering without food
or water, he managed to locate the fifth government watchtower.
Xuanzang was recognized, but the head sentry, a Buddhist, ig-
nored the order to send Xuanzang back to his monastery and
gave him provisions to continue his journey.[12]

Within days, Xuanzang's fortunes turned. Tang control apparently ended at the seventh watchtower. Less than 200 miles west
of Lanzhou, Xuanzang reached a Buddhist monastery in an independent kingdom located along the caravan route on the southern
rim of the Gobi Desert. Although politically independent, King
Qu-wentai had traveled to the court of the dynasty that preceded
the Tang and had heard lectures on Buddhism in monasteries. His
own country supported several hundred monks. The king knew
how to honor a learned Buddhist monk from China.

> When [Xuanzang] entered the city, the king, surrounded by his
> attendants in front and rear, bearing lighted torches, came forth
> in person to meet him. . . . [Xuanzang,] having entered the inner
> hall, took his seat beneath a precious canopy in a pavilion. . . . [In

---

*To the east of these watchtowers is Dunhuang, one of the most famous Bud-
dhist sites along the Silk Road. Located in western China where the northern
and southern routes around the Taklamakan Desert converged, the thriving
monastery was patronized by kings, nobles, and wealthy travelers. Abandoned
several centuries after Xuanzang, it was rediscovered in the twentieth century
and has proved an incredibly rich source of both paintings and books of the
period. Current research projects include reuniting texts that went to various
libraries in Europe and America.

the morning, the king] ordered food to be provided according to the rules of religion. Moreover by the side of the palace there was an oratory to which the king himself conducted [Xuanzang] and installed him there. Moreover, he commissioned certain eunuchs to wait on him and guard him.[13]

King Qu-wentai intended to keep Xuanzang, by force if necessary, in his country as a teacher, but the monk refused.

[S]eeing that he would be detained by force in opposition to his original design, [Xuanzang] declared with an oath that he would eat nothing, in order to affect the king's heart. So he sat in a grave posture, and during three days he neither ate nor drank; on the fourth day the king seeing that the Master was becoming fainter and fainter, overcome with shame and sorrow, he bowed down to the ground before him and said "the Master of Law has free permission to go to the West."[14]

This strikingly early example of successful personal nonviolent resistance strengthened Xuanzang's moral authority with the king.

In the Buddhist tradition, one gained great personal merit by furthering Buddhist teachings. At this time kings, nobles, and wealthy traders across much of Asia regularly patronized monasteries and rest houses for traveling monks, and supported the production of objects used in teaching, such as sacred texts, bells, and paintings.[15] King Qu-wentai decided to outfit fully Xuanzang's expedition to India. The king made arrangements to ordain four novice monks to be Xuanzang's attendants and had thirty robes stitched.

As the climate in the western countries was cold, he made for him also face-covers, gloves, stockings, and boots. A total amount of one hundred taels of gold, thirty thousand silver coins, and five hundred rolls of silk were provided for him as traveling expenses to last twenty years. Thirty horses and twenty-five carriers were allotted to him.[16]

Xuanzang received a royal escort to the next kingdom and twenty-four letters of introduction to kingdoms on his route. During the next fourteen years of his travels, Xuanzang, accompanied by this entourage, was a notable teacher wherever he went.

This was the way to travel in the steppe of the seventh century. Distances were long, winters cold, water scarce, and people even scarcer, but with the right institutional support, travel—from court to court, monastery to monastery, and oasis to oasis—was possible, if not easy.* Xuanzang's entourage was the core of a large caravan. Within days of leaving King Qu-wentai, Xuanzang sadly observed the massacred bodies of a small group of traders who had pushed ahead alone in hopes of reaching the next capital before the main caravan. On the borders between kingdoms, travel was safe only in an organized caravan.

When the caravan did reach the capital, Xuanzang found several dozen monks there. During the troubles some years earlier, they had fled west from their home monastery when he fled south to Sichuan.[17]

In the next stage of his journey, Xuanzang traveled north of the Taklamakan Desert. Mountain stretches in this region were dangerous and cold. For a monk raised in the land of Henan, the cold must have been a test of his resolve.

[The snow] has been changed into glaciers which melt neither in the winter nor summer: the hard frozen and cold sheets of water

---

*Caravans traveling east from the oasis cities carried horses and high-value goods, including jade, but especially glassware, from as far away as the Middle East.

rise mingling with the clouds: looking into them the eye is blinded by the glare. The icy peaks fall down sometimes and lie athwart the road. . . . Moreover the wind, and the snow driven in confused masses make it difficult to escape an icy coldness of body though wrapped in heavy folds of fur-bound garments; twelve or fourteen of the company were starved or frozen to death, whilst the numbers of oxen and horses that perished was still greater.[18]

Two hundred miles further west at a kingdom on the north shore of Lake Issy Kul [Oz Issy-Kul] in what is now Kirghizstan, a king invited Xuanzang to his camp. This well-watered region drained a broad area of mountains and thus had a permanent water supply in the generally dry steppe and grasslands, so it could support a myriad of grazing animals. Such a site was the heartland of some of the steppe's large kingdoms. Six centuries after Xuanzang, Kublai Khan, the great Mongol king visited by Marco Polo in 1275 CE, centered his empire on Lake Issy Kul.

In spite of religious differences, this semi-nomadic king and the Chinese Buddhist monk shared a common understanding of elite culture. One of the ceremonies that demonstrated nobility and bound together people of high rank was the wearing and sharing of silk. The king and his nobles wore Chinese silk robes in the royal tent of audience, where the king received Xuanzang's credentials and read his letter of introduction with obvious pleasure. The king then honored the monk with thirty silk robes.

These robes of Chinese silk were highly significant. A few centuries before Xuanzang's arrival at Issy Kul, silk had become a universally accepted currency between China and the nomads west and north of the Great Wall. Silk was so important because of the ecological differences between the sedentary agriculture of China and the grasslands of the nomads to the west. The steppe nomads raised horses that were in constant demand by the Chinese elite and the army; their cattle were equally essential for sedentary agriculture.

China raised grain, and only China produced silk. These four items were the main spoils of war. Successful Chinese armies seized cattle and horses from nomads they defeated, just as successful nomad raids on China brought back grain and silk. When China occasionally tried to end nomad raids through a marriage alliance with a nomad leader, silk and grain formed the dowry.[19]

For the steppe nomad confederations, grain and silk were important for holding together fragile alliances. Grain allowed a band to stay together through the lean times of a long winter. Silk was more complicated. Nomad leaders traded some of the precious fabric for necessities like iron, but its main use was to reward and retain the loyalty of followers. The presentation of silk robes was an important occasion for nobles to acknowledge their solidarity under a powerful leader. "Robes of honor" came only from the hand of the leader and defined a man as suitably attired at court. In subsequent centuries, the ceremony spread widely through Asia and was used by kings both west and east of the steppe. Even at this early date, Xuanzang and the semi-nomadic king both knew the meaning and importance of robes of silk. When Xuanzang returned to China from India many years later, the emperor would honor Xuanzang with elegant robes. The Tang emperor, too, belonged to the same broad system of honor.

While the nobles feasted on meat and wine, the king prepared special vegetarian food for Xuanzang: butter, honey, grapes, rice, and sugar. Rice and sugar, though found at this royal table, grew nowhere in the steppe. Rice likely came from China by the same route Xuanzang had followed. In Xuanzang's time, sugarcane was grown and processed only in India. It likely came over the Khyber Pass and north through Afghanistan, then east along the caravan routes.

It is not known exactly what dish the king served Xuanzang, but sugar, butter, rice, and fruits suggest what is known as a pilaf. Such a dish was prepared all along the routes from China to Turkey and was known by a closely associated group of words in many languages: *pilaf* in Iraq and Turkey, *polow* in Iran and southern Russia, *pilavi* in Armenia, *pilau* in Afghanistan, *palau* in Uzbekistan, and *pulao* in northern India. Similarly, filled breadlike dumplings are called *mantou* in China, *mantu* in Afghanistan and Iran, *mandu* in Korea, *manti* in Central Asia, and *momo* in Tibet.[20] Pasta and biscotti also came along the caravan routes from the Asian world and found their way to Italy when the cities of Venice and Genoa were western termini. Traders brought flavorings such as saffron and such fruits as the bitter orange to Europe and spread cuisines that used them.

Xuanzang and his entourage traveled west along the caravan routes through a variety of language regions: Turkic, Mongolian, and Uighur. This was yet another reason to travel with a large caravan, which surely had guides and multilingual interpreters. One incident at the Issy Kul court suggests that not only specialists learned more than one language at this time. In the king's entourage was a "young man who had spent some years in Chang'an and could speak Chinese." He became Xuanzang's interpreter.[21]

The monks eventually reached the cities of Tashkent, Samarkand, and Bukhara. Along the way, they were occasionally welcomed at monasteries, and Xuanzang met monks who had made the trip to India in search of knowledge. He regularly engaged in theological discussion and debate. Xuanzang next followed the Amudarya River [Oxus] upstream. From there the monks pushed overland southeast to Balkh, then south through Afghanistan. This portion of the journey was Buddhist territory, complete with monasteries, statues, and relics.

> In the hall of Buddha, there is the water-pot of Buddha . . . there is also here a tooth of the Buddha. . . . There is also here the sweeping brush of the Buddha, made of Kasa grass. . . . These three things are brought out every feast day, and the priests and

laymen draw near to worship them. The most faithful behold a spiritual radiancy proceeding from them.[22]

Xuanzang was awed by massive figures carved into the face of the mountain at Bamian in northern Afghanistan. "Northeast of the capital, on the declivity of a hill, there is a standing stone figure about 150 feet high. To the east of the figure there is a [monastery], to the east of which is a standing figure of Sakya [Buddha] ... in height one hundred feet."[23] These figures were, alas, destroyed in 2001 CE by the Taliban.

Xuanzang's party proceeded over the Khyber Pass and east into Kashmir and the valleys of the Himalayas. Besides worshipping relics, listening to teachings, worshipping at shrines, and observing footprints of the Buddha, Xuanzang regularly debated doctrine. Kings often sponsored and listened to these debates. In a monastery west of Kashmir, "the discussion meeting lasted for five days and then the people dispersed. The king was highly pleased and separately presented five rolls of pure silk ... as a special honor" to Xuanzang.[24]

During the millennium from 500 CE to 1500 CE, the highest mountains on earth, the Himalayas, which Xuanzang crossed to get to India, did not form a religious, political, or economic boundary. Regions on both sides of the mountains were part and parcel of the same world. Both had similar Buddhist monasteries and welcomed travelers. Theological discussions included Brahmans from India, Zoroastrians from Persia, and people with other beliefs. Large kingdoms regularly encompassed portions of Central Asia, Afghanistan, and the northern plains of India. Trade passed over the mountains in both directions.

There were good reasons that Xuanzang found Buddhist kings from China to India. At this time, a king's most vexing problem was building loyalty beyond ethnic or language ties. Buddhism could help.[25] Its beliefs appealed to a universal humanity and bridged kinship or ethnic differences. Buddhism made the king and his Buddhist subjects joint supporters of the spiritual work of monks and monasteries but gave the king great status and merit as the largest endower.

Buddhist monasteries also provided practical benefits for both a king and his subjects. The chain of monasteries was an infrastructure that promoted trade. Wherever Buddhism flourished, traders were prominent patrons of shrines and monasteries. One incarnation of the Buddha, the compassionate Avalokiteshvara, became a kind of patron saint of traders and travelers. In a world of disease and death, monasteries were also repositories of medical knowledge. The monks often treated both kings and ordinary laity.

On the Jumna-Ganges Plain in northern India, Xuanzang found the heartland of Buddhism that he had so long sought. Here, 1,000 years before Xuanzang, the Buddha and his disciples had walked, taught, and meditated. Pillars celebrated events from the Buddha's life. Relics of the Buddha formed the core of hundreds of shrines. Thresholds and steps were already deeply worn by the bare feet of thousands of pilgrims. As his biography noted, Xuanzang found many flourishing monasteries with thousands of monks: "From ancient days 'til now, royal and noble personages endowed with virtue and love, in the distribution of charitable offerings, have resorted to this spot for the purpose."[26]

Through the center of the plain, however, many ancient Buddhist sites were deserted. Xuanzang discovered that "[t]here was formerly a Sangharama [monastery] here, but now it has been overturned and destroyed."[27] Shrines that held relics of the Buddha were unattended. The ancient Buddhist kingdom of Kapilavastu was "all waste and ruined."[28] Xuanzang acknowledged competition not only between the two major schools of Buddhism, known as the Great Vehicle and the Small Vehicle, but also with non-Buddhist Brahmanic sects that he termed "heretical." They had lived side by side in competition, not always friendly, for 1,000

years. At Bodh Gaya in present-day Bihar was the tree under
which the Buddha had found enlightenment, but Xuanzang noted
that as "wicked kings have cut it down and destroyed it, the tree is
now only fifty feet high."[29]

After three years of mountains and rivers, kings and hospitality,
Xuanzang arrived with great ceremony at the renowned Nalanda
monastery (located in the eastern Ganges valley), which at the
time housed 10,000 monks in a variety of residences.[30] The monastery provided Xuanzang with quiet quarters, more than ade-
quate food, and a novice to assist him. He found the teacher of the
texts he sought and stayed for five years. Xuanzang's routine included studying and copying manuscripts, listening to teachings
both Buddhist and Brahmanic, participating in the rituals and
discussions, and visiting Buddhist sites throughout the region. After five years at Nalanda, Xuanzang traveled for four years to
monasteries in Bengal, south along the eastern portion of peninsular India, north through the western region of India, and back
to the Nalanda monastery.

Xuanzang's story is one of success. After two more years of
study, he decided to return to China.

> I have visited and adored the sacred vestiges of our religion, and
> heard the profound expositions of the various schools. My mind
> has been overjoyed, and my visit here, has, I protest, been of the
> utmost profit. I desire now to go back and translate and explain to
> others what I have heard. . . .[31]

King Kumara, from the region of the Nalanda monastery, provided the funds for a major return expedition across Central Asia
that carried 657 books, plus several dozen relics and statues, each
of which would become the center of a shrine in China. In keeping with the monastic commitment to medicine, Xuanzang also
carried many plants and seeds from India.

South of the Taklamakan Desert, Xuanzang wrote a contrite letter to the emperor of China. He apologized for leaving illegally seventeen years earlier, but summarized his trip with some pride.

> I accomplished a journey of more than 50,000 li; yet notwithstanding the thousand differences of customs and manners I have witnessed, the myriads of dangers I have encountered, by the goodness of Heaven I have returned without accident, and now offer my homage [to the Tang emperor] with a body unimpaired, and a mind satisfied with the accomplishment of my vows. I have beheld the Ghrirakuta Mountain, worshipped at the Bodhi tree: I have seen traces not seen before; heard sacred words not heard before; witnessed spiritual prodigies, exceeding all the wonders of Nature. . . .[32]

The reply—three months in coming—forgave Xuanzang and provided an imperial escort for the remainder of the trip.

In all, Xuanzang traveled more than 15,000 miles and still stayed within the institutional support of Buddhism. Through personal experience Xuanzang knew of the monasteries and rest houses in the cold dry world of the steppe and heard reports of the monasteries and numbers of monks in the warm ocean world of Southeast Asia. Everywhere Buddhism flourished it was supported by royal and noble patronage, supplemented by pious women and traders.[33] Across the chain of Buddhist institutions moved teachers, ritual objects, texts, medicines, ideas, and trade. Curiosity and hospitality were hallmarks of the system. Although specific practices might differ, all Buddhist travelers, whether monk or layman, found similar settings and symbols in Buddhist monasteries and rest houses.

Xuanzang's journey coincided with the vigorous beginning of the Tang dynasty in China. Chinese influence soon extended not just to the seven watchtowers of Xuanzang's journey but west more than 2,000 miles along the caravan routes, as well as east to

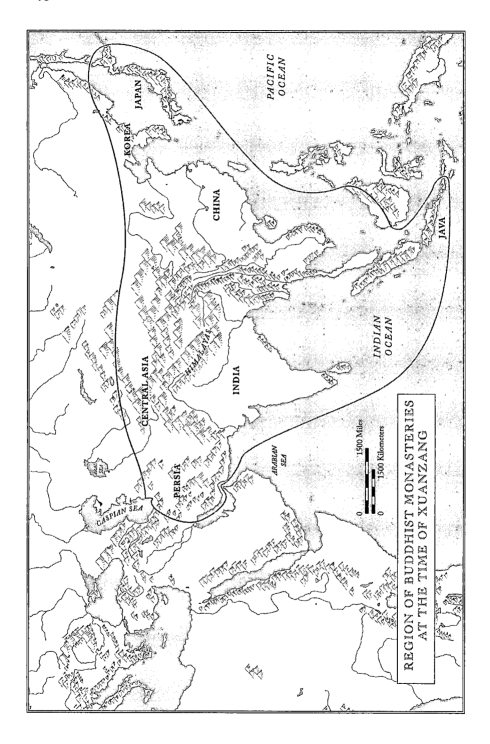

REGION OF BUDDHIST MONASTERIES
AT THE TIME OF XUANZANG

Korea and Japan. In a long, touching passage, Xuanzang recounted the virtues of China to monks of the Nalanda monastery
and the virtues of the Tang emperor to King Kumara of India.[34]
In several portions in his memoir, Xuanzang described kings he
met as urbane, sophisticated, and spiritual. Foreign places and
foreign things fascinated the Tang emperor, who commanded
Xuanzang to recount his travels.

Xuanzang's pilgrimage set off a flurry of diplomatic missions
between China and India, more than fifty in the next century.
Many were couched in Buddhist terms: to donate a particular
Chinese robe to an Indian monastery or to receive the ambassador
from an Indian king thanking the Chinese emperor for the donation. However, these contacts between various kings in India and
the Chinese court had functions quite beyond Buddhism. Kingdoms in India and the Tang emperor, for example, explored their
mutual interest in keeping a rising Tibet in check.[35] Both sides
learned of trade possibilities. Foreigners were welcomed at the imperial capital, and their clothes influenced fashions at court.[36]*
Less than a decade after Xuanzang's journey, the second Tang embassy to India brought back both sugarcane and the technology to
press it. Within the context of Buddhist donation and pilgrimage,
frequent diplomatic contacts between India and China continued
for more than four centuries.

Buddhism changed China in profound ways. The heartland of
Buddhism was India, not China. All the sacred places were thousands of miles away from China. The largest monasteries, the least
corrupted texts, the most famous teachers were all in India. Those
texts were in Sanskrit, not Chinese. Buddhism stood as a spiritual

---

*Official documents and literature recount exotic goods of every sort arriving
at the Tang court: dwarfs and dancers, lions and elephants, hawks and pea-
cocks, date palms and narcissus, lac and lapis lazuli.

and intellectual challenge to the recurrent Chinese attitude of self-sufficiency and self-importance. Buddhism connected China to the outside world in ways even deeper than trade.

Buddhism competed with Taoism and Confucianism in China, but it also competed with Zoroastrianism in Central Asia and Brahmanism in India and Southeast Asia. Xuanzang stood ready to debate texts and practices of other sects and religions just as he frequently debated his rivals within Buddhism, followers of the Little Vehicle. Courts of kings across Asia were often the venue for such debates, and the participants vied for truth, honor, and patronage.

The rise and fall of competing religions was an expected phenomenon. Xuanzang observed the decline in patronage for Buddhist monasteries in the Central Ganges Valley. Two Chinese monks who traveled to India a century after Xuanzang found that more and more, Indian kings patronized Hindu gods and temples; Buddhism slowly disappeared in much of India.[37] At the same time, it remained strong in Bengal and Sri Lanka, and expanded in Southeast Asia. Centuries later, when Buddhism was almost gone from its Indian heartland, there was a mass conversion to Buddhism in Tibet. In spite of these regional advances and declines, the power of Buddhism to promote universal ideas and institutions that altered local cultures and promoted trade was proven. Asia was transformed and connected in ways previously inconceivable.

And what of Xuanzang after his return to China? In spite of several requests by the emperor to become a high official, Xuanzang chose to stay a Buddhist monk. He found his brother still alive and still a practicing monk. Xuanzang spent the rest of his life supervising a team of translators and teaching Buddhist texts in the city of Chang'an, the very city in which he and his brother had sought refuge from robbers and bandits in their youth. He became abbot of a newly dedicated monastery and designed and helped build a library for the texts. The seven-tier pagoda-shaped building exists to this day.[38]

2

CALIPH AND CARAVAN

Ibn Fadlan, 921–922 CE

In the spring of 921 CE, Almish, king of a large tribe of nomadic Bulgars located near the Volga River in current-day Russia, requested that the caliph of Baghdad "send him someone who would instruct him in religion, acquaint him with the laws of Islam, raise a pulpit for him from which he would speak his [the caliph's] name in the city and throughout his kingdom."[1] Thus, Almish asked to become not only a Muslim but to enter into formal subordinate alliance to the caliph, political ruler of the Islamic Empire. The reading of the caliph's name in Friday prayers would publicly acknowledge this relationship. Almish also asked for funds to "build a fortress to defend himself against rival kings."[2] The caliph acceded to Almish's requests and chose one Ibn Fadlan to head the expedition from Baghdad to the Bulgar camp.

Islam, in its early decades (620–680 CE), defined admission into the *umma*, the community of the faithful, by the required behavior of a Muslim: a monotheistic statement of faith, in addition to prayers, fasts, pilgrimage, donations to poor Muslims, proper food and clothing, and personal appearance.[3] One proven attraction of Islam was the idea that before God, all Muslim worshippers were equal, regardless of clan, family, or region.[4] Rule of law governed the *umma* and covered a host of moral and functional relationships: between man and wife, owner and slave, and trader and consignee. It was forbidden, for example, for a Muslim to kill or enslave another Muslim or even to feud with other Muslims.

This legal code offered the possibility of ending the frequent blood feuds among the nomad clans of Arabia.[5] Islam had a larger vision that transcended loyalty based only on kinship and thus paralleled what Buddhism offered to kings along the trade routes in Central Asia, Southeast Asia, and China. This same set of laws defined a position for nonbelievers that was, on the whole, far less onerous than prior empires.[6] On payment of specific and limited taxation, non-Muslims could go on with their lives. In Islam, the political was never separated from the religious. From the time of Muhammad, Islam was at the same time a religion of personal belief, a community of believers, and an expanding conquest state that encompassed great numbers of nonbelievers.

At the time of Ibn Fadlan, Islam was less than three centuries old, but its ruler controlled vast territories. Baghdad, the Abbasid dynastic capital of this empire in the tenth century, ranked with Delhi, Beijing, and Constantinople as one of the largest, wealthiest, and most sophisticated cities in the world. Founded in 750 CE as a new, circle-shaped, fortified city, Baghdad's gardens and palaces soon spread outside the walls and across the Tigris River. Its bazaars, libraries, and banquets were the stuff of legend in Europe.[7] At court, silk robes were the norm and the caliph had a storehouse attached to the palace to store the garments that he bestowed on the worthy.[8] Nobles supported all sorts of learning and innovation, including the translation of Greek texts on science, mathematics, geography, astronomy, agriculture, and medicine. Religious commentary flourished.[9]

Politically, however, the situation of the caliph was insecure. There were always problems with the outlying provinces. Distances were long, communication slow, and rebellion frequent. Closer to home, most caliphs had rival relatives waiting for their opportunity. Factional, sectarian conflict began in the early decades of Islam and continued unabated three centuries later at the time of Ibn Fadlan. Because Islam merged secular and religious leadership, the issue of who would lead the Islamic Empire was not only a matter of effective policy, it was a matter of who was the correct moral leader to lead the faithful to paradise.

Because no method of choosing a leader had been set before the death of Muhammad, the leadership issue generated feuds between clans, between Arabs and non-Arabs, and between nomads and townspeople. The result of these feuds was differing interpretations of Islam.[10] Three of the first four caliphs were murdered. Wars followed.[11] The first century after Muhammad saw the emergence of the main sects. Sunnis believed that all caliphs, in spite of dynastic change and other conflicts, were the legitimate spiritual and temporal successors to Muhammad. Shias favored a line of succession through Muhammad's cousin Ali, who was murdered in 661 CE. Some Shias accepted only the first five or seven caliphs as legitimate; others accepted the first twelve caliphs. Sects that rejected Sunni interpretation tended to be strong in outlying provinces, such as Persia.[12]

Caliphs were always looking for new allies, especially new converts who would fight and die for Islam and could balance the less-than-reliable forces around Baghdad. By 800 CE, the Abbasid caliph replaced clan troops around the capital with slave soldiers whom he thought would be more loyal. The policy unfortunately backfired. The slave army soon emerged as a political force of its own and by 850 CE regularly promoted or displaced rulers.[13] The caliph needed all the allies he could muster and occasionally sent out ambassadorial missions to nonbelievers beyond the borders of Islam. This is the story of one such difficult, dangerous mission.

Ibn Fadlan, whom the caliph chose to head the embassy to the Bulgars, was most likely a middle-level courtier used to a comfortable life in Baghdad. He goes unmentioned in biographical lists of the time or surviving government documents and was certainly not

a great figure on the historical stage.[14] We know him only through
the memoir he wrote of his mission—but what a memoir it was.
Ibn Fadlan was a curious and careful observer of customs and
people he saw along the way. He was interested in climate, crops,
food, and trade. He sometimes described his feelings in response to
unfamiliar situations. Although some comments in the memoir
suggest Ibn Fadlan was trained in Islamic law, he never reacted le-
galistically. He was rather like an anthropologist, inquisitive and
attentive, recording what he saw for an audience back in Baghdad.
He probably knew that geographic knowledge was flowing into
the capital and intended the memoir to add to the knowledge of
the lands he saw along the way.

In mid-June 921 CE, Ibn Fadlan left Baghdad with a small entourage that included a religious instructor, a jurist, and an ambassador. Among the gifts for Almish, the Bulgar king, were elegant
silk robes, banners, and a decorated saddle.[15] Trusted retainers
carrying enough silver currency to build a modest fortress were to
catch up with him on the road.

Political and religious realities made it impossible for Ibn Fadlan to take a direct northerly route to Almish. That way lay across
Christian Armenia and portions of the Byzantine Empire, both
bitter foes of Baghdad. Instead, Ibn Fadlan was forced to add
thousands of miles to the mission, first traveling east, then north,
then back west to circumvent these enemies.

The mission, on camels, left the lush agriculture of the valley of
the Tigris, climbed onto the drier plateau of western Persia, and
"traveled the direct route" northeast through Kermanshah, a rich
agricultural district, over the mountains of Hamadan to Reyy
(close to current-day Teheran).[16] They were part of a large caravan
that, almost certainly, rose pre-dawn to the sound of camel bells
and the curses of drivers, assembling for the day's journey. Such
caravans had hundreds if not thousands of camels and stretched a

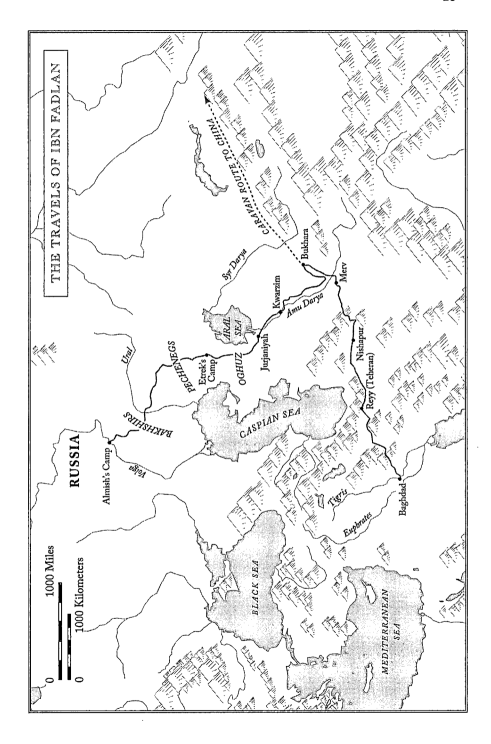

THE TRAVELS OF IBN FADLAN

mile or more along the worn track. Caravans like this typically covered about twenty miles a day from oasis to oasis, usually stopping by midafternoon to avoid the heat of the day.

The embassy passed into drier grazing lands and pushed east across Persia via Nishapur, Sarkh, and Merv, all oasis and trading cities on the caravan routes. Persia, at the time, was a patchwork of religious beliefs, generally closely intertwined with local political power. There were pockets of Zoroastrianism and a variety of non-Sunni sects, including early forms of Shia Islam. Ibn Fadlan reported that as Sunni Muslims traveling through a territory held by one of these sects, known as the Zaidi, "[we had to] conceal our identity in the caravan."[17]

By the fall of 921, Ibn Fadlan and his men had crossed 200 miles of desert, ferried the Amudarya River, and arrived at Bukhara, regional capital of the nearly independent Islamic province of Khurasan. Ibn Fadlan notes that the emir "saw to it that a house was secured for us, and appointed a man to take care of our needs."[18] While he waited for the courier and the cash for Almish's fort, Ibn Fadlan learned what was ahead—an immense expanse of largely empty grassland and a brutal steppe winter. The huge low-rainfall grassland of the steppe extended from the border of China west to the Caucasus and Russia, south to Persia and Turkey. By trade and conquest, the steppe's influence extended into North China, the plains of India, the Middle East, and the eastern Mediterranean. He would have to cross more than 2,000 miles of its western reaches.

In the fall, even though the cash for the fort had not yet arrived, Ibn Fadlan decided to push into the steppe.[19]* The mission

---

*Frye presents a plausible explanation for the missing money. It was to come from estates confiscated in the swirl of courtly politics at Baghdad. The estates were located a thousand miles from Baghdad in Khwarizm, along Ibn Fadlan's route. The bailiff of the estates, however, refused to turn over anything and remained loyal to the ousted noble.

returned to the Amudarya River. He hired a boat and traveled more than 400 miles north to the city of Khwarizm [on the site of the modern city of Khorezmskaya], commenting about this part of the journey, "We used to travel only part of the day due to the severity of the cold." At the north edge of the Islamic world, his party met resistance. The emir of Khwarizm warned Ibn Fadlan, "Between you and this land that you mention, there are a thousand tribes of unbelievers."[20] He told Ibn Fadlan that the caliph had been deceived and Almish's letter was merely a trick to lure a vulnerable entourage into dangerous territory.

Khwarizm, though formally a province of the caliphate, was in fact independent. The Khwarizm ruler had little use for a new ally of the caliph anywhere in his region. With Almish as an ally, it might be possible for the caliph to attack Khwarizm from both the north and the south simultaneously. It is understandable that the Khwarizm ruler wanted Ibn Fadlan's mission to go no farther. In a succession of interviews, Ibn Fadlan begged, pleaded, and finally convinced the emir to let his party leave.

What did it mean that Ibn Fadlan was leaving the territory of Islam for lands of "unbelievers"? The capital of Khwarizm was no Baghdad, but its legal, religious, and physical structure would have been familiar to Ibn Fadlan and similar to dozens of other Islamic cities of the time. Its center was the main mosque. Friday prayers were the most heavily attended and the presiding cleric blessed the name of the ruling king, an act central to kingly legitimacy. Ibn Fadlan might have found a cleric from Mecca or Baghdad. These two cities had the best religious training, and clerics regularly traveled from them to outlying congregations across the Islamic world. Close by the mosque was the king's palace with guards and stables. Muslim cities like Khwarizm included a broad open area near the palace that could be used for military practice and ceremony. The Muslim community was mixed, including descendants of the original Arab Islamic conquerors, Arab traders, and local converts such as landholders, shopkeepers, craftsmen, and laborers. Khwarizm, like other Muslim cities, included a common bathing building *(hamam)* and a central bazaar for both daily necessities and imported items. The city included one or more caravan serais where caravans stopped, traders stayed, and goods in transit were stored. Khwarizm had a legal structure that would have been familiar to Ibn Fadlan, including professional, trained jurists who presided over courts of both civil and criminal Islamic law and a professional class of administrators who served the governor.*

In late fall, Ibn Fadlan left Khwarizm and traveled north along the Amudarya River. He arrived at Jurjaniyah as winter closed in.[21] Jurjaniyah was a small town on a tributary of the Amudarya but still well within the Muslin world. Ibn Fadlan noted how cold it was in winter: "When I used to come out of the public bath and enter my house, I would look at my beard and find it to have been frozen into a piece of ice."[22] However, he found firewood inexpensive and readily available in Jurjaniyah. The steppe was not undifferentiated grassland. Along perennial rivers fed by snowpack from distant mountains were, as here at Jurjaniyah, forests and irrigated fields of millet, sorghum, and wheat.

Late in February, the Amudarya River thawed. Ibn Fadlan then purchased camels, had collapsible boats built for crossing rivers, and hired a local guide. The jurist, the ambassador, and the religious instructor were too frightened to go on, though perhaps it was more than the cold and the distance that scared them. Beyond Jurjaniyah, there would be no more communal baths, no bazaars, no mosques, no legal protections of Islamic law, and no protection of an Islamic king. For someone raised within the Islamic world, the world beyond could, indeed, be a frightening place.

---

*The population of most "Islamic" cities at this time was predominantly non-Muslim and remained so for centuries.

Ibn Fadlan pushed on alone. Provisioned "with bread, millet, and jerked meat, enough for three months," he joined a caravan of more than 1,000 men and 3,000 animals, heading north.

> Those of the people of the town with whom we were on friendly terms . . . [stressed] the grimness of the undertaking, and magnified the [dangers of the] affair. When we experienced it, it was many times worse than what had been described to us.[23]

Two centuries before Ibn Fadlan traveled through this region, the overall borders of the Muslim world had been set in one of the fastest, broadest conquests in human history. Between 630 CE and 680 CE, Islamic armies swept north from Mecca across what is present-day Jordan, Palestine, and Syria and east across Iraq, then fought in Persia and attacked south into Yemen. By 720 CE, Muslim armies had successfully attacked Egypt, North Africa, and Spain and had conquered several caravan cities: Samarkand, Tashkent, Bukhara, and Khwarizm. There, however, the conquest stopped.[24] Like Buddhism before it, Islam was successful in the caravan cities but singularly unsuccessful in converting the clans and families of the steppe nomads.

These dramatic Islamic conquests took place mainly in the lifetime of Xuanzang, the Buddhist pilgrim of Chapter 1. Palestine, Jordan, and Syria fell while he was peacefully copying texts at the Buddhist monastery of Nalanda in eastern India. It was less than a century after he passed through Bukhara and Tashkent that Islamic armies conquered these caravan cities.

From a scattering of tenth-century documents, modern scholars now know more of the political situation on the steppe than Ibn Fadlan knew. Some sort of tribal union had emerged among Oghuz Turks in the previous three decades. None of the Oghuz had converted to Islam, though it had attracted some interest among other tribes. Some branches of the Oghuz had recently fought Almish, to whom Ibn Fadlan carried diplomatic papers.[25] Beyond the Oghuz was the Khazar kingdom, which probably began as a coalition of Turkic tribes about two centuries before Ibn Fadlan's journey and steadily expanded in size and power. The Khazar kingdom was strongly opposed to Islam. Some elements of the aristocracy had converted to Judaism, but scholars have been able to discover very little about its government or institutions. Almish's kingdom lay deep inside Khazar territory. It is clear that he was a vassal of the Khazars, and his request for money from the caliph for a fort was an attempt to break free from Khazar vassalage. Ibn Fadlan would later learn that at the time of his trip, the Khazar court held Almish's son as a hostage.[26]

Ibn Fadlan's caravan pushed into the "uninhabited, mountain-less steppe" and "experienced adversity, exertion, and extreme cold which made the cold of Khwarizm seem like the days of summer." The pattern of caravan travel probably hadn't changed much since the days of Xuanzang three centuries earlier. Caravan travelers still put up with angry, biting camels, welcomed arrival at an oasis, and enjoyed a variety of cooking smells in camp.

On the fifteenth day after leaving Jurjaniyah, they came upon "tents made of hair," the camp of a tribe of Turks, a branch of the Oghuz, which Ibn Fadlan termed the Ghuzz. Like all nomad groups Ibn Fadlan encountered, these people raised "camels, horses, cattle, and goats." "They remain in a place for awhile, then move on. You see their tents in one place, and then you see others similar to them at another place, in keeping with the practice of nomads and their wanderings."[27]

Ibn Fadlan probably noticed similarities to the desert areas of Arabia. Although Arabia was hot and the steppe cold, both areas had scant populations and daunting ecologies that took great skill and toughness to survive. Both regions had an economy based on flocks and a clan structure based on lineage. Riding, hunting, and war skills were taught from childhood. Blood feuds, and war over pasture and water holes, were common. Like the nomad herders of Arabia, those of the steppe had an uneasy relationship with oasis towns and sedentary agriculture. Both needed the towns for iron, cloth, and food. The towns needed the nomads' animals for meat and draft. Town dwellers manufactured the hair of the nomad animals into felt and fabric. In spite of this mutual dependency, war was frequent between nomads and the towns in both Arabia and the steppe.

The political problems of assembling a kingdom in Arabia before Muhammad's creation of the idea of the *umma* were similar to those of the steppe three centuries later in Ibn Fadlan's time. The only basis of loyalty among nomad and town dweller was kinship. Any noble had a host of rivals with equally legitimate claims. Two clans that wanted an alliance might find or create a common ancestor, but these were fragile and tenuous ties for keeping an alliance together. Among nomads, alliances shifted virtually from year to year.

Bands generally consisted of a leader, his family, and male relatives—brothers, sons, uncles, nephews—and their families. The band included some families that were not relatives, often survivors of a defeated band that sought refuge. A successful band tended to grow until summer and winter pastures could no longer sustain it, at which time it would divide. There was incessant competition for better-watered grasslands, making war endemic; wholesale displacement and slavery of the defeated was common. Leaders of bands often faced coups engineered by relatives whose wealth (in animals) and claims to leadership were equal or nearly equal to theirs. The result of this pattern of ecology and male lineage was a series of loosely related bands scattered across thousands of miles of steppe. Generally, these related bands competed with each other as much as they did with other bands.

Even before Ibn Fadlan's time, there were leaders who were able, through personal charisma, to unite bands into formidable

fighting forces. The Chinese chronicles of the first century recount the incursions of the Hsiung-nu, a confederation of nomad
clans of the eastern steppe.[28] More well known is the ravaging of
Europe in the fifth century by the steppe nomad army of Attila
the Hun.

For Ibn Fadlan, Turks, not Huns, were the problem. Over the
next three months, Ibn Fadlan cajoled and bribed his way north
and west around the Caspian Sea through what is today Kazakh-
stan and into southern Russia. One bribe to a clan leader named
Yinal the Little consisted of an inexpensive caftan, a piece of Persian cloth, some "round, flat loaves of bread, a handful of raisins
and a hundred walnuts."[29]

In his memoir, Ibn Fadlan described, as an anthropologist
might, the typical pattern by which a Muslim Arab trader survived in these hostile nomad regions. A trader needed a local Turk
sponsor and friend. When passing through the sponsor's territory,
the Muslim trader stayed with the Turk and gave him a robe, "a
veil for [the Turk's] wife, and some pepper, millet, raisins, and
nuts."* The Turk might advance the trader money or horses if he
ran short, which the trader repaid on his return.

Turk sponsors treated all Muslim traders as if they belonged to
a single clan, the clan of Muslims, and assumed that the clan had
joint responsibility for their members, including loans. For example, if a trader died on the road or did not return, his Turk sponsor collected—by force if necessary—outstanding loans from the
richest trader in any returning caravan. The Turk sponsor un-
packed the rich merchant's goods and took "from him his money

---

*These gifts were a mixture of the exotic and the mundane. Pepper came from
India, raisins possibly from Persia, and nuts from the Middle East; robes and
veils, depending on their pattern and style, might have come from as far away
as India or as close as the weavers of Baghdad. Millet was grown in the Caucasus and Persia.

an amount equal to that which he had with the [deceased] merchant, without taking a single additional grain."[30]

Ibn Fadlan arrived next at the camp of Etrek, whom he termed the commander of the army of the Ghuzz Turks. His gifts to Etrek were precious: "[F]ifty dinars [silver coins] . . . three mithqals of musk [about fifteen grams], pieces of tanned leather, and cloth from Merv from which we cut for him two tunics, tanned leather boots, one brocade garment, and five silk garments," and to his wife a veil and a ring.[31] Etrek put on the robes Ibn Fadlan presented him but would not commit either to Islam or to the caliph. Over the next few days Etrek's nobles, generally anti-Muslim and opposed to Almish, debated Ibn Fadlan's fate. They looked for advice to one Tarkhan, the oldest noble at court, who said:

> This is something we have never seen, nor heard of. No envoy of a Caliph has ever passed through our country in our time or the time of our fathers. I cannot but think that the Caliph has resorted to a ruse by sending these [men] to the Khazars with the object of raising an army against us. The thing to do is to have these envoys cut in half and possess ourselves of what they have with them.[32]

One noble suggested that the thing to do was to strip them naked and send them back the way they came; another wanted to exchange them as slaves for captives held by the Khazars. After seven days in a "deathlike state," Ibn Fadlan heard that the nobles would let the mission proceed. Ibn Fadlan then gave robes to all the nobles, along with gifts of millet, pepper, and flat bread. He departed with the caravan, which had apparently waited for him.

Although Ibn Fadlan found these nomads uncouth, the peoples of Arabia and the steppe had for centuries used the same presentation of robes to show honor and establish political relationships. Three centuries before Ibn Fadlan, a king in the eastern steppe honored Xuanzang, the Buddhist pilgrim, with silk robes. During the same period, Muhammad honored one of his successful generals in Arabia with elegant robes in a similar public ceremony. By the time of Ibn Fadlan, the caliph, as well as the Christian king of Constantinople, regularly used the ceremony to establish political relationships, just as kings across the steppe did. Both Etrek and Ibn Fadlan knew perfectly well the implication of putting on robes from the caliph. Etrek prevaricated, however, saying only that he would give an answer on Islam and an alliance when Ibn Fadlan returned. Both men understood that Etrek's acceptance of the robes, but his refusal to acknowledge the sovereignty of the caliph, was a violation of the system.

Through the spring, another thousand miles of traveling with the caravan across the treeless steppe brought Ibn Fadlan west across both the Ural River and the Volga River to Almish's capital. Compared to what he had seen while traveling, Almish's grazing lands looked good, the grass green from spring rains. In early May, Almish sent his "brothers and his sons to meet us . . . with bread, meat, and millet," then came himself, showered the party with money, and had tents pitched for them. In spite of his considerable experience at the court of Baghdad, Ibn Fadlan found Almish formidable. "He was a man of striking appearance and dignity, stout and broad, who sounded as though he were speaking from inside a large barrel."[33]

On May 20, 922 CE in Almish's tent of audience, large enough to house 1,000 men and with a floor covered with Armenian carpets, Ibn Fadlan presented honorific robes, banners, and the decorated saddle, and finally, through an interpreter, read out the caliph's letter. Things started very well, with a diplomatic banquet at which Almish fed tiny bits of meat to Ibn Fadlan. Ibn Fadlan presented perfume to Almish for his wife. The next Friday, Almish's public profession of subordination to the caliph was read out in a mosque near the court. Even this reading required delicate negotiation. In the Baghdad tradition, Friday prayers call down blessings on both the reigning king and his father. Almish's father had been an unbeliever, and Almish did not want him mentioned. Ibn Fadlan acceded to this request. Also, Almish carried the name of his father and asked for a new Muslim name for Friday prayers. He took the name of the reigning caliph.

Three days later, however, the situation began to sour. Almish discovered that there was no money, though money for the fort was mentioned in the caliph's letter. Almish was furious, threw the letter of the caliph at Ibn Fadlan, and demanded the money. Ibn Fadlan replied, "It was impossible to collect it. Time was short. . . . We left the money behind to catch up to us later." Almish accused Ibn Fadlan of stealing the money and betraying the caliph, saying, "You who eat [the caliph's] bread and wear his clothes and see him at all times have betrayed him with regard to the mission . . . which he sent you to me . . . and you have betrayed the Muslims." Ibn Fadlan left his audience with the king "frightened and distressed."34

Equally distressing to Ibn Fadlan was the discovery that there had been some dissembling by King Almish. He and the court were already practicing Muslims, but had not told the caliph of this in their letter. Their customs of worship were those of Khurasan, already quite independent of the caliph. These "Khurasani" practices signaled that the king was fully aware of the current politics of the Islamic world and was looking for an ally—if not the caliph, then possibly Khurasan.

Almish refused all religious advice and effectively revoked Ibn Fadlan's ambassadorial status. Ibn Fadlan knew that without the silver for the fort, his mission was doomed. Late in his memoir, he wrote that a Jewish faction at the court of the caliph favored the Jewish Khazars, Almish's enemy, and had held up the money. At this historical distance, it cannot be known whether these charges are true. The mission failed; Almish received no money for his fort and the caliph got no new ally. Almish found Ibn Fadlan's stories of Baghdad amusing, and this storytelling ability probably saved his life.

Even though the political purpose of the mission was in ruins, Ibn Fadlan remained a keen observer of everything around him: clouds, snakes, local fruits and cuisine, clothing, and the complexities of the five required daily Muslim prayers during long summer days. The later portion of the memoir includes an account of a people he terms the Rus (probably Norse, though the issue has been debated by scholars for more than a century) when they arrived to trade at Almish's capital. Ibn Fadlan also relates that he exhorted local women at the capital "to cover themselves while swimming, but I did not succeed in my endeavors."[35]

The tenth-century Asian world was one of various religious worldviews competing for patronage and followers. Whether it was the movement of Buddhism into Tibet or Islam into Central Asia, there were generally long periods of a mixture of local practice and the new religion. Conversion was complex, splits common, and backsliding frequent. Within Islam, the new religion was often expressed in local sects that challenged practices from older centers, both religiously and militarily. Local kings and local people made very real judgments on the possible benefits of converting, judgments frequently tied to alliances, trade, taxes, and the benefits of a wider network. Religion and politics were intimately intertwined, both in the big metropolitan centers like Baghdad and in smaller courts such as Almish's. Kings, big and small, in the Middle East and Central Asia already shared a set of ceremonies and symbols with subtle degrees of political alliance and subordination. Both the caliph and Almish knew the meanings of a common courtly language of banners, decorated saddles, prostration, silk robes, Armenian carpets, banquets, and formal letters.

While Islam could offer new beliefs, ceremonies, and symbols, Ibn Fadlan offered precious little of what Almish apparently wanted. There was no money, no trade benefits, and no functional connections to a larger world. Perhaps Ibn Fadlan thought he was bringing Islam and civilization to the far reaches of the Volga River, but he could not have been more wrong. King Almish was already connected to the Asian world. His capital was on the Volga. Norse boats passed regularly, trading slaves for food and gold. Almish sought to control the valuable trade in sable, fox, and other furs highly prized for court dress at Baghdad and Constantinople. He probably needed to displace his overlord, the Khazar king, from his capital on the lower Volga to accomplish this aim. Recall that the caravan that Ibn Fadlan joined consisted of more than 1,000 men and 3,000 animals. Almish knew of the fracture between the caliphate and Khurasan and was already involved in warfare between the Rus people and his overlord, the Khazar king. He was connected by alliances to a political system that spread across 2,000 miles of the western steppe and included Persia, Constantinople, and Baghdad. Trade connected him north to Scandinavia.[36]

A few months after Ibn Fadlan's arrival, Almish's son-in-law rebelled. Almish sent a very telling letter to the faction that supported his son-in-law.

> God—Might and Majesty be His—has bestowed upon me the blessings of Islam and the power of the Commander of the Faithful [the caliph]. I am his servant, and this nation has invested me with authority. Whoever opposes me, him I shall meet with the sword.[37]

Almish invoked the very relationship with the caliph that he had apparently rejected only weeks earlier. Ibn Fadlan recounted that the strategy worked. When Almish "sent his letter to them, they were awed by this, and all of them journeyed with him. . . ."[38]

In a poignant passage late in the memoir, Ibn Fadlan, who at last understood how large an area Almish ruled and the extent of his contacts, finally asked the king if the money for the fort was really all that important. Almish said:

> I found the Empire of Islam to be prosperous, and recourse may be had to its lawfully-derived revenues. I sought these funds for this reason. Had I wanted to build a fortress of silver or gold with my own money, the attainment of such an objective would not have been difficult for me. I merely sought to benefit from the blessing that attaches to the money of the Commander of the Faithful [the caliph], and for which reason I asked him for it.[39]

Ibn Fadlan's mission was about political and religious alliances that stretched across the entire western half of the Asian world. The fort was only a concrete symbol of the caliph's commitment to Almish. Because the caliph had not produced the money for the fort, it was Almish who controlled the relationship. With impunity, he soon invoked the name of the caliph in local disputes, but he knew that the caliph was weak and he would never have to fulfill his side of implied obligations. Indeed, even though a royal Bulgar pilgrimage to Mecca passed through Baghdad about ten years later, the travelers brought no tribute.

And what of Ibn Fadlan? Nothing is known of him beyond his own narrative. It is clear he made it back safely to Baghdad because his memoir survives. In the whirlwind of caliphal politics, it is not known whether his mission was considered a failure, whether the caliph was merely testing the waters for a possible inexpensive alliance, or whether the new geographical and political information was worth the cost and risk of the embassy.

3

PHILOSOPHER
AND PHYSICIAN

Ibn Sina, 1002–1021 CE

Two hundred miles northeast of Baghdad in the Persian city of Hamadan almost exactly a century after Ibn Fadlan's expedition passed through, Ibn Sina, already a famous philosopher and physician, was on his way to prison. As the guards led him away, he quipped to his student:

> That I go in you see, that's without a doubt
> What's uncertain is whether I ever come out.[1]

Ibn Sina spent the next four months in confinement in a castle outside Hamadan. He wrote two important works while in jail: an allegory on human intellect and a medical treatise entitled "Colic." Prison turned out to be only a way station on Ibn Sina's journey. His books had travels of their own as part of the wide movement of ideas at the time.

Both the style and substance of what Ibn Sina wrote connected him to three centuries of extraordinary concentration of human learning and thought. In 750 CE, a Central Asian dynasty, the Abbasids, swept into power in current-day Iraq, replacing an Arab dynasty, the Umayyads, at the center of Islamic power. The Abbasids founded Baghdad as the capital of the Islamic Empire. This dynasty soon initiated a massive translation project of Greek and Latin works into Arabic that included tens of thousands of books, from philosophy to mathematics, plays to medicine. The early translators were non-Muslim scholars of the conquered lands: Jews, Nestorian Christians, and Zoroastrians.[2] This project brought together the intellectual output of a vast world that included Persia, India, the Middle East, Greece, Egypt, and Rome.

Sponsorship of learning at Baghdad quickly went beyond simply translating classics. Scholars soon built on this body of knowledge. Every important breakthrough in science in the ninth and tenth centuries was made by researchers and scholars in Asia, mainly at Muslim courts.

Early Abbasid kings invited Hindu mathematicians from India to teach at court, and they brought the notation system known as Arabic numerals. By 850 CE, the master mathematician al-Khwarizm and his students combined Euclid's theories with Hindu mathematics and produced rapid developments in algebra and trigonometry: linear and quadratic equations; geometrical solutions; tables of sines, tangents, and co-tangents. Al-Kwarizm's name is the basis for our word *algorithm*, the step-by-step solution to a problem. Within the same century, zero—either a local invention or an import from India—appeared for the first time in Baghdad mathematical books. Interchange between later court mathematicians led to the addition and subtraction of radicals, the solution to the area of a parabola, developments in the mathematics of conic sections, solutions to higher-degree equations, and explorations of spherical geometry. These mathematical advances formed the basis for complex, beautiful patterns on Islamic tiles. Within a couple of centuries, these tiles appeared across the Asian world and were an implicit statement of the superiority of mathematical knowledge in the Middle East.[3]

There were breakthroughs in navigation, particularly invention of the plain and the spherical astrolabe and development of more accurate star charts. The Abbasids established a royal observatory at Baghdad. Geographic description flowered as knowledge came in from Muslim armies, embassies, and traders. By 850 CE, the first Arab accounts of China circulated through the Middle East. At the time of Ibn Sina, the early eleventh century, there were no fewer than eleven geographers writing and circulating descriptions of the Asian world. Several scholars produced broad histories based on this new information.[4]

Medical research was equally impressive. At the Baghdad court, some scholars translated the Greeks, such as Galen and Aristotle. Others wrote treatises based on their working knowledge as practicing physicians. The greatest of these was al-Razi, a Persian, who was by all estimates the greatest clinician of the Middle Ages. His medical encyclopedia circulated in Europe and Asia for centuries.

Baghdad's fame was as great in Asia as it was in Europe. Al-Yqubi wrote glowingly of it in the ninth century:

> There is none more learned than their [Baghdad's] scholars, better informed than their traditionalists, more perspicuous than their grammarians, more accurate than their readers, more skillful than their physicians, more melodious than their singers, more delicate than their craftsmen, more literate than their scribes, more lucid than their logicians, more devoted than their worshippers, more pious than their ascetics, more juridical than their judges, more eloquent than their preachers, more poetic than their poets, and more reckless than their rakes.[5]

In this fertile atmosphere, there were also important philosophical speculations, most based on interactions between Islamic thinkers, Greek translations, and beliefs from conquered and surrounding peoples. Many books were commentaries on and extensions of the ideas of classic Greek authors such as Aristotle, Plato, and Ptolemy.

Copies of the important books circulated outward to courts in Persia, the caravan cities of the Silk Road, east as far as Afghanistan and west to North Africa and Spain. By about the year 900 CE, the movement of both books and scholars had produced an extraordinary intellectual network. Treatises and letters went from Persia to Cairo, and debate raged from Damascus to Morocco.

The importance of paper to this process cannot be overestimated. Papermaking originally came from China. The basic technology passed down the Silk Road into the Middle East with the Abbasids in about 750 CE. With royal support at Baghdad, the process was reinvented to suit local conditions. Chinese paper manufacture used tropical plants that did not grow in the Middle East. It was soon discovered that linen and cotton fibers produced a supple, smooth paper. Within a century, there was a flourishing paper market and many paper mills in Baghdad. The earliest surviving paper document from the Middle East is an official Jewish letter from Baghdad to Egypt.[6]

Other capitals such as Damascus and Fustat[7] soon competed with Baghdad, offering alternate sizes and compositions of paper. Paper made possible not only the hundreds of thousands of volumes of the Baghdad Imperial Library, but circulation of these texts to multiple capitals in the Middle East, Persia, Central Asia, and Spain. As the fifteenth century historian Ibn Khaldun put it in his *Muqqdima:*

> Thus, paper was used for government documents and diplomas. Afterwards, people used paper in sheets for government and scholarly writings, and the manufacture reached a considerable degree of excellence.[8]

In the century before Ibn Sina, this vast intellectual network had even developed a core curriculum for teaching. There were certain books, read in a certain order, that were mandatory—without this course of study, one was simply not considered educated. Teachers of this required reading circulated through Muslim cities across the Middle East, some cities in Persia and Central Asia, and as far west as Spain.

Ibn Sina's father came from Balkh in northern Afghanistan and belonged to the educated administrative elite. Before Ibn Sina was born, the king posted his father to administer a town near Bukhara, 200 miles northwest, in present-day Uzbekistan. At Bukhara, Ibn Sina's father readily found good teachers for the Quran and the widely used books of the standard curriculum. Ibn Sina finished the first phase of his education by age ten.[9]

Where Ibn Sina's family differed from the standard educated elite was in its attraction to Ismaili beliefs, as Ibn Sina recalls in his autobiography:

> From them [the Ismailis], he [father], as well as my brother, heard
> the account of the soul and the intellect in the special manner in
> which they speak about it and know it. . . . There was also talk of
> philosophy, geometry, and Indian calculation.[10]

Who were these Ismailis in eleventh-century Bukhara? Since the 1980s, scholars have been able to locate many more Ismaili texts than were previously available and have pieced together the beliefs and development of the sect. In Islam, the close association of political power, moral authority, and religious beliefs made legitimate authority its most central issue. Shias questioned the succession of all caliphs not of Muhammad's family; almost by definition, therefore, Shia sects were centers of rebellion because they questioned the legitimacy of the caliphs who ruled from Baghdad in the eleventh century as well as those prior to the

Baghdad caliphate. Some Shias preached and practiced overt rebellion, while others sponsored covert political resistance. Shia sects tended to develop away from Baghdad, the caliph's capital.

The Ismailis were a Shia sect that emphasized particularly the "hidden" nature of the truths written in the Quran and the importance of a highly spiritual teacher, an imam, in learning those hidden truths. Ismailis also believed in reason and intellect as a way to understand spiritual truth and in the basic rationality of the world.[11] At the time of Ibn Sina's youth, Ismaili sects sent educated spiritual leaders, in secret, to provincial towns to spread the message. They were often successful in converting upper-class families, who risked their position in government by holding these views. It appears that Ibn Sina's family was one of those that quietly and privately discussed Ismaili rationalism with teachers in Bukhara.[12]

According to Ibn Sina's autobiography, when he was a youth, his father sent him to be tutored in "Indian calculation" (the use of zero) from a local grocer, philosophy from a noted teacher, and Islamic law from a local judge.

Like al-Khwarizm (the famous mathematician a century earlier) and thousands of others across the Asian world, Ibn Sina continued his education with Porphyry's *Isagog*, an introduction to Aristotelian logic taught from Persia to Spain. Ibn Sina—clearly brilliant—suggested elegant, unexpected solutions to standard problems. He next disposed of Euclid's *Elements of Geometry* in short order and quickly surpassed his teacher's understanding. He recalled this time: "As for its deeper intricacies, he had no knowledge of them. So, I began to read the texts and study the commentaries by myself."[13]

Ibn Sina then moved on to more complex material, more of the Greek and Roman classics that had been translated at Baghdad. He tackled Claudius Ptolemy's book of astronomical mathematics, solving the figures one by one, and consumed texts in natural sciences and metaphysics.[14]

An important point is that these books were quite easy to locate and buy in Bukhara, more than 1,000 miles east of Baghdad, where they had been translated. This anecdote from the autobiography describes a lively book market:

> One day in the afternoon when I was in the bookseller's quarter a
> dealer approached with a book in his hand which he was calling
> out for sale. He offered it to me, but I refused it with disgust, be-
> lieving that there was no merit in this science. But he said to me,
> "Buy it, because the owner needs the money and so it is cheap. I
> will sell it to you for three dirhams." So I bought it.[15]

Next, he read medicine and picked it up quickly. The texts were mainly from Greece and Rome, translated into Arabic and Persian. Ibn Sina found that

> [medicine] is not one of the difficult sciences and therefore I ex-
> celled in it in a very short time, to the point that distinguished
> physicians began to read the science of medicine under me. I
> cared for the sick and there opened to me some of the doors of
> medical treatment that are indescribable and can be learned only
> from practice.[16]

Ibn Sina was sixteen years old. He then struggled full-time with philosophical texts, mainly Aristotle's *Metaphysics.*

A few months later he was in for a rare opportunity. The king summoned him to treat his illness, which baffled the court doctors. In gratitude for his complete recovery, the king gave Ibn Sina the run of the royal library.

> I was admitted to a building which had many rooms; in each
> room there were chests of books piled one on top of the other. In
> one of the rooms were books on the Arabic language and poetry,

in another, on jurisprudence, and likewise in each room a single science. So I looked through the catalogue of books by the ancients and asked for whichever one I needed.[17]

Recall that this was Bukhara, an important regional city, but by no means Baghdad, Damascus, or Delhi. And the king had rooms full of books, thousands of texts, all arranged and catalogued. From this simple paragraph in Ibn Sina's autobiography, we get a glimpse of the depth and extent of the intellectual network of his time.

For the next four years, Ibn Sina served as a court physician and wrote steadily. His first book, *Good Works and Evil*, was on ethics. Two other books followed, both responses to requests by educated men in his neighborhood. Even in cities far from Baghdad, an educated literate elite cared about the sciences and philosophy. Familiarity with and ownership of these books was an important sign of status. Officials and kings gave positions to researchers and teachers who traveled to spread aspects of this knowledge. Ibn Sina's early philosophy teacher moved on to Jurjan, a small but sophisticated court near the eastern shore of the Caspian Sea.[18]

In this period, Ibn Sina established both the basic philosophical framework and the working methods that he used for the rest of his life. He believed in direct insight into the rational working of the world around him and used wine, prayer, and directed dreaming to solve recalcitrant questions.

The scattering of books that Ibn Sina mentioned in his memoir and his subsequent writings place him squarely in the philosophical traditions of Neoplatonism. To understand Ibn Sina's travels and dangers, we must wrestle a bit with this approach to philosophy, which flourished in Rome from about 300 CE to the closing of its academy in 529 CE. Its adherents were called "Neo"-platonists because they revived and reconsidered Plato's writings which date from more than 700 years prior to the founding of the academy in Rome.

Central to understanding this vein of philosophic thinking is Plato's concept of Forms. Forms were changeless, ideal types, not tainted by the messy specifics of a day-to-day actual world. Take a chair, for example. There are thousands of specific types of chairs, yet they are all somehow chairs, sharing some characteristics, differing in others. The Form of a chair is the perfect ideal that expresses and encompasses all specific chairs.

For the Neoplatonist, as well as for Ibn Sina, the core philosophic problem was to explain the relation of an eternal and unchanging God to a changing and flawed world. Plato's Forms were seen as a bridge or intermediary between God and the world. From Spain through North Africa, Egypt, the Middle East, Persia, and Central Asia at the time, there was widespread agreement on the terms of this central problem and common understanding of approaches to its solution. In the two centuries between the early translations of the Neoplatonists into Arabic and Ibn Sina, three towering figures of Arab philosophy—al-Kindi, al-Razi, and al-Farabi—attacked this problem within the same general framework.[19]

Discussion centered on the relation of God to the Forms and to the changing material world. These relations were generally conceived not in just a logical way but also in a material way. God (or the One, or the Intellect in some writings) was the furthest from earth. The activity of the One produced the Forms that were closer to earth. The individual soul was still closer to earth and could contemplate both the perfect Forms and the changing earth. The body resided in the here and now of politics, war, evil, and death. For Ibn Sina, just as for the Neoplatonists, the higher and lower realms all reflected God and were proper subjects for philosophic inquiry. It was important to understand the Forms, but it was equally important to know the workings of politics, society, rocks, plants, and the human body.[20]

This Neoplatonist schema generated many questions. How involved was God in the creation of Forms? Where did the soul fit in? What was the role of individuals in the translation of the Forms into the imperfect material world? Did the soul demand proper moral behavior? For Muslims, there were several additional problems: how to reconcile statements in the Quran of God's direct involvement with the world with Plato's separation of God from the world; how to reconcile the God of the Quran who sits upon a throne with Plato's god, which was shapeless and formless; and how to reconcile knowledge based on reason with the revelations of the Quran.

Although it might seem that these philosophical researches were frivolously removed from the real world, they were not. They were the freight and baggage underlying the politics of the day. For example, one solution to the central question—widely discussed at the time—posited that God created everything, down to atoms, at every moment. The implications were enormous. Since God could change his pattern of creation at any time, there was no point in reasoning, studying nature, or trying to understand patterns of human behavior. There was no free will, and man had no particular importance. Another position was that God created everything. Once that process started, everything had a cause and effect and was changeable. Thus, nothing man sensed had permanent patterns. The implications were the same. Man's reason was helpless to understand the world around him. A third position held that man was simply incapable of understanding God, the Forms, and God's relation to earth. Man's task was to accept a transcendent, unknowable God, to obey God's laws, pray, and hope for God's mercy. Each of these philosophical positions promoted "authority" over reason and obedience over questioning. All three of these positions had the support of sects, kings, and armies. All played their part in the religious wars of Ibn Sina's time.

Ibn Sina rejected all of these positions at great personal cost. He wrote letters to fellow scholars across the Asian world and put forth his position in books and treatises. Ibn Sina believed in the power of man's reason, both his capacity to understand the world around him and his ability to understand the relation of man to the Forms and to God. He argued that man's task was to understand patterns in nature and society in what was a comprehensible and rational world and thereby understand the immanence of God in the world. It was man's obligation to explore the most difficult questions in the clearest possible way and use reason and intellect to arrive at the best answer. Mankind as a whole could advance via breakthroughs in understanding.

Even a broad discussion of Ibn Sina's philosophical explorations is not possible here except to note that his writings delved into the entire range of the Neoplatonist schema, from God to the pulsing of human blood. Ibn Sina wrote at least fifty books, which are listed in the "Shorter Bibliography" attached to his autobiography, and possibly more than 100 books, listed in the "Longer Bibliography," attached to other versions of his autobiography. More than two-thirds of the books are on metaphysics, ethics, and logic. Ibn Sina also wrote several studies on specific medical subjects, such as cardiac remedies, colic, and lovesickness, as well as a major medical encyclopedia. He also wrote poetry, several books on astronomical instruments and geometric problems, and one volume on the management of troops.[21]

Ibn Sina's medical books drew on both his experience as a doctor, medicines he saw in use around him, and Greek and Roman knowledge from Galen and Aristotle. His great compendium, the *Canon of Medicine*, began with the physician's task: first to understand the individual patient, then to analyze symptoms and causes of the illness, and only after that to initiate treatment. Analysis began with the four humors: fire, air, earth, and water. In a healthy, balanced person, the humors stayed mainly within their appropriate organs. People differed in the predominant influence of one humor or another—hot, cold, dry, or moist. A trained physician could understand a patient's emotions, for example, by examination of the breath or even the hair color, either of which categorized a patient as mainly hot or cold, moist or dry. Illness could be an imbalance among the humors, blockage of the breath moving through the body, or restriction of energy flows in and around the organs. Treatments were designed to boost or suppress the humors, stimulate certain organs, or change the nature of the breath and its action. Treatment also placed the body in a better alignment with the larger Soul or Spirit of divine nature, which was both within and outside that body.[22] Ibn Sina explains how to strengthen the breath:

> Wine, for instance, restores the breath by nourishing it; pearl and silk (which counteracts disagreeable things) supply the breath with brilliance and luminosity. Embolic myrobalan, amber, and coral concentrate the breath and prevent it from dissipating rapidly: doronicum modifies the temperament of the breath by giving it heat.[23]

One striking feature of Ibn Sina's *Canon* is the sheer number of tropical plants and derivatives that appear in a long section on mixed remedies. Three dozen are easily identified, though there are undoubtedly more. Here Ibn Sina drew on the practical trade network that brought these medicines, and knowledge of how to use them, to the Middle East, Persia, and Central Asia. To the formulations of Galen and Aristotle he added medical knowledge developed and refined in the great Asian world. But Ibn Sina was hardly the first to notice and utilize such tropical medicines, which had been in use for more than a century. Most of those Ibn Sina described appear, for example, in a book of medical remedies from ninth-century Baghdad.[24]

So why was this brilliant philosopher and physician in prison in a castle outside Hamadan? While he wanted a peaceful life to study and write, he was swept into dynastic conflict and politics far beyond his control. His autobiography says simply, "Necessity led me to move to Nasa, from there to Baward, and then to Tus, then to Samaqan, then to Jararm at the extreme limit of Khurasan, then to Jurjan."[25]* Other sources give a fuller picture. Ibn Sina fled the rapidly expanding kingdom of Mahmud of Ghazni, king of Afghanistan. Mahmud sent letters to the kings who harbored Ibn Sina, proclaiming that he wanted the philosopher as an ornament to his court. Ibn Sina knew better. Mahmud's orthodox court would hardly welcome his brand of humanist, rationalist thinking.[26] Ibn Sina suspected that he would likely "ornament" Mahmud's court as a prisoner.

From 1010 to 1017 CE, Ibn Sina and his faithful student, Juzjani, stayed just ahead of the edge of Mahmud's empire, moving from capital to capital, further west and south. With his usual clarity, Ibn Sina understood that he was both an asset and a liability to any court.

> I grew so big that no city could hold me
> But my price went so high every buyer has sold me.[27]

In spite of all the dangers and flights, Ibn Sina continued to write, discuss philosophy, and correspond wherever he went. He stayed at Reyy near present-day Teheran, which held off Mahmud for a number of years, then moved west to Qazvin and finally south to Hamadan, where he became a close companion of and administrator for the ruler Shams al-Dawla, brother of the ruler of Reyy. Ibn Sina accompanied the king on military campaigns. This experience inspired him to write *The Management of Troops*.

---

*Except for Jurjan, these were names of relatively small places even in Ibn Sina's time. Some have disappeared. The reader is referred to the map within the chapter for their approximate locations.

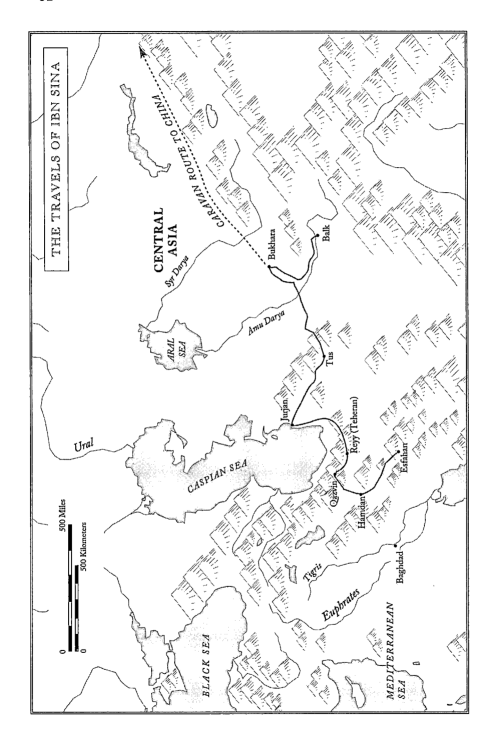

THE TRAVELS OF IBN SINA

CENTRAL ASIA

CARAVAN ROUTE TO CHINA

Syr Darya

ARAL SEA

Amu Darya

Bukhara

Balk

Tus

Jurjan.

Reyy (Teheran)

Ural

CASPIAN SEA

Qazvin

Hamdan

Esfahan

Tigris

Euphrates

Baghdad

BLACK SEA

MEDITERRANEAN SEA

500 Miles

500 Kilometers

0

Even at the friendly court of Shams al-Dawla, Ibn Sina had his enemies. Once, when enemies defeated the king at some distance from the capital, he appointed Ibn Sina to lead civil and military administration. However, the troops mutinied against his leadership.

> They surrounded his house, took him off to prison, ransacked his goods, took everything he owned, and even demanded his execution by the Amir. He refused to execute him, but compromised by banishing him from the state, since he desired to satisfy them.[28]

Ibn Sina escaped the order of banishment by hiding in a friend's house for forty days. The king rescinded the order when he needed medical treatment.

Shams al-Dawla died in 1021 CE, and Ibn Sina doubted that his young heir could protect him from either elements at court who opposed his rationalist thinking or Mahmud. The philosopher opened secret correspondence with the king of Esfahan, 200 miles to the southeast, an archrival of Hamadan. When Ibn Sina's enemies at court revealed this correspondence, the king arrested him for treason and sentenced him to prison. Four months later, Ibn Sina and Juzjani managed to flee to Esfahan disguised as Sufi mendicants.

As Ibn Sina knew, his world was changing. Gone were the days of a unified caliphate, lavish patronage for translations from the Greek, wide-ranging philosophical debate and scientific inquiry. Orthodoxy was the order of the day in many of the caliphate's successor states, not inquiry and philosophical discussion. Finding humanist and rationalist patrons became harder and harder.

Ibn Sina spent the last fifteen years of his life at Esfahan under the patronage of a prince, Ala al-Dawla, whom he liked and openly praised. He stayed through victory and defeat and a celebration of Mahmud's death in 1031 CE. As the autobiography says, he received "numerous robes of honor" for his service and his writings.[29]

It was in Esfahan, accompanied by his brother and Juzjani, that he completed his medical encyclopedia and his most encompassing philosophical work, entitled *Shifa* (Healing—of the Soul), a monumental response to errors he saw in the Baghdad version of Aristotelian thinking. He also wrote *The Book of Hints and Pointers*, a mature statement of his philosophy. Particularly interesting is a book of science Ibn Sina wrote for the prince in simple, elegant Persian rather than the Arabic of the rest of his books. His familiarity with both languages anticipates by two centuries a time when Persian was the recognized language across Central Asia and into India.

We can sense the breadth and connectedness of this intellectual world by the spread of Ibn Sina's ideas after his death in 1037 CE. By 1100 CE, prominent philosophers in Persia were commenting on Ibn Sina's works. Ibn Sina was just as well known to Muslim and Jewish thinkers in Spain, at the western end of the Islamic world. In the early twelfth century, the writings of Moses Maimonides, one of the great Jewish thinkers, showed familiarity with Ibn Sina's writings.

By 1200 CE, Latin translations of Ibn Sina's *Shifa* appeared in Spain, and shortly thereafter, these and other translations reached Italy, generating commentary in philosophical works. One of the translators renamed Ibn Sina "Avicenna," a name more acceptable to Christian Europe than an obviously Muslim one. Many in Europe thought Avicenna was from Spain rather than from the far reaches of Persia.

Ibn Sina's books soon spread north. The writings of an eminent thinker of the time, William of Auvergne, bishop of Paris (1228–1249 CE), show considerable familiarity with Ibn Sina. Two major figures of European medieval philosophy, Albert the

Great, who traveled the roads of present-day France, Belgium, and Germany in the second half of the thirteenth century, and Thomas Aquinas (1225–1274 CE), also knew and commented on portions of Ibn Sina's work. On the continent, Ibn Sina's medical encyclopedia, the *Canon*, became the standard medical book for 400 years. His book on minerals was the main source for European geology until the thirteenth century.

Ibn Sina's writings also circulated in Britain, especially at Oxford and the court of King Henry II. At the time, there were close connections between thinkers in Paris and at Oxford, and several men could have brought Ibn Sina's books from France to England. Later in the thirteenth century, the important British philosopher Roger Bacon (1214–1292 CE) knew of the writings of Ibn Sina.[30] Adelard, one of the early British translators of Arabic texts, wrote this touching recognition of the place of Arabic philosophy:

> Hence it comes about that in the first climes [near the Equator], they say, the home of philosophers has its natural position. For there all seeds spring up spontaneously and the inhabitants always do the right thing and speak the truth.[31]

Through the Middle Ages, Ibn Sina's writings remained important in philosophy. More than twenty nearly complete medieval collections still exist, some in Arabic, more in Latin. His medical encyclopedia was one of the first books printed in Europe (in 1485, only twenty years after the Gutenberg Bible). Even today, Ibn Sina remains a towering creative figure in philosophy. His work has generated more than 2,000 scholarly articles in English, French, Turkish, Arabic, Persian, German, Russian, Italian, and the Scandinavian languages in the last three decades of the twentieth century alone.[32] There is good reason for this scholarly interest.

For anyone believing in God, the questions considered by Ibn Sina are as central today as they were a millennium ago. What is the relation of a perfect God to the complex, changing universe and this manifestly imperfect world? Almost every logical argument in today's discussions of "intelligent design" was analyzed and discussed by Ibn Sina and the Neoplatonists centuries ago.

Ibn Sina's life and writings illustrate the depth of commitment to learning of Muslim elites from Spain to Central Asia. After the fall of Rome, learning moved to the Asian world, where Greek knowledge was translated, commented on, developed, and ultimately surpassed. Ibn Sina, philosopher and physician, was a brilliant member of a whole class of scholars who moved from court to court, participating in scholarly debate, writing and giving practical advice. The broad schema of Neoplatonism allowed debate to cross religions, sects, and individual kingdoms. The inclusiveness of this intellectual world is astonishing and includes books by Jews in Spain, letters from Christians in Baghdad, and commentary by Persians in Central Asia. The range of curiosity was wide at this time and included research on plants, medicines, customs, governance, mathematics, geography, minerals, and the fundamental philosophical questions of human existence.

4

INGOTS AND ARTIFACTS
The Intan Shipwreck, circa 1000 CE

About the time Ibn Sina studied philosophy in Bukhara, roughly 6,000 miles to the southeast a ship sank in the Java Sea. At a historical distance of a thousand years, it is not possible to know for certain what happened. Some hazards can be ruled out. The ship was forty-five miles off the coast and there were no rocks in the vicinity. In fact, the sea floor is flat, featureless clay. The most likely disaster was a sudden storm. Perhaps the ship was aging and it broke rather than flexed. The unknown sailors and merchants were only 150 miles from their port in western Java. They left no memoirs, only their bones and their belongings. Recent research, however, allows us to read the wreck rather like a memoir and follow the goods to their origins, some as far away as the Middle East of Ibn Fadlan and Ibn Sina.[1]*

What sort of a ship was it? It was wood and of Southeast Asian timber and design. The craft was about ninety feet long and twenty-five feet across, perhaps 300 tons, with a V-shaped keel rather than the flat bottom typical of Chinese ships. The ship's most striking feature was that its builders used no iron.

---

*The results of the Intan excavation with much background material and additional research were written first as a doctoral dissertation and later published by Michael Flecker.

They first carved a keel, then carved and stacked curved planks to form the hull. Dowels on the edges joined the stacked planks. On the inside of these planks, the builders left matched projections that were then drilled. Cross members (thwarts) rested on and were lashed to these projections with palm fiber rope. Vertical lashing between these thwarts kept the planks tight. These ships usually had three or four sails and a large rudder about three-quarters back along one side. There were hundreds, if not thousands, of such ships plying the islands and mainland ports of Southeast Asia in the tenth century.[2]* These ships used local materials in a light, elegant design that allowed them to flex and not break in heavy seas.[3]

There was no salvage at the time. Even the most valuable of the cargo lay on the floor of the Java Sea for a thousand years. Torpedo worms ate the exposed timbers. The cargo spilled out, the heaviest staying close and lighter objects drifting further away. The wreck, even though decomposed, protected the underlying clay from erosion by water currents and eventually formed a mound on the seabed.

Birds located the wreck. Local fishermen habitually watch for concentrations of diving birds, because where there are birds, there are fish. Fish concentrate around anything sticking up from the seabed. Indonesian fishermen know that wherever they catch reef fish in the open ocean, there is probably a wreck below, and they know its ceramics and artifacts are worth much more than fish.

---

*More than a dozen wrecks have been alluded to or identified in the last few years. An auction at Sotheby's of more than 30,000 prime Chinese ceramics was based on about fifteen wrecks in Philippine waters. In 2004, a German news weekly reported a Tang dynasty wreck in the same area as the Intan wreck. It contained a large horde of Chinese ceramics, in addition to Chinese gold vessels and panels.

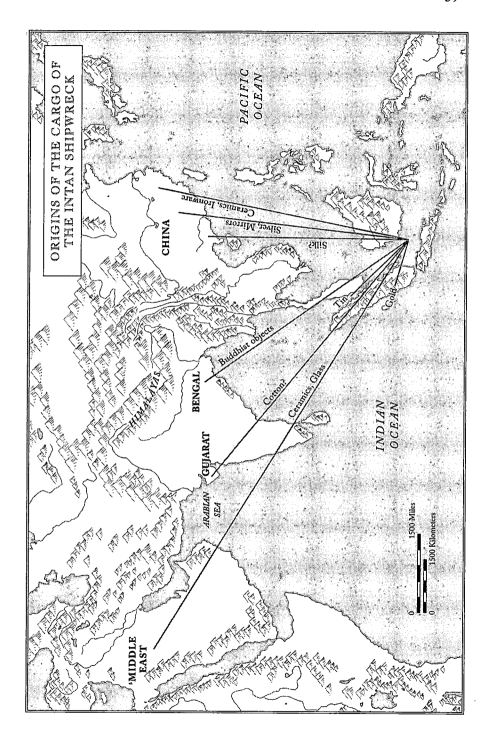

ORIGINS OF THE CARGO OF
THE INTAN SHIPWRECK

PACIFIC OCEAN

CHINA

Ceramics, Ironware

Silver, Mirrors

Silk?

Gold

Tin

HIMALAYAS

Buddhist objects

BENGAL

Cotton?

Ceramics, Glass

GUJARAT

ARABIAN SEA

INDIAN OCEAN

MIDDLE EAST

1500 Miles
1500 Kilometers

In 1996, the appearance of a cache of antique ceramics in Jakarta antique shops alerted government authorities that a wreck had been located. The depth of the wreck, seventy-five feet, and the relatively short dive season slowed looting and allowed time for the navy to arrest the divers. The Indonesian government shipwreck committee sanctioned a local salvage company in partnership with a German excavation team to undertake a full archaeological expedition. The team made a grid of the site and systematically brought up more than 2,700 historically important artifacts.[4]

In the bottom of the ship were thousands of pounds of tin, formed into similar-sized, marked, squat pyramids from the Kedah region of the western Malay Peninsula. In the tenth century, tin was mined much like gold. Tin-bearing ore was ground, probably by hand, and washed. The heavy tin oxide settled to the bottom of sluices. Miners also panned for tin pebbles in rivers. From either source, the tin oxide was then smelted into tin ingots. The tin ingots of the shipwreck were bound for Java, which was devoid of the metal.

Tin was important as a component of bronze, a metal in extraordinarily wide use at the time of the shipwreck. Bronze was cast into statues and religious objects, simple domestic objects such as mortars and door hinges, jewelry, and weapons. Bronze coinage with high tin content was minted in India and the Middle East as well as in Southeast Asia. Arabs in the Middle East knew Kedah well. Abu Dalaf, a geographer, in 940 CE wrote, "In the entire world there does not exist a tin mine as this one in Kalah [Kedah]."[5]

Aboard the ship were many items made in part from tin. Two separate caches of mirrors lay on the sea floor. One, of lower quality, was characteristically Indonesian in design. The other, of higher quality, was of Chinese origin. Tin was an important component of both. The Chinese mirrors were 25 percent tin, alloyed with copper and lead.[6] This mixture yielded a brittle metal that took a lustrous, reflective polish. It is likely that Malay tin was shipped to China in ingot form, melted into this special alloy, and cast into high-value items such as mirrors, some of which were then reexported to Southeast Asia.

There were a number of large kingdoms in tenth-century Southeast Asia. On the mainland, there were four: Pagan was just emerging in upper Burma, Angkor in Cambodia, Champa in southern Vietnam, and, slightly later, Dai Viet in northern Vietnam.[7] These kingdoms were based on intensive rice cultivation and dense population in areas close to the capitals, and were places of sophistication and courtly ritual.[8] In the islands, Srivajaya, a shadowy entity probably based in Sumatra, dominated trade. Current-day scholars are deeply divided about the strength and size of Mataram, a state in central Java, which was apparently based on non-irrigated rice and produced Borobudur, a small mountain faced with carved stone panels on Buddhist themes.[9] On one panel at Borobudur, a sophisticated court woman is pictured using just the sort of mirror found in the shipwreck to apply makeup and comb her hair.[10] She wears elaborate jewelry similar in style to the more than thirty gold rings and numerous gold earrings, pendants, and beads found at the wreck site. Tin and gold were, thus, essential to the expression of courtly culture throughout Southeast Asia in this period.

The Chinese mirrors only hint at the complexity of the tin trade and the importance of bronze in the expression of ideas and culture. The salvage divers brought up a small bronze standing Buddha statue. The style is much like that of eastern India at the time.[11] Bengal has no tin, so it is likely that traders brought Kedah tin to Bengal, where it was alloyed and cast into this image. The ship also held several molds for Buddhist miniature shrines. These tiny shrines, in bronze or terra-cotta, were locally produced in Java for Buddhist worshippers and appear, like the lady with her mirror, in the carved stone panels on Borobudur.

The Buddhist statue found on the shipwreck embodied a very long tradition. By the tenth century, Buddhist and Hindu objects

and ideas had been moving along the trade routes into Southeast
Asia for at least 500 years. A century before Xuanzang's trip to
India, a Chinese pilgrim named Fa Xian went to India in a similar search for sacred books and returned to China on an Indian
ship via the water route through Southeast Asia. If he had explored Myanmar, Indonesia, Thailand, Vietnam, Cambodia, and
Laos, he would have found well-established monasteries, shrines,
and rest houses much like those on the Silk Road and in India.[12]
By the tenth century, the great kingdoms of Southeast Asia had a
distinctly Buddhist or Hindu cast. Like the kings along the Silk
Road, kings in Southeast Asia found the same benefits in Buddhism—a new vision of kingship that transcended ethnic loyalties and chains of institutions that promoted trade.[13]

Just as along the Silk Road and in India, Buddhism melded
with local tradition. For example, though the buildings at Angkor
(c. 900–c. 1200) in Cambodia have many stylistic similarities to
Buddhist buildings in India, their purpose was different. They
were not shrines built over a relic of the Buddha such as a tooth, a
bit of his robe, or a piece of his begging bowl. Most of the large
structures at Angkor were built as monuments to dead kings, usually by the dead king's heir. The inscriptions praise the deceased
king and only tangentially the Buddha. This sort of ancestor worship was characteristic of Southeast Asia but was not practiced in
India, the heartland of Buddhism.[14]

Southeast Asia was connected to all branches of Buddhism at
the time.[15]* The salvage divers brought up a hoard of ritual objects associated with Vajrayana Buddhism: bells and the distinctive spear-shaped scepter. This form of Buddhism was well

---

*Northern Vietnam, for example, had been a province of the Tang Chinese
Empire, and its Buddhist institutions were closely tied to Chinese sects.
Around the time of the shipwreck, Vietnam successfully rebelled from China
and developed its own local variants of Buddhism.

developed in eastern India but was also strong in Southeast Asia in the tenth century, competing for patronage with other more established Buddhist sects. At this time, Vajrayana Buddhism also moved into Tibet. Patrons commissioned images of exactly this sort of scepter on several panels of the ninth-century Buddhist monument of Borobudur in Central Java.[16]

Other artifacts aboard the ship seem connected to forms of ritual from India: a bronze lion's head finial, a bronze lotus bud, and ceremonial spears, vessels, and trays. The most striking of these objects is a set of incised and carved brass hinges and door decoration. The wood has rotted, but the scale of the brass fittings is far too large for a house.[17] The doors were probably intended for a well-endowed religious site on Java, where various Hindu and Buddhist sects were in competition for royal patronage and followers.* This intertwining of religious practice and political rivalry seems similar to the tension between the Islamic sects that both Ibn Fadlan and Ibn Sina experienced.

Lastly, tin appears in the alloy of more than 1,000 pounds of bronze ingots originally in the hold of the ship. All are dome-shaped but lack standard size or weight. The bronze was melted and poured into simple depressions in sand. Archaeological evidence suggests that these ingots were not produced from new ore but were instead made from melted-down bronze objects. Next to these bronze ingots in the hold were a number of broken bronze fragments. Perhaps this scrap had yet to be melted down into ingot form. The bronze was possibly on its way to Java, probably for reworking into a variety of domestic and sacred objects.

---

*Following heavy-handed government suppression of many Buddhist monasteries in China in 841 ce, most sects had fewer contacts with Central Asian, Indian, or Southeast Asian Buddhism. The most successful sects, such as Pure Land and the Chan School, were those that adopted the most local culture.

The true complexity of the tin trade involved the original mining and smelting, but also the gathering of broken objects, melting
them into ingots, shipping the ingots all over the Asian world, and
recasting new objects, perhaps again and again over centuries. The
sheer human labor represented in each pound of bronze made it
valuable enough for recycling to be an economic imperative.[18] In
addition to bronze, scrap brass, an alloy of copper and zinc, was
also well represented in the ship's hold. Recycling and recasting of
objects makes it difficult to know whether any object from that
time was from far away or locally made.

Another metal in ingot form found on the seabed was silver
from China. Inscriptions on some of the silver ingots read, "Sword
office high grade silver of 52 *liang* certified by officer Chen Xun."
Unlike the tin, which was concentrated close to the center of the
wreck site, silver was found in many sectors of the grid, suggesting
that it was not a single hoard; perhaps several traders on board
kept a few ingots.[19] The divers found a scattering of Chinese silver coins and less than a handful of gold coins. Traders apparently
did not need large quantities of Chinese coinage to conduct trade.
Absence of hordes of foreign coin suggests that traders traded in
the currencies of the large and relatively stable local kingdoms.

The iron aboard was also Chinese: ingots, cooking pots, and
spearheads. Only China, at the time, had a highly efficient two-
stage smelting process that successfully competed with local
manufacture in iron-producing areas of Southeast Asia. Archae-
ologists have found Chinese cast-iron cooking pots in most precolonial shipwrecks in Southeast Asia and many sites on land.[20]*
Java, for example, produced no iron for many centuries after the

---

*At the time of the shipwreck, the south of China was the political and eco-
nomic center. The north had been generally ravaged by warfare and competing
warlords. Unification came with the Song Dynasty in the late decades of the
tenth century.

Intan shipwreck. It simply imported what it needed, in spite of some iron ore deposits on the island.[21]

The divers brought up more than 245 glass beads, similar in size and style, and especially interesting because they are "eye" beads. One method of manufacture was to form molten glass into a small globe. While still soft, the glass worker pushed several small drops of another color glass into the surface, creating dots. He finished the bead by pushing a tiny droplet of still another color into the center of each dot. In the wreck horde, the base color of the beads was green, blue, or in a few cases, brown. The dots were white with blue centers. The chemical composition of the glass and the colors suggest an origin in Persia, rather than China or India, the only other glass-manufacturing regions at the time.[22] Glassmaking had been entirely lost in Europe for centuries and would not be recovered for more than two centuries. Eye beads of this type from around the time of the shipwreck have been found in several archaeological sites in Thailand.[23] They are particularly common in archaeological sites near Kedah, the region of the Malay Peninsula associated with tin. These long-traveled eye beads were one of the kinds of objects purchased with the profits from tin and the tin trade.

The bead trade, like the tin trade, was quite complex and already long established at the time of the shipwreck. Beads are among the earliest foreign items found in Southeast Asian archaeological digs. Distinctive carnelian stone beads from India have been excavated at sites that date from before the Common Era.[24] Throughout the millennium before the shipwreck, such beads show up in most digs in capital cities and many more prosaic sites. There is good archaeological evidence that by the tenth century, centers in Southeast Asia were making glass beads, even eye beads. These manufacturing centers, however, seem to have melted imported glass to make beads, but could not make glass. Evidence from the shipwreck supports this viewpoint. Not far from the beads, the divers found many pieces of glassware, only a few still intact. When the archaeological team tried to reassemble the glass vessels, it became clear that most of the glass had been shipped as broken pieces. Perhaps this was raw material for the bead works of Southeast Asia.

The ceramics in the shipwreck suggest the importance of objects of everyday use in this ocean trade. A relatively small number of fine Chinese domestic ceramics were found: jars, pots, and bowls. Their numbers are overwhelmed by 7,000 pieces of coarse domestic ceramics. Most of these were originally in closely nested and bound packages of bowls, ware now known as Yue, from a variety of kilns in the coastal province now known as Zhejiang. An earlier wreck of a vessel in the same trade yielded 60,000 ceramic pieces, mainly simple bowls from the same geographic area.[25]

What of the perishables on board the shipwreck? There were thirty-two large copper cooking cauldrons. Seawater easily corrodes copper, so only the handles remain. Also suggestive of the prosaic nature of much of the cargo was a load of tough oily candlenuts, still intact after 1,000 years in the ocean. Similar nuts are still pressed today for lamp oil.

Unfortunately, there are no traces of two fabrics that other archaeological evidence suggests were probably a valuable part of the cargo. Silk, bound for the elegant courts of Java and Sumatra, was almost certainly on board. In the tenth century, at the time of the shipwreck, silk was the cloth of choice for courtly life from China to Spain. Along with ceramics, silk was the pivotal export of China. Although silk's origin was China, by the time of the shipwreck there were other centers of production. The nascent silk industry of Europe died around 500 CE. In the oasis towns of the Silk Road, Persia, and cities of the Middle East, however, knowledge of the cultivation of silkworms and production of the fiber continued. In spite of this competition, China still dominated much of the silk trade, especially in Southeast Asia. China produced luxury fabrics carefully targeted to a variety of local tastes, climates, and uses. In many panels carved on the Borobudur monument, the fabric's drape suggests silk. In Java at the time of the shipwreck, nobles at court wore silk. When rich commoners bought silk, the king found it necessary to pass laws restricting the use of silk and certain colors of cloth to the nobility.[26] The purpose of these regulations must have been to maintain easily visible distinctions between nobility and commoners and prevent blurring of status distinctions.

Cotton was a major export from India and almost certainly would have been on board. Many documents that date from the period of the shipwreck, from the Middle East to China, concern the trade in Indian cotton. Recently discovered archaeological evidence is more direct, specific, and exciting. Several digs in the garbage dump of the old city of Fustat, south of Cairo, have turned up hundreds of fragments of printed cotton fabric that date as far back as the eleventh century, though many of these pieces are from the subsequent two centuries. The dry climate of the Cairo area has preserved these fragments for nearly 1,000 years. Analysis of the twist pattern of the yarn, the selvage style, and the wood-block printed patterns places their origin in Gujarat on the western coast of India. These small pieces of cotton were from simple, functional clothing, quite different from the use of silk in Indonesia. As with the ceramics industry in the Chinese province of Zhejiang, Gujarat had many specialized centers of cotton cultivation, dyeing, and weaving spread through the countryside.[27]

By the time of the shipwreck, the ports of Gujarat had a long tradition of exporting cotton fabric. Like silk manufacture, cultivation of cotton and its weaving had spread along the trade routes in the Asian world. Tenth-century Java, for example, grew and wove cotton. Much like China, Gujarat became subtly responsive to distant market demand. Researchers have recently located large intact cloths in the islands of Southeast Asia that are virtually exact matches in weave and selvage to small pieces found in Egypt. The only differences are in color and block-printed pattern. Apparently red patterns sold well in Indonesia. Blue, being an inauspicious color in Southeast Asia, never appears. Green patterns sold well in Egypt. Animal patterns were sent to Southeast Asia, but not to Islamic Egypt. These archaeological finds suggest that traders did not simply take Gujarati cotton out to distant lands hoping to sell it. Instead, there was a sophisticated return flow of information from traders to manufacturers on what sold well and what did not. There is even some archaeological evidence that Indonesian patterns were brought back to Gujarat and copied to meet market tastes.[28]

Perhaps the most evocative of the usually perishable artifacts was a rare find of forty-four human bones, from different skeletons. When a small ship sinks, the crew and passengers usually try to escape; the bodies of those who do not are generally carried far away from the site of the wreck by currents. Why didn't these unfortunate people get off the boat as it sank? Perhaps they were just asleep below deck, but equally likely they were slaves, confined below deck. Slavery, in many forms and for many purposes, was common. In Southeast Asia, like the steppe region discussed in Chapters 1 and 2, land was plentiful and people were scarce. Enslaving the conquered or defeated was an ancient, widely practiced way for any tribe or kingdom to increase population. Slavery in Asia encompassed an extraordinary variety of legal and practical relationships between owner and bondsman or bondswoman—in households, businesses, armies, and courts. Like pilgrims, traders, and ambassadors, slaves moved in large numbers throughout the Asian world.

Of other people on board, there are only hints. The divers found many well-used sharpening stones that probably belonged to sailors who passed the time sharpening their swords and knives. In Southeast Asia, as on both coasts of India, there was little distinction between a sailor and a pirate. All were armed, and the difference between pirate and sailor depended on who owned the cargo or the ship. Piracy was such a continuing problem that it even shows up in some of the Southeast Asian inscriptions contemporary to the shipwreck.[29] Some well-used cooking pots, a fishhook, and three mortars and pestles are other traces of the crew.

A few peculiarly shaped bronze finials are characteristic of the kind of staff that certain sects of Buddhist monks carried. As in the time of Xuanzang, monks moved from monastery to monastery in search of learning. Recent research has established a circulation at this time between Bodh Gaya in northern India, Myanmar, and Sri Lanka.[30] Individual gold rings scattered over the whole site and the occasional find of small scales for weighing precious metals suggest the presence of wealthy traders on board. There is no direct evidence of who these traders were, but they were probably of Southeast Asian origin. Possibly there were traders from further afield, because near-contemporary inscriptions from Java mention Cambodians and Burmese in addition to traders from several regions of India.[31] It is likely that both monks and traders were literate, though the only direct evidence is that some of the rings the divers found were seals with script on them.

Where did this vessel take on this extraordinary variety and origin of goods? It seems clear all of the goods were loaded at an entrepôt in Sumatra, probably Palembang. Goods came from all directions to a single port, where traders stored and reassembled them into cargoes bound for many different ports. This was the nature of seaborne trade across all of Asia in this period. In western Southeast Asia, the favored position of the entrepôt shifted in response to developing naval technology. Around 400–600 CE, the time of Xuanzang, sailors apparently did not have the tools or skills to navigate the shoals of the coast of Sumatra or overcome the pirates of the Straits of Malacca. They landed cargo bound for the Indian Ocean at a narrow point of the Malay Peninsula known as the Isthmus of Kra; goods were then shipped overland to the western side.

By the tenth century, navigational technology had developed, causing routes and ports to shift. Aboard the shipwreck, divers found a compass bowl. This technological breakthrough came from China but had spread throughout Southeast Asia and along the shipping lanes to India by this time. The compass consisted of a natural fragment of magnetite, the magnetized form of iron, which was mounted on a small wooden disk. This lightweight apparatus was then floated in a special bowl with incised markings on the inner surface. Like a modern compass, the magnetite always pointed to magnetic north, so sailors could set their course from the incised lines on the bowl. The compass was common enough that there was one aboard the wrecked ship, an otherwise undistinguished cargo carrier.[32] It is likely that the crafting of both sails and rudders had also improved considerably in the centuries before the shipwreck.

In island Southeast Asia, kingdoms competed to develop and control the dominant port, and thereby accrue the wealth from taxes on commerce. At the time of the shipwreck, Srivajaya, on Sumatra, was the most powerful maritime realm and controlled the dominant entrepôt. A raid on Srivajaya by a South Indian empire in 1025 ended its domination of trade. For several centuries, multiple ports competed for the entrepôt trade. Eventually, Melaka emerged as the dominant port of the fourteenth and fifteenth centuries.[33]

Java, the apparent destination of the Intan ship, was well set up to distribute imported items. Although it had no large cities, the towns and villages of Java had regular markets on designated days. Inscriptions from the period list traders, items of trade, and the kinds of taxes paid and suggest that groups of professional traders worked more than one circuit and several towns. In the local economy, agricultural taxes were paid in cash, which suggests that enough local currency circulated for people to buy imports. It was regional traders working these regular markets who brought the Chinese cooking pots and everyday ceramics, both Chinese and Javanese, deep into the interior of the island. Like other places in the Asian world, local entrepreneurs produced cheaper copies of foreign imports. Local Javanese pottery closely followed Chinese styles.[34]

What about balance of payments? Suppose the ship had not gone down; what might it have carried back to the entrepôt and perhaps on to other ports to pay for the ceramics, silk, tin, cotton, and other items? Chinese government documents of the time describe an almost insatiable demand for Southeast Asia's many varieties of aromatic resins, spices, and woods. Government officials were so concerned with the drain of Chinese silver to pay for these forest products that they suggested development of ceramics to sell in Southeast Asia. The large quantity of simple ceramics on board the shipwreck suggests that this policy was not only implemented but also successful.[35]

Aromatics were essential commodities across the Asian world. Such resins and woods were the basis for the incense required in China and India for religious and domestic ceremonies at home, in court, in temples, and in graveyards. Aromatics from Southeast Asia were important components of drugs and medicines of the time, as well as perfumes and oils for the body. They were high-value trade commodities all the way to the Middle East and filled the censers of the churches of Europe. At the shipwreck site, the only suggestion of this important trade was twenty-four small pieces of benzoin, a Southeast Asian tree resin widely used in Buddhist monastic and home ritual.[36] There may have been more, but the ocean current probably carried away these lightweight objects.

The farthest-traveled artifacts of the wreck were a small group of ceramics, all broken. The turquoise blue glaze and the incised patterns were certainly Islamic and could only have come from the Middle East, possibly Ibn Fadlan's Baghdad. It was not only Islamic artifacts that traveled the sea routes to Southeast Asia. In the ninth and tenth centuries, before the shipwreck, Arab sailors reached Southeast Asia and China, leaving several extant accounts. Within two centuries, Muslim traders had established small resident communities in ports along the way and had built mosques. Gradually, Muslim clerics and jurists moved to these ports to serve congregations. Islam found converts along the maritime routes: on the west coast of India, in the ports of Southeast Asia, and in southern China. At the same time, Islam found converts in the caravan cities of Central Asia and in northern China. The pattern by which Islam followed the trade routes seems very similar to the spread of Buddhism.

What do the ingots and artifacts of this tenth-century shipwreck suggest about trade along southern water routes of the great Asian world? The development of large kingdoms with relatively sophisticated urban populations in the Middle East, India, and China produced demand for high-value goods such as gold, ivory, silk, spices, and pearls—the signature items of the "riches of the East."[37]* Equally important on the trade routes were objects of religious faith: texts, statues, paintings, bells, and such. Specialized centers produced these goods. It was often monks who carried them thousands of miles, supporting intellectual and spiritual ties that spanned continents. Prosaic regional goods were, however,

---

*Between 750 and 1100 CE, the population of China doubled and the size of the bureaucratic-literary elite probably kept pace. The demand for luxury goods, many of them foreign, thus grew substantially in this period.

probably more economically valuable than either the luxury trade or the trade in religious objects. Ships carried fish paste, rice, ordinary ceramics, iron pots, and tin.

Luxury, religious, and prosaic goods affected large numbers of people well beyond urban centers and courts. Demand reached deep into the hinterland forests of India and Southeast Asia, the pearl fisheries of Sri Lanka, and the cloth production centers of rural Gujarat. Trade did not follow the contours of religions. Incense from Buddhist and Hindu Southeast Asia moved easily to the Muslim Middle East and Confucian China. Trade goods were integral to the practice of religion. The high-value doors on board the shipwreck suggest the prosperity, strength, and vitality of the Buddhist monastic orders in island Southeast Asia at the time. The Vajrayana Buddhist ritual objects suggest a new sect on the move. Islam was new, and spreading along the very same routes. Finally, trade was essential to the everyday practice of culture in the Asian world. The Chinese needed Southeast Asian incense for their rituals, just as imported gold was used in the courts of Java.

5

PEPPER
AND PARTNERSHIPS
Abraham bin Yiju, 1120–1160 CE

In 1138 CE, Abraham bin Yiju, a Jewish spice trader, waited anxiously at the port in Mangalore for a shipment of cardamom he was expecting from inland. He had paid a large advance and the delay meant serious trouble. If he missed his ship to the Middle East, Abraham bin Yiju's cardamom would reach Aden at the worst possible time, after other merchants had sold their cardamom and glutted the market.[1] Soon, it became clear that the cardamom was not late; it was never going to appear. A local supplier had defrauded Abraham bin Yiju and there would be no cardamom shipment.

Mangalore was typical of ports on the southwest coast of India. The harbor was at the mouth of a river, and a narrow sandbar parallel to the coast protected a shallow lagoon from the Indian Ocean waves. Lush tropical greenery, particularly coconut trees, spread up the hills behind the harbor. The fortified houses of the merchants also served as warehouses and clustered close to the beach.[2]* The port was otherwise unprotected by a wall, guns, or other defenses.[3]*

---

*The first detailed description of Mangalore is by Ibn Battuta, subject of Chapter 6 in this book, in about 1340 ce. Today the harbor is a sleepy fishing port below the city of Mangalore.

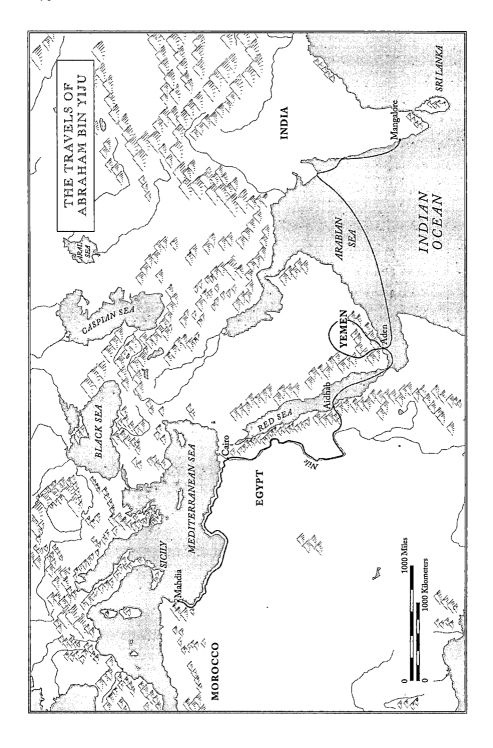

THE TRAVELS OF
ABRAHAM BIN YIJU

A heterogeneous community of Arabs, Gujaratis, Tamils, Jews, and others might have numbered between 2,000 and 3,000.

The profits of this port, like other competing ports up and down the coast, began far inland in the green hills of the Western Ghats. Here grew spices. Black pepper was native to these hills and grew in few other places on earth. The hills also produced cardamom, coriander, ginger, turmeric, cloves, nutmeg, and more than a dozen other spices. These nuts and plants, some gathered, some cultivated, were used in lotions for the body, in medicines, and as flavors for food.

Abraham knew that he had a ready market for his spices if only he could get them to market. Many were in regular use in the Asian world. The cardamom would have gone to Cairo and from there would have found markets throughout the Middle East, North Africa, Spain, and Europe. For example, a thirteenth-century recipe for meat patties *(isfiriyâ)* from Muslim Spain uses several Indian spices:

> Take some red meat and pound as before. Put it in some water and add some sour dough dissolved with as much egg as the meat will take, and salt, pepper, saffron, cumin, and coriander seed, and knead it all together. Then put a pan with fresh oil on the fire, and when the oil has boiled, add a spoon of *isfiriya* and pour it in the frying pan carefully so that it forms thin cakes. Then make a sauce for it.[4]

Elegant cuisine was part of the courtly style in the Baghdad of Ibn Fadlan, just as it was in the regional capitals he visited in the tenth century.

For Abraham and the other traders at Mangalore, black pepper was the core of the spice trade, both as flavoring and medicine. A

---

*The general pattern of unfortified ports was the norm on the Indian coast and throughout Southeast Asia.

thousand years before bin Yiju, traders on the Malabar Coast had shipped pepper to Rome. It was pepper, 3,000 pounds of it, that Alaric demanded and obtained as part of the ransom of Rome in 408 CE.[5] Recall that Ibn Fadlan used pepper to bribe his way to his destination in the eastern steppe.

More important than their use as flavorings for food, tropical plants constituted staple medicines. As noted in Chapter 3, Ibn Sina's *The Canon of Medicine,* which was the standard medical encyclopedia across much of Asia and Europe, listed more than thirty-six tropical plants in its remedies. Kings across Asia used and stockpiled spices and tried to grow them. Most attempts failed because the plants grew only in specific tropical microclimates.

A good deal is known about Abraham bin Yiju, his missing cardamom, and the details of his life, because miraculously, more than seventy letters and accounts to or from the trader survive, as well as many letters from his circle of business friends. How the letters survived from the twelfth century to today is a fascinating story. In the twelfth century, many Jews believed (as many Jews believe today) that if any form of the word *God* appeared on a written document, it was sacrilege to destroy it. What to do with old, worn, or unneeded documents that happened to have "God's blessings upon you" or "Praise God . . . " in them? One solution was a room, called a *geniza,* generally built next to a synagogue. It had no door and no windows, merely a ladder leading up to a large slot in one wall. Members of the congregation wishing to dispose of unneeded documents that contained some form of the word *God* threw them through the slot.[6] Bin Yiju's daughter apparently belonged to a synagogue near Cairo with just such a geniza. She disposed of her father's correspondence and some business records through the slot in the wall.

For centuries, members of the congregation filled this geniza with tens of thousands of documents. They remained intact because of Egypt's dry climate. In the late nineteenth century, scholars became aware of this uncataloged and untouched treasure. Several libraries bought large lots of the papers, by the pound, and the collection was dispersed. Termed the "Cairo Geniza" papers (hereafter, "Geniza"), the horde is now divided between Russia, England, and the United States. In the first half of the twentieth century, scholars worked mainly on versions of religious texts that were found in the collection.[7]

Since the 1950s, scholars have turned to the many letters and accounts, patiently cross-referencing traders, relatives, shipowners, and ships. The work goes slowly, however, because crucial family collections are now scattered between England, Russia, and the United States. An additional problem is the language and script. The Geniza documents are in Arabic but written in the Hebrew script. Few scholars today know the medieval form of both languages well enough to read the Arabic and script. Still, the documents already catalogued and translated yield a rich picture of the trading life in the twelfth century.

Abraham bin Yiju, whose father was a rabbi, was from a family that lived in the port of Mahdia in Tunisia.[8] There are no documents that fix his date of birth, but 1098–1102 CE seems likely. Mention of two brothers and a sister appear in Abraham bin Yiju's letters, but there may have been other siblings. None of the three brothers opted to become rabbis. Instead, all chose trade. There seems to have been no conflict over this decision because his father, with crucial letters of introduction, helped Abraham in his youthful hopes. His brothers, Yusuf and Mubashshir, and sister, Berakha, married and stayed in Tunisia. These three families remained in the Mediterranean Sea trade.

Sometime around 1120 CE, Abraham set out on the road to fortune. He first traveled the caravan route from Tunisia to Cairo, carrying precious letters of introduction from his father to prominent Jewish traders of the city, probably fellow Tunisians.[9] Through them, he found a junior position and perhaps small partnerships.

Within a few years, he was off again, this time to Aden at the mouth of the Red Sea. Again, he carried letters of introduction to prominent Jewish traders.

Abraham bin Yiju's travels suggest the larger politics of the Mediterranean at the time. Turkish forces in Anatolia wiped out the Peasant Crusade in 1096 CE, shortly before bin Yiju's birth. During his childhood in Tunisia, the First Crusade fought its way through Palestine and took Jerusalem. In his teenage years, crusaders established kingdoms over much of the coast of what is today Israel and Lebanon. The holy wars hardened attitudes toward non-Christians in Europe and made it difficult for Jews to work there. Anti-Semitism was rampant. None of Abraham's family considered moving to Europe to work.[10] Waves of warfare in Syria (current-day Israel, Palestine, Jordan, Syria, and Lebanon) made trade to that region not impossible but difficult. The situation on the Mediterranean was equally grim. Venice and Genoa attacked fleets from Cairo and other Muslim ports and fought for the seaborne trade. The attention of many Jewish traders, both refugees from Europe and those resident around the Mediterranean, turned away from these conflicts and toward other opportunities, especially the spice trade from India.[11]

In Aden, the major crossroads for the India trade to Egypt, Abraham formed a relationship with Madmun ibn Bandar, the most powerful and influential trader in Aden at the time.[12]* Like his father before him, Madmun was known as the *nagid*, the "trustee" of the Jewish Aden traders. Much is known of this Madmun because his many letters, like Abraham's, were preserved in the Cairo Geniza, apparently the home synagogue of

*Apprenticing in a firm that resulted in long-term ties with the head of the firm was a common pattern even in an earlier period.

Madmun's children. His network of correspondence extended from India to Spain.[13]

Madmun, like others in the India trade, formed long-lasting trading partnerships among the many communities at Aden. Typical was his venture of 1230 CE with a Muslim. "After asking God, the exalted, for guidance, I constructed a boat in Aden and sent goods in it to [Sri Lanka] in partnership with the illustrious Sheikh Bilal."[14] He also regularly sent Sri Lankan goods from Aden to Egypt. "On my own account I sent with him sixty bags of Seli [Sri Lankan] cinnamon, each bag weighing 100 pounds. Kindly take delivery of one-half of this and sell it for your servant [Madmun] for any price God, the exalted, may apportion."[15]

Madmun's letters confirm that the basic divisions of the maritime trade remained as they had a century and a half earlier at the time of the Southeast Asian shipwreck, discussed in Chapter 4. The Mediterranean sector included Cairo and the Mediterranean. The Indian Ocean sector included the Red Sea, the Persian Gulf, the west coast of India, and Sri Lanka. The Bay of Bengal sector included the east coast of India, Bengal, Myanmar, and the west Malay coast. The Java Sea sector included the rest of Southeast Asia and coastal China. Ports vied with one another to dominate trans-shipping between sectors. In the early twelfth century, the main port of Sri Lanka dominated the trade between the Indian Ocean and the Bay of Bengal sectors. Even the rich and powerful Madmun did not send ships beyond Sri Lanka.[16]*

Although ships at the time were capable of longer voyages, division of the maritime trade into sections probably reduced the

---

*There were at least one or two fabulously wealthy traders who traded all the way to China. One was a Muslim named Ramisht. He made so much profit on one voyage that he personally provided a Chinese silk covering for the entire Ka'aba at Mecca.

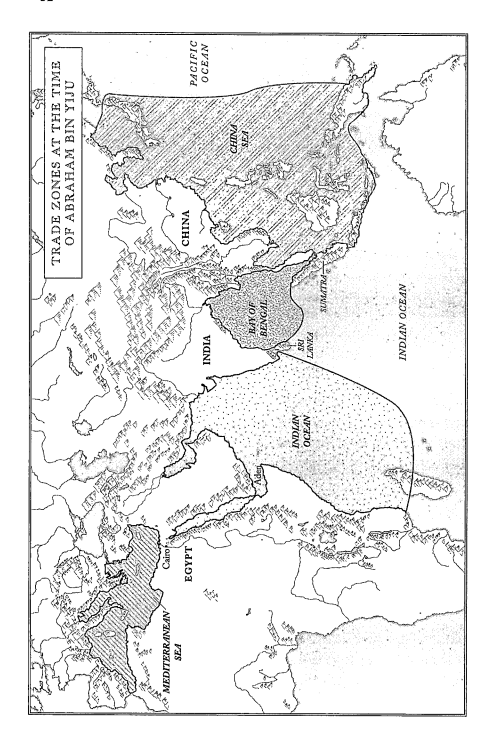

TRADE ZONES AT THE TIME
OF ABRAHAM BIN YIJU

risk of loss at sea. Captains and pilots needed to know the monsoon winds, the dangerous shallows, and navigational features of only one-fourth of the route. Even trading along a single section was a dangerous business. Any ship could encounter bad weather; many were lost to pirates.

Merchants found any way they could to reduce risk. Partnerships, such as that between Madmun and Sheik Bilal, spread the risk, as did many other business activities mentioned in letters of the Cairo Geniza. Traders sent their goods via reputable shipowners and divided their goods among several ships in case of loss at sea. They divided their goods among several recipients, sealed the packages while in transit, and wrote the name of the consignee on the outside. Traders dealt in a variety of goods to cover unknown fluctuations in distant markets. They wrote ahead to a consignee and described in detail what was coming.[17] All of these risk-reducing measures depended on trust between a merchant, his partners, shipowners, and distant consignees.

Long-distance trade thus relied on trust and a reputable name. Unlike later times, in the twelfth century there were no brokerage firms to receive goods from overseas, warehouse them until a consignee arrived, and charge a fee to anyone needing the services. Traders were wholly dependent on the goodwill of friends and business contacts. In distant places, friends received the goods, sold them, kept accounts, bought specified items to send back for a profit, but took no commission for this work.[18] Their frequent and detailed letters make clear the importance of trusting colleagues to do business.

> I am asking you now, relying on your favors, when this shipment, God willing, safely arrives, to kindly take delivery of one-half of the aforementioned bales and sell them for me for whatever God will apportion and grant. After the price is agreed upon, turn

everything into gold and silver—nothing else—and distribute it among various merchants, coreligionists, or others, if they are known as reliable, and send it on.[19]*

In Aden sometime in the 1120s, Madmun ibn Bandar took young Abraham bin Yiju into his firm and put him to work keeping accounts in his warehouse. After an apprenticeship of about three years, Madmun encouraged the young trader to move to Mangalore on the southwest coast of India to enter the spice trade. Through senior-junior partnerships, Madmun almost certainly provided working capital. Madmun wrote soon after Abraham bin Yiju arrived in Mangalore that a shipment of areca nuts and other goods had arrived safely, suggesting both that the capital that Madmun had provided was making money and that Abraham was doing good work. His letters are full of timely market advice from Aden, news of other traders, political events, and tips on trading. The partnership rarely shipped anything to Mangalore except cash to buy spices.[20]** In later centuries, there was an active trade to India in horses, slaves, weapons, and ceramics, but it apparently had not yet begun in the twelfth century.

Most goods from India bound for Cairo went first to Aden and then to a bleak port called Aidhab on the western shore of the Red Sea. Three years into his work at Mangalore, Abraham consigned a large shipment for transport through Aidhab but apparently refused to pay the man who unloaded his goods and reloaded them onto a caravan headed west for the Nile. The complaint went to Madmun, Abraham's senior patron.

---

*The ideal was to keep capital moving. A trader relied on the consignee to dispose of his goods and buy goods that could, in turn, be sold at a profit in the trader's home city.

**Ordinary silk was used throughout the Asian and the Islamic world as currency. Its price was steady and its demand regular for centuries.

Every time I see him [Abraham bin Yiju] he crosses words with me so that I have become frightened of him. Each time he says to me, Go, get out, perish . . . a hundred times. . . . [I ask] of you Exalted Presence [Madmun] to act in this matter until you reclaim the [money]. . . . Stand by me in this and strengthen your heart, Oh my Lord and master . . . and extend your help to me.[21]

Power clearly lay with Madmun, the senior partner in Aden. A letter from him a few months after the complaint tersely noted a debit of 300 dinars from Abraham bin Yiju's account to settle this affair.

Personal gifts reinforced the mutual obligations of a trader's network of relationships. A consignment worth thousands of dinars from Madmun to Abraham included items that he particularly liked, goods that he termed, with the self-effacing tone of so many of these letters, "items of no importance or value," such as white sugar, "a bottle, in a tight basket, entirely filled with raisins," eye makeup for his wife, and several pounds of kosher cheese from Europe.[22]

Trade partners also regularly sent household goods at the request of traders, especially luxurious metropolitan items that reflected the lifestyle of larger cities. Madmun ordered from Egypt good quality "bowls, dishes, and cups," also "good rose marmalade, such as one prepares for the household."[23] Abraham bin Yiju, from Mangalore, ordered a leather table cover of the type used for playing chess, which was popular all over the Asian world. For Abraham, the most precious of these goods was quality paper, not available in India.[24] In spite of paper's appearance along the Silk Road more than three centuries earlier, little paper was produced in India and scribes in India continued to write on palm leaf fronds.

Relationships were also reinforced by explicit greetings to the trader's partners, as well as to close relatives. The following quote is from a Geniza document written between 1080 and 1100 CE.

Accept my best greetings, and likewise my best greetings to the elder Abu 'l-Hasan [a trading partner]; if he needs anything, let him write to me about it. Greetings to Rachael [his wife] and her mother and to everyone in the house . . . and to the son of my paternal aunt, and his sons. And Peace. And may your life be prolonged.[25]

Trade and family were closely related. Madmun, the trustee of the Jewish traders at Aden, married the sister of his counterpart, the trustee of Cairo.

In 1138 CE, Abraham agonized over his missing cardamom because it threatened the trust that was at the core of all his trade relationships. He had used money from his Aden partners as an advance for the spice shipment. In all of Abraham's surviving correspondence, this is the only occasion that caused him to call down God's curse on another man.

The kardar [manager], may God curse him, owed . . . 14 mithqals [of gold] for two bahars of cardamom [about 600 pounds]. He did not deliver the cardamom, so I bought . . . two bahars from Fandrina [a port further down the coast] as a substitute, for 17 mithqals.[26]

When the cardamom dealer defaulted, Abraham's partners in Aden made clear their displeasure. The formal language of their business letters does not mask that this bad debt was to be Abraham's, not the partnership's.

Only by resolving this misuse of the Aden money could Abraham bin Yiju restore the trust that made the spice trade possible. This displeasure of the Aden partners would have stopped his credit and his news of the markets in Aden and Cairo. Although the partners recognized that Abraham bin Yiju had himself been defrauded, they had no means, legal or otherwise, to recover a bad debt in Mangalore. All they could do to help was to threaten the reputation of the dealer who defaulted. Madmun's cousin suggested this sort of censure in a letter to Abraham.

Perhaps you should threaten him that here in Aden we censure anyone that owes us something and does not fulfill his commitments. Maybe he will be afraid of the censure. If he does not pay, we shall issue an official letter of censure and send it to him, so that he will become aware of his crime.[27]

The partnership survived the cardamom incident, though the documents are silent on the outcome. It is most likely that Abraham quietly paid the partnership its losses.

The cardamom incident suggests the degree of freedom of trade along the water routes of the Asian world. In comparison, in Abraham bin Yiju's time, in Europe guilds set the times and places of trade, controlled prices and quality of goods, and specified who could trade by means of apprenticeships and member rolls. Kings chartered guilds and thus had a hand in trade and quality of goods. Abraham was subject to none of these limitations. He simply searched for replacement cardamom where he could and paid what he had to. Documents mention the "trustee" of Jewish traders for several Malabar ports, but this official had little actual power to control ventures or venues of trade. Further east in the wider Asian world, there is some evidence of guilds in South India, but none indigenous to Southeast Asia.[28]* China, however, was more restrictive. Boats and cargoes had to register with port officials. Port officials tended to treat the various types of traders—Arabs, Jews, Tamils—as members of an ad hoc guild.

---

*The inscriptional evidence for "guilds" in South India at this time is actually quite vague. Some sort of corporate entity of traders made donations to temples, but there is no direct evidence of how these traders worked together, whether they set prices, controlled quality, or even collaborated on shipping.

Bad behavior by one member was referred to the group. Illegal activity, however, meant Chinese courts and quite possibly prison.

Abraham bin Yiju's letters demonstrate little involvement in local politics and his letters never mention connections to the local Hindu court. There were twelve Hindu kingdoms along the coast, each consisting of a portion of the narrow coastal plain and a port, such as Mangalore, Beypore, Cochin, Cannore, and Kalikut. The main source of income for these kings was taxes on trade, and the wealthier ones financed trading ships. The king's troops provided some protection from pirates while ships were in port. A few of these local kings kept war fleets to attack pirates and force merchant fleets to come to their port and pay duty.

One of the Geniza letters of Madmun's family reveals the constant dangers of piracy. Madmun was married to a sister of Judah bin Joseph ha-Kohen, a prominent trader in Cairo. Pirates seized the ship on which Judah sailed with his goods and cast ashore the traders and crew on the Gujarat coast. The letter is from a ship captain who plied the India-Cairo trade and was married to another of the unfortunate trader's sisters. The captain pleaded with Judah to join him in Mangalore.

> In all circumstances, please come quickly to Mangalore and do not tarry, for I am waiting here in Mangalore and—if God wills—we shall embark on our way home as soon as possible. It is better for you to travel from Mangalore with me than to travel in the ships of foreign people. Please remember that there is no difference between us, my money is yours, it is just the same. . . .
>
> And again, my lord, do not take to heart what you have lost; you have, praise be to God, plenty to have recourse to and be compensated with. When life is saved, nothing else matters.[29]

It perhaps needs to be emphasized that in his years at Mangalore, Abraham bin Yiju, though a Jew, neither lived nor worked in an isolated enclave of Jews. The Mangalore trading society included local Hindus, resident Gujaratis, and local Muslims, in addition to periodic arrivals of Middle East Muslims. Abraham bin Yiju regularly formed partnerships with Gujaratis and local Hindus that were essential to the development of his business. These sorts of partnerships were entirely common for Jewish traders and appear all through the Geniza documents. Ties of trust also went inland to the dealers and suppliers of spices. The documents show that Abraham never traveled inland to the sources of the spices. He relied on local Hindus for cultivation, processing, assembling, and transport to Mangalore.

A decade after Abraham bin Yiju arrived in Mangalore, he was wealthier, more his own man, and no longer just an agent for Madmun. His letters imply a comfortable lifestyle. He imported for his family's use special soap and sugar from Egypt, pots and sieves from Aden, mats from Somalia, and a carpet from Gujarat. His regular clothing included imported robes from Egypt and fine turbans and shawls.[30]

The letters often refer to Abraham's male slave, Bamah. He was no ordinary household slave. Rather, he was a trusted agent in all of Abraham's business dealings. He carried money to and from Aden and purchased goods. He was so well known that Madmun explicitly greeted him in letters, along with Abraham's son, Surur.[31] In general in the Geniza documents, the acquisition of a male slave was cause for celebration. Like Bamah, many other slaves traveled the trade routes for their masters.[32] This is another aspect of the complex bondage relations found in Asia at the time.

During this period, Abraham bin Yiju saw an opportunity among the skilled metalworkers of the Malabar Coast. In a port somewhat south of his home, he set up a metal works, but not for new production. From his widespread contacts, he received damaged and worn vessels: lamps, dishes, and such from as far away as Spain. With them came instructions for the new items:

I am sending you a broken ewer and a deep wash basin weighing seven pounds less a quarter. Please make me a ewer of the same measure from its bronze as it is good bronze. The weight of the ewer should be five pounds exactly.[33]

Here is an example in the twelfth century of international outsourcing and recycling that carried goods thousands of miles and relied on skilled Indian metalworkers.

Abraham bin Yiju was a successful trader and a rich man, but he had family problems. In his first Mangalore years, he had formed a liaison with a local slave woman named Ashu. Such liaisons were common among traders at the time. The problem arose because Abraham bought her, freed her, married her, and lived with her during his entire two decades in Mangalore. The formal deed of manumission, found among the Geniza documents, indicates that on October 17, 1132, Abraham bin Yiju publicly granted freedom to a slave girl named Ashu. With her, he had a son named Surur and a daughter.[34]

His partners, however, disapproved and signaled their disapproval by their silence toward Ashu. The standard greeting between business partners wished peace on everyone in the household, by name. Although the letters from Madmun and other partners greeted and wished peace to Abraham bin Yiju's children, they never mentioned his wife. Such a wife would not have been welcome in Aden or Cairo. The real problem, however, was the children. Jewish law assigned children the religion of the mother, but Ashu was not a Jew. Abraham bin Yiju hoped, prayed, and worked so that his daughter might, perhaps with a substantial dowry, find a husband in the Jewish community.

Who was this Ashu? There is only one ambiguous reference in all of Abraham bin Yiju's letters that identifies Ashu as a Nair. This stray bit of information creates more questions than answers. Nairs, along with Brahmins, were generally the elite of Malabar. Nairs were, first and foremost, warriors. A few Nair families headed local kingdoms, but many families were tenant overseers of lands held by Brahmins or temples. Some Nair girls married "up" into Brahmin families. Later evidence suggests that some Nairs were merely menial servants of Brahmin families and relatively poor.

Among the Nairs, a common form of marriage was known as *sambandham*. A woman married several men either at the same time or serially. The family consisted of a woman and her children, regardless of who the father was. Property was inherited in the female line, passing from mother to eldest daughter. Typically, several generations of women and their children lived in a large, fortified house. The only resident male of the female-centered household was the woman's brother. The Nair social structure is one in which women were relatively powerful.[35]

It thus seems unlikely that a woman from this wealthy and powerful caste would be a slave and need manumission. Modern anthropological research has collected stories of "olden times," and from this research comes a strong suggestion of how a Nair woman could become a slave. After a puberty ceremony, a Nair woman could receive men from outside her lineage as long as they were of higher status. If, however, she formed a liaison with a Nair of lower status or a man of lower caste, the family was deeply shamed. They could only remove this blot on their honor by killing the woman or giving her as a slave to the king. The king regularly sold these slaves to foreign merchants. This is likely Ashu's story.[36]*

Abraham bin Yiju's family troubles only hint at the complexity of the relationship between foreign traders and local women.

---

*The Geniza documents have several cases of marriage between a freed slave woman and her former owner.

Foreign traders along the water routes of the Asian world rarely if ever brought their wives. Some married before they left their homeland and later formed more or less temporary liaisons with local women during their travels, fathering two sets of children.[37] Another pattern was common to Chinese traders in Southeast Asia. They married local women and became integrated into the local society. Their children were seen as full members of the local community. A third pattern was for the trader to marry a local woman and convert her to his own faith. From these unions grew small local communities. This pattern is embedded, for example, in the tradition of the Navayaths, a Muslim community located in several towns and cities along the Malabar Coast. They trace their origin to Muslim traders of Arab descent who married and converted local women. Communities like the Navayaths probably grew through conversion of both men and women.[38]

In the twelfth century, there were many Jewish communities—mixtures of traders and local converts—across Africa and Asia. A community of several thousand Jews centered in Cochin, another of the Malabar ports. Abraham bin Yiju chose not to marry a Jewish girl from this community but instead opted for the Nair girl. The documents are silent on why. Perhaps he did not like local Jewish women because they were from Syria rather than his homeland of Tunisia. Perhaps he did not find someone he liked among the daughters of his business partners. Perhaps he fell hopelessly in love with Ashu.

Abraham bin Yiju's later years were profoundly sad as family troubles mounted. His siblings, based in Tunisia, were swept up in the crusader wars of the Mediterranean.[39] Christian fleets and armies attacked many non-Christian targets, including Jews living among Muslims. Abraham wrote to his business partners in Cairo:

> I heard what happened on the coastland of [Tunisia]. No letter, however, from which I could learn who died and who remained

alive, has arrived. By God, write exact details and send your letters with reliable people to soothe my mind.[40]

In 1148 CE, the Christian forces of Roger II of Sicily attacked Tunisia for a second time, kidnapped Abraham bin Yiju's whole family, and took them to Sicily. No documents give any clear indication of why the family was kidnapped. Roger II may have wanted the family as traders. Trade ceased during the war, however, and the family was soon destitute, "reduced to a single loaf of bread."[41] Abraham intended, if he could, to save his brothers and his sister and wrote to them, desperately hoping that the letter would reach Sicily and that they would join him in Cairo:

> By God, and again by God, do not delay your coming here, take this dirhem, which I have earned, and buy and sell with it, if God will—saying less about this would have been enough. Would I try to write all that is in my heart, no letter could contain it and no epistle could comprise it.[42]

With his children, Abraham bin Yiju left Mangalore and Ashu forever in 1149 CE, and from that point in his life there are fewer Geniza letters. He met his unmarried brother, but it was a bitter encounter. The scoundrel defrauded Abraham bin Yiju of 1,000 silver dirhams and disappeared.[43] Abraham's siblings survived the war but remained in poverty in western Sicily. His son died shortly after his return to Aden, and he wrote, "I know not what to describe of it." Madmun, his mentor and senior partner, died two years later. Abraham wrote to his elder brother, "I am sick at heart."[44]

After his return from Mangalore, Abraham did not stay long in Aden. Following a trip to Egypt, he moved to southern Yemen and took up trade there. In the twelfth century, Yemen had a more benign climate than now and there were many relatively prosperous villages and towns. For centuries Jews had migrated south from the Middle East into Yemen. They lived in Muslim towns and worked in crafts, producing decorative leather, metalwork, or jewelry.[45] With some capital from his Mangalore years and experience in metals, perhaps Abraham exported metalwork. With his Aden connections, perhaps he imported sugar or even staples like rice. One can only speculate; the letters are silent.

Abraham bin Yiju left his daughter in Aden in the household of one of his partners. Three years later, he received a marriage proposal from the son of this Syrian Jewish partner, but he rejected it, hoping for a marriage within his Tunisian Jewish community. The solution was close to home. Abraham bin Yiju proposed marriage between his daughter and a son of his elder brother. This arrangement had benefits for all. It kept Abraham bin Yiju's wealth in the family, provided for the impoverished relatives, and placed the daughter in the community Abraham bin Yiju wanted. Both of Abraham bin Yiju's nephews soon arrived from Sicily, and Abraham bin Yiju married his daughter to his elder brother's son as planned.

The last trace of Abraham bin Yiju is an account written in Egypt in an unsteady hand. After all the sorrows and disappointments, he apparently chose to live out his life close to his daughter rather than return to his wife, Ashu, in Mangalore.[46]

Although Abraham is but one life, his story reveals a great deal about trade in the great Asian world in the twelfth century. The business model was based on trust and reputation, family and personal ties. A career began with a father recommending his son as an apprentice to a senior trader. The young man learned the yearly pattern of trade, made connections, and gained knowledge of markets. Risk was spread by dealing in a variety of commodities, using several ships, and forming partnerships. The system of trust depended on a relatively reliable mail system. Abraham bin Yiju's letters reached Aden and Egypt in a month and contained specific instructions, gossip, general news, and personal affection. Within communities there was some degree of self-regulation via, for example, Jewish courts or Sharia courts, but partnerships were often conducted across religious lines. It seems that the possible loss of reputation was a stronger bar to shady practices than legal repercussions. There is no evidence of a guild structure that regulated prices and terms of trade for members, as there was in Europe at the time.[47]

Traders competed continuously with each other, and over the longer term, the rise and fall of various groups of traders is also evident. The strong position of Jews in the Malabar spice trade of Abraham bin Yiju's time lasted only another two centuries, until about 1300 CE. Thereafter, a cartel of substantial Muslim traders from Egypt largely muscled them out—but not entirely. A congregation of several thousand Jews continued in the spice trade in Cochin until they migrated to Israel between 1970 and 2000. Their restored synagogue retains its beautiful original blue-and-white Chinese floor tiles, reminders of the waterborne trade—from China to Spain—that sustained the Jews on the Malabar Coast.

6

NOBLES AND NOTABLES
Ibn Battuta, 1325–1356 CE

In 1332 CE, the public area of the sultan of Delhi's palace consisted of several courtyards and a vast hall called Hazar Ustan, or Thousand Pillars. A contemporary observer noted, "The pillars are of painted wood and support a wooden roof, most exquisitely carved. The Sultan sits on a raised seat standing on a dais carpeted in white, with a large cushion behind him and two others as arm-rests on his left and right."[1] A hundred guards flanked him on the left and a hundred on the right. Immediately in front were his highest officials and behind them, more than a hundred nobles—all in silk robes. On each side was a row of judges and Muslim teachers of the city. Further back in the hall were distant relatives of the sultan, lower-ranked nobles, and military leaders.

In this setting was one whose special duty was to introduce foreigners to the sultan, Muhammad Tughluq. On this day, recently arrived Ibn Battuta from Morocco and his companions came forward with their gifts for the sultan. In the subsequent decade, Ibn Battuta saw this ceremony many times and described it in his memoirs:

> The Sultan then addresses him in person with the greatest courtesy and bids him welcome. If he is a person who is worthy of honor, the Sultan takes him by the hand or embraces him, and

asks for some portion of his present. It is then placed before him, and if it consists in weapons or fabrics he turns it this way and that with his hand and expresses his approval of it, to set the donor at ease and encourage him by his gracious reception. He gives him a robe of honour and assigns him a sum of money . . . proportional to the donor's merits.[2]

It was a good day for both Ibn Battuta and his companions. The sultan treated them as notables and suggested suitable employment in his government. Seeing the sultan was a high-stakes gamble for Ibn Battuta. From a moneylender, he had borrowed the money for the very expensive gifts he offered the sultan and had no way to repay the loan other than the employment he sought. Still, funding of expensive presents to the sultan prior to employment was a familiar form of risk capital for traders.[3] Thousands of men had preceded Ibn Battuta in just such a venture.

Not yet thirty, Ibn Battuta arrived in Delhi with an entourage of nearly forty people, including male and female slaves, servants, and traveling companions. He had more than 1,000 horses, chests of fine clothes, and a string of pack animals, including camels. He had come a long way in the seven years since leaving Morocco in June 1325 CE, passionately sure that he wanted to go on pilgrimage to Mecca.

I set out alone, having neither fellow-traveller in whose companion-ship I might find cheer, nor caravan whose party I might join. . . . Both [my parents] and I were afflicted with sorrow at this separa-tion. My age at the time was twenty-two years.[4]

Ibn Battuta set out from Morocco, fearful of the journey and in danger. Nomad bands from central Morocco and Tunisia regu-larly attacked caravans and even cities. Racked by fever, he joined a small group that traveled fast to Tunis, a haven of safety. No one greeted him when they arrived.

> I felt so sad at heart on account of my loneliness that I could not restrain the tears that started and wept bitterly. But one of the pilgrims, realizing the cause of my distress, came up to me with a greeting of friendly welcome, and continued to comfort me with friendly talk.[5]

At Tunis he joined a large caravan of pilgrims organized by one Abu Yaqub al-Susa. The coast still suffered from raids by Christian armies, as it had in the time of Abraham bin Yiju two centuries earlier. Ibn Battuta quotes a poet of the time: "How many there are who wander distraught on the land, despoiled of their goods! How many who spend their nights at sea bewailing captivity and perdition!"[6] The raids ruined the economy of Tunisia, and bandits were everywhere. Fortunately, the caravan included a troop of archers and was accompanied part of the way by more than 100 horsemen.

From the first, Ibn Battuta seems to have had a talent for self-promotion. Within the caravan, he managed to gain the position of *qazi,* judge and adviser on Islamic law, to a large group of Moroccan pilgrims.[7] Ibn Battuta came from a family of judges. He had the education and native intelligence to take advantage of such opportunities. He was not rich, but he clearly was also not poor. He contracted to marry the daughter of a magistrate from Tunis who was on the pilgrimage. She joined him at Tarabulus as the caravan continued along the North African coast. In what is now eastern Libya, he "became involved in a dispute with my father-in-law which made it necessary for me to separate from his daughter." He married again almost immediately, this time to the daughter of a scholar from Fez, presumably also in the caravan. When his bride joined him in coastal Egypt, Ibn Battuta "gave a wedding feast, at which I detained the caravan for a whole day, and entertained them all."[8] Neither this wife nor any children by her appear in the remainder of Ibn Battuta's four-volume autobiography. Perhaps she was another youthful folly sent back with her father to Fez.

Cairo, almost two centuries after Abraham bin Yiju settled there in his old age, remained a great metropolis.

> It is said that in Cairo there are twelve thousand water-carriers who transport water on camels, and thirty thousand hirers of mules and donkeys, and that on its Nile there are thirty-six thousand vessels belonging to the Sultan and his subjects, which sail upstream to Upper Egypt and downstream to Alexandria and Damietta, laden with goods and commodities of all kinds. On the bank of the Nile opposite Cairo is the place known as al-Rawda which is a pleasure park and promenade, containing many beautiful gardens. The people of Cairo are fond of pleasure and amusement. I once witnessed a fete there. . . . All the merchants decorated their bazaars and had rich stuffs, ornaments and silken fabrics hung up in their shops for several days.[9]

On horseback, Ibn Battuta explored the towns of the Nile Delta and then, by boat, went up the Nile expecting to cross the Red Sea and complete the hajj to Mecca. It was a leisurely trip that ended at Aidhab, the same dusty port where two centuries earlier, Abraham bin Yiju disputed a 300-dirham bill from his consignee. Unfortunately, the ruling family of the Aidhab region was at war with the forces of the sultan of Cairo and regularly sank ships on the Red Sea. Ibn Battuta could go no farther and returned to Cairo by boat.

Ibn Battuta already knew that he loved travel at least as much as religious learning. During the Cairo trip, he evolved a pattern that accommodated both passions. On arrival at a city or town, he

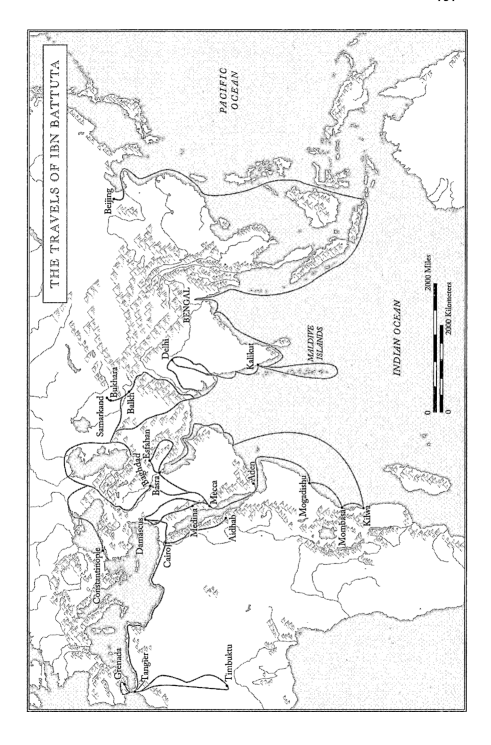

THE TRAVELS OF IBN BATTUTA

PACIFIC
OCEAN

Beijing

BENGAL

Delhi

Kalikut

MALDIVE
ISLANDS

INDIAN OCEAN

Bukhara

Samarkand

Balkh

Esfahan

Baghdad

Basra

Mecca

Medina

Aidhab

Aden

Mogadishu

Mombasa

Kilwa

Damascus

Constantinople

Cairo

Grenada

Tangier

Timbuktu

2000 Miles

2000 Kilometers

0

sought out the well-known clerics and spent a few hours with them. He did not stay for months, as was common among those traveling in search of learning, but instead just listened to a sermon or had a conversation. Typical was this encounter in El Bahnasa on the Nile: "Amongst those I met there was the learned Qadi, Sharaf al-Din, a noble-minded and worthy man, and I met there also the pious sheikh Abu Bakr al-Ajmani, with whom I lodged and who made me his guest."[10] Ibn Battuta particularly treasured a set of letters of introduction that he received from a well-known cleric in another town along the Nile. As he traveled, Ibn Battuta kept his eyes open and learned much more than religious doctrine. He met as many of the local elite as possible, gathered stories of those he could not meet, and used everything for later stories and parables. He observed local shrines, architecture, products, and customs. Of the towns along the Nile, he noted that Bush was "the chief center of the Egyptian linen industry and exported it hence to all parts of Egypt and to Africa."[11] El Bahnasa was the center of the woolen industry. The town of Mallawi had eleven functioning sugar presses. "It is one of their customs never to hinder an indigent person from going into any pressing shed, so that a poor man will come with a piece of warm bread and throw it into the vat in which sugar is being cooked, and then pick it out again soaked with sugar and go off with it."[12]

After he left the caravan in Alexandria, Ibn Battuta entered the network of donation-supported hostels and colleges (madrassas) found in all Muslim cities of the time. For the Muslim elite, facilitating trade, travel, and pilgrimage were pious, prestigious, and sometimes profitable acts. On the Nile trip, Ibn Battuta praised the hostel of Sahib Taj al-Din ibn Hanna south of Cairo that was endowed to provide food for all learned travelers. And at Halab in Syria, Ibn Battuta described the mosque as "one of the most splendid buildings of its kind, its pulpit inlaid with ivory and ebony," and the adjacent school corresponded to it "in beauty of plan and execution."[13]

This system of elite-supported institutions for travel and study sounds strangely like the Buddhist monasteries visited by Xuanzang (Chapter 1) and may have been modeled on them. This Islamic system of supporting those traveling in search of learning originated in Central Asia, the very area where Buddhist monasteries had supported travelers in similar pursuits for 1,000 years.[14] Like Buddhism, Islam demanded personal travel for spiritual development and learning.[15*] Serious study meant not just the one-time pilgrimage to Mecca required of every Muslim but learning from a variety of scholars and clerics in different cities and schools.

After Ibn Battuta made his return trip down the Nile, he stayed only one night in Cairo and then set off for Mecca by the northern land route along the coast of present-day Egypt, Israel, and Lebanon. On the way to Damascus, Ibn Battuta visited Akko, Sour, Saida, and Trablousi, as well as the inland holy city of Jerusalem. By 1325 CE, Turkish forces had retaken all the crusader states along this coast, though many places were still in ruins from the wars between Christian and Muslim armies. Ibn Battuta noted the manufactures and the specialties of the towns he passed through.

> We traveled next to the town of [Beirut]. It is a small place, but with fine bazaars, and its congregational mosque is of striking beauty. Fruit and iron are exported from there to Egypt.[16]

In his memoir, Ibn Battuta wrote eight pages describing the architectural wonder of the main mosque in Damascus, but he

---

*At the time, there was a parallel tradition of Jewish scholars wandering in search of knowledge.

wrote many more pages on the people of his developing network: imams of the mosques, and teachers and notables.

> There are in this mosque several "circles of instruction" in the various branches of [sacred] knowledge, while the traditionalists read the books of Tradition, sitting in high chairs, and the Qur'an-readers recite in pleasing voices morning and evening. It contains also a number of teachers of the Book of God, each of whom leans his back upon one of the pillars of the mosque, dictating to the children and making them recite. . . .[17]

In Damascus, Ibn Battuta attended lectures on *Sahih* (a book of the sayings of the Prophet written around 850 CE) and proudly noted that he had been formally licensed to teach the book.

If the dates given in the memoir are accurate, Ibn Battuta was a busy man. He was in Damascus for only twenty-two days. Besides listening to lectures, he married again. This union produced a son, mentioned in a chance reference later in the memoir. Ibn Battuta left his pregnant wife in Damascus and joined a huge pilgrim caravan bound for the holy cities of Medina and Mecca.

From the time of Muhammad, one pilgrimage to Mecca, known as the hajj, was an obligation of every Muslim. By the fourteenth century, the hajj was a fully organized tour. The journey from Damascus started with well-provisioned rest stops and sites associated with Muhammad but included several days of desert travel and some danger from heat and sandstorms. The caravan stopped for four days at the city of Medina, where Muhammad had preached and lived. Days were spent in visiting holy places.

> We halted at the Gate of Peace to pay our respects, and prayed at the noble Garden between the tomb [of the Apostle] and the noble pulpit. We kissed the fragment that remains of the palm-

trunk that whimpered for the Apostle of God . . . which is now attached to a pillar. . . .[18]

Nights were spent in the city's mosques, listening to recitations of the Quran by candlelight. Incidentally, Ibn Battuta's memoir tells us that the ceiling and the gilded trim of the main mosque at Medina were made of teak, undoubtedly from the Malabar Coast of India.[19]

After seven days of travel with nights in well-watered villages, the caravan arrived at Mecca. Each day of the hajj had specified sacred activities in and around Mecca. Ibn Battuta and his traveling companions first went to the Ka'aba, the holiest site in Mecca.

> We made around it the [sevenfold] circuit of arrival and kissed the holy Stone; we performed a prayer of two bowings at the Maqam Ibrahim and clung to the curtains of the Ka'ba . . . between the door and the Black Stone, where prayers are answered; we drank the waters of Zamzam. . . .[20]

Including his side trips and excursions, it had taken Ibn Battuta sixteen months to reach Mecca.

On the hajj, Ibn Battuta met men from all over the Muslim world. He met one Mansard bin Shaik of Medina, whom he encountered twice subsequently, once in Syria and once in Bukhara. Another fellow pilgrim was named Ali bin Hujr al-Umawi. He came from Granada in Spain, and later Ibn Battuta offered him patronage in Delhi.[21]

Most pilgrims returned to their lives after the week of holy activities at Mecca. Ibn Battuta, however, stayed, studied, and made contacts. During his year in Mecca, Ibn Battuta met the man who served as senior ambassador from the sultan of Delhi and regularly traveled between India and Mecca with donations from the Indian court. He also came across a fellow jurist who was a friend of his father's from his hometown of Tauja, Morocco. These men were only a sample of tens of thousands who traveled far and found employment as teachers, judges, clerics, administrators, and soldiers.

By the twelfth century there existed—for the first time—a world largely without borders for educated men. These were men who felt at home everywhere within the vast region stretching from Spain to the port cities of China. Their skills in law and religious teaching were equally applicable and equally desired across the whole Muslim world. Many cities attracted these learned travelers, and they made their mark in their adopted homes. Ibn Battuta found that the "controller of the judicial administration" at Medina was from Tunis, where his own family was still well connected. Scholars at Medina included men from Fez, Cairo, and Granada. Among the notable scholars of Damascus, one was from Seville, Spain, and another from Marrakech, Morocco. At Mashed, in southern Iraq, the religious and political head of the city had a brother who lived and worked in Spain and Gibraltar. Near Shiraz, in Persia, Ibn Battuta visited the hostel of Shaikh Abu Iasq, which received money from patrons ranging all the way from the Middle East to coastal India to China.[22]

Overall, the number of people who traveled to find employment was large, probably in the hundreds of thousands. At the time, there were more than a dozen Islamic capital cities and hundreds of smaller cities, any of which might offer employment.

After a year in Mecca, Ibn Battuta joined the caravans again, consumed by the desire to "travel through the earth."[23] Soon he spent less time in donation-supported hostels and more in the company of kings and nobles. He learned courtly manners and customs. He left Baghdad and joined the entourage of Sultan Abu Sa'id, in order "to see the ceremonial observed by the king of al'-'Iraq in his journeying and encamping."[24] This sultan was a fifth-generation descendant of the empire builder Genghis Khan (1162–1222) and ruled much of the Middle East at the time. Ibn

Battuta watched the daily ceremony of this great Mongol king: the processions, musicians, soldiers, banners, and ritual of attendance by the nobles, noting their "handsome robes."

He accompanied the king for almost two weeks, next traveled with one of the king's nobles for ten days, then returned to the king's camp, "where the amir told the sultan about me and introduced me into his presence." Ibn Battuta was ready with a stock of stories when "he asked me about my country." Ibn Battuta came away from the interview with "a robe and a horse" and "provisions and mounts" for the whole of his next trip.[25] More important, the sultan wrote letters of introduction to the governors of Baghdad and two other cities on his route.

Ibn Battuta was suitably impressed by the ceremony of the camp and train of Sultan Abu Sa'id.

> [On setting out] each of the amirs comes up with his troops, his drums and his standards, and halts in a position that has been assigned . . . either on the left wing or the right wing. When they all have taken up their positions and their rank are set in perfect order, the king mounts, and the drums, trumpets, and fifes are sounded for departure.[26]

Over the next six years, Ibn Battuta honed his courtly skills in Persia, Constantinople, the Crimea, the Caucasus, and what is today Uzbekistan and Afghanistan. He learned how to make a courtly greeting from horseback and on foot. He knew the names and origins of the fine fabrics of the day, which is evident in such descriptions as "a tunic of Egyptian linen, a furred mantle of Jerusalem stuff" and "kamkha, which are silken fabrics manufactured at Baghdad, Tabriz, Nishapur, and in China."[27]* Kingly

---

*Ibn Battuta was upset when he met a king who was not attired in suitably luxurious clothes.

presents of fine robes made him suitable for court. He found that whether he attended a Muslim, a Christian, or an animist court, courtly presents were similar across much of Asia. Such gifts included silk robes, jeweled weapons, gold, horses, and slaves. In a year or two, Ibn Battuta became something of a connoisseur of horses—and slave girls. He received and gave several slave girls as gifts and bought several more on his circuitous route from Damascus to Delhi. The purchase of concubines for personal pleasure was yet another aspect of slavery in the Asian world. The memoir names none of these girls, nor do they seem important to Ibn Battuta's entourage. He described his traveling companions with more detail and more affection.

In Damascus, across Turkey and Persia, and in India, Ibn Battuta occasionally stayed in guesthouses of various Sufi orders. Who were these Sufis? Unlike other Muslims, Sufis believed (and still believe) that there is the possibility of direct, ecstatic experience of God and that their special practices—dancing, chanting, poetry, numerology, and mystical allusions—put one in a state where this might happen. This direct experience of God was more important than daily prayers and Sharia law, though most Sufis follow convention as a practical requirement of living in a Muslim world.

In the beginning, Sufi centers consisted of single teachers who took up residence at an existing guesthouse or caravan stop and instructed men who came and went in search of knowledge. A few of these teachers developed their own methods, which students maintained and developed after the teacher's death. Soon, in various cities where students settled, one found places where the method was taught, including rest houses for students. As might be expected, a bureaucracy quickly developed to support these institutions, giving rise to endowments, officials, initiation, rules and regulations, and ties to a designated center of the teachings. Many offices became hereditary and their endowments became government sponsored.[28] Well before Ibn Battuta's time, Sunni branches of Islam accepted Sufi teachings as complementary (rather than threatening) to their own more legalistic approach. By the fourteenth century, some Sufi orders were more than five centuries old, but new ones occasionally appeared around a particularly dynamic teacher.

Some Sufi orders developed only regionally, such as in North Africa or Persia, but many spread to cities of the Middle East, Central Asia, and into India. The Sufi orders really came into their own after the fall of Baghdad to the Mongols in 1258 CE. The caliphate, the central institution of Islam, was no more. Seventy-five years later, when Ibn Battuta traveled, chains of Sufi rest houses and schools were the strongest remaining large-scale institutions of Islam.

In his travels, Ibn Battuta soon discovered that like kingly presents, much of kingly ceremony was shared across Asia, and even beyond. In several courts he noticed the custom of presenting and chewing betel leaf and areca nut. Although the leaf and nut were native to India, the custom had spread through all courts of the Middle East and the east coast of Africa. Betel from the hand of a king was one of the highest honors a man could receive.[29] Ibn Battuta would later encounter the kingly presentation of betel throughout Southeast Asia and southern China. Kings were also surrounded by a host of common royal symbols, such as the parasol, the fly-whisk standard, and drums. These symbols and ceremonies transcended language, region, and religion.

Soon, Ibn Battuta was able to tell one king about another, information kings eagerly sought. Every king was surrounded by rivals, factions, squabbling nobles, and a necessary but unwieldy bureaucracy. Kings particularly wanted to know about the successful strategies, symbols, and ceremonies in other courts. Ibn Battuta's conversations with kings were, in a sense, the management seminars of the day; Ibn Battuta was a particularly successful management consultant. The king of Yemen asked Ibn Battuta about the sultan of Morocco, "and about the king of Egypt, the king of al'-'Iraq, and the king of Lurs, and I answered all the questions that he asked concerning them. His vazier [the vizier, a high executive officer] was in his presence, and the king commanded him to treat me honourably and arranged for my lodging."[30]

Ibn Battuta also traveled to the east coast of Africa and found it connected by religion, trade, and custom to the Asian world. The main cities were Mogadishu, Kilwa, Mombasa, and Zanzibar and all were Muslim. Their economies were based on the export, mainly to India, of slaves, gold, and horses and the import of Indian cotton. African ivory was imported all over the Asian world. Ibn Battuta found the people exotic, but the customs were familiar. The sultan of Mogadishu presented betel and robes of honor to Ibn Battuta, about which he noted:

> [T]heirs consist of a silk wrapper which one ties around his waist in place of drawers (for they have no acquaintance with these), a tunic of Egyptian linen with an embroidered border, a furred mantle of Jerusalem stuff, and an Egyptian turban with an embroidered edge.[31]

Deep in Central Asia, Ibn Battuta met a sultan and received similar gifts for his stories of kings.

> After I had saluted him he sat down and asked me about myself and my journey, and whom I had met of sultans; I answered all of his questions and after a short stay he went away and sent a horse with a saddle and a robe.[32]

It was from kings that Ibn Battuta gradually acquired horses, robes, gold, and furs. His entourage grew as he received slaves and accepted companions into his train.

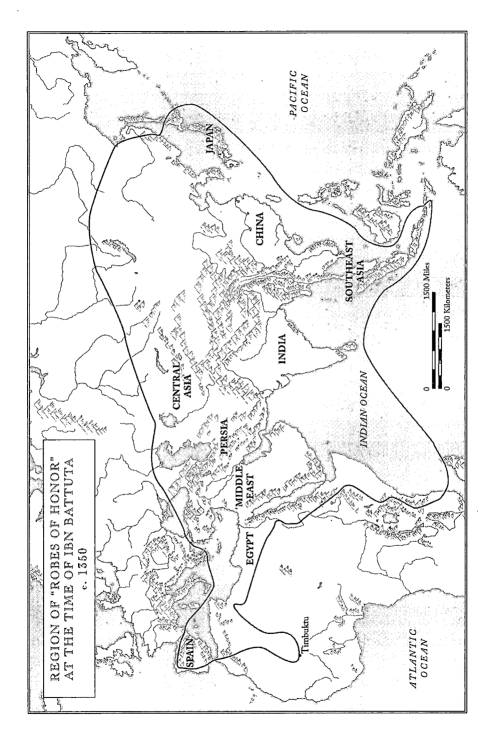

REGION OF "ROBES OF HONOR"
AT THE TIME OF IBN BATTUTA
c. 1350

JAPAN

CHINA

SOUTHEAST
ASIA

CENTRAL
ASIA

INDIA

PERSIA

MIDDLE
EAST

EGYPT

SPAIN

Timbuktu

PACIFIC
OCEAN

INDIAN OCEAN

ATLANTIC
OCEAN

1500 Miles

1500 Kilometers

0

0

This, then, is the background to Ibn Battuta's entourage of forty people, over 1,000 horses, and chests of fine robes with which he arrived at Delhi. He had become a "notable," had stories to tell, ceremonies to describe, and reasonable expectations of kingly patronage. Ibn Battuta was, at that point, 55,000 silver dirhams in debt for his gifts to the sultan, but the gamble was beginning to look like it would pay off. In India, like many other soldiers, clerics, and judges, Ibn Battuta found more than patronage—he found employment. The sultan of Delhi hired him as one of the chief judges of the city, and he filled this well-paid post through famine, factional conflict, and court intrigue for nine years.[33] Ibn Battuta could fill this post, though he knew no local language, because Sharia law across the whole of the Muslim world was essentially the same.[34] His duties to the king also included management of the benevolent endowment of a prominent mausoleum.[35]

In 1341 CE, Ibn Battuta left Delhi for the last time on a diplomatic mission to transport robes, gold, slaves, and other presents from the sultan of Delhi to the emperor of China. The entourage traveled southwest across India to Cambay, a major port in Gujarat. Ibn Battuta reports that the presents were lost in a shipwreck. Present-day scholars doubt the authenticity of this mission; there is no corroborating evidence in Chinese or Indian records.

Ibn Battuta, for whatever reasons, could not return to Delhi and traveled down the west coast of India to Malabar. At Cambay, Honar (near Mumbai), Kalikut, and Cochin, he found branches of Sufi orders. Local followers and their lay supporters used these cities as a trading network to the Middle East. At Mangalore, he found the spice trade just as active as it was two centuries earlier in the time of Abraham bin Yiju (Chapter 5). "This is the town at which most of the merchants from Fars [Persia] and al-Yaman [Yemen] disembark, and pepper and ginger are exceedingly abundant there."[36] Unlike Abraham's letters, Ibn Battuta's memoir

A nineteenth century engraving of the Bamian Buddhas showing the sculptures largely intact. They were destroyed by the Taliban in 2001 CE. (Alexander Burnes, *Travels into Bokhara* [London: J. Murray, 1834])

Ruins of the Nalanda Monastery, where Xuanzang studied and copied texts for five years. The small cubicles are monks' cells. (American Institute of Indian Studies. AR 020800)

A wall painting of Xuanzang's expedition on its way back to China. Note the white elephant carrying precious Buddhist texts. Located on Xuanzang's route in a cave at the Dunhuang Buddhist monastery, the scene was probably painted within a century after his travels. (The Lo Collection)

The Wild Goose pagoda built in 652 CE at Changan to house the texts Xuanzang brought from India. (Asian Studies Program, University of Florida)

An elegant glass flask of the type used by courtiers like Ibn Fadlan in sophisticated Baghdad. (*Glass Flask*, Eastern Mediterranean, 11th Century, Los Angeles County Museum M.45.3.44)

Tomb of Ismaili Samani in Bukhara. It was standing when Ibn Fadlan's entourage passed in 921, when Ibn Sina studied there in the eleventh century, when Ibn Battuta visited in the fourteenth century, and when Babur attacked the city in the fifteenth century. (Photograph by Galen F. Frysinger. USED BY PERMISSION.)

A bathhouse typical of Muslim cities across the Asian world, from Spain to India. Ibn Fadlan appreciated one in the far reaches of the Caucasus, even though his beard froze from cold on his way back to his lodgings. (*Firdawsi Receiving Wages in a Bathhouse, Page from a Manuscript of the Shahnama [Book of Kings*, c. 1550–1575], Los Angeles County Museum M.73.5.591)

The Astrolabe of Ahmad and Muhammad of Esfahan, dated 984 CE. The earliest extant astrolabe, it calculates the position of thirty-seven stars for five different latitudes. Similar tenth century instruments are known from the Middle East and Spain and are typical of the flowering of scientific knowledge in the ninth through the thirteenth century Asian world. (The Museum of Science, Oxford)

Written on paper, rather than older materials, this beautiful Koran is from the time of Ibn Sina. Paper had arrived from China only two centuries earlier, but local inventors quickly discovered that pounded linen made a superior product—smooth, supple, and tough. (*Koran transcribed by Ibn al-Banwab,* Baghdad, 1000–1001 Chester Beatty Library, Dublin Is. 1431, fol. 286r)

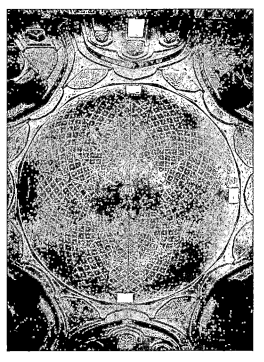

The dome of the Ardestan mosque
built around the time Ibn Sina was in
Hamdan, some 400 miles to the west.
The dome is a superb early example
of complex brickwork, probably based
on the new mathematics developing
in the region. (Photograph by
Sussan Babaie, University of Michigan.)

Ibn Sina's *Cannon* of medical information, in Latin translation, was
one of the most widely used books in medieval Europe. This version
was printed in 1476 CE, less than thirty years after the Guttenberg
Bible. Note the handwritten commentary in the margins by a
medieval doctor. (University of Michigan. Special Collections. Incum.129)

The decorated reverse side of a Chinese mirror which lay on the floor of the Java Sea for a thousand years before being excavated from the Intan Shipwreck. (Photo by Michael Flecker.)

Buddhist Tantric ritual object known as a Vajra (handheld lightning bolt). This and other Buddhist objects were on the way from Bengal to Java and formed part of the Intan shipwreck horde. (Photo by Michael Flecker.)

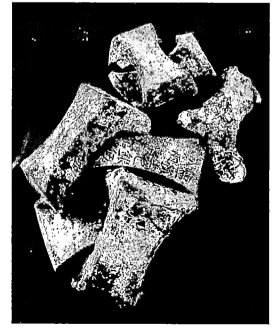

Chinese silver ingots from the Intan shipwreck. Note the Chinese characters on the central piece, which give a government guarantee of the purity of the silver. (Photo by Michael Flecker.)

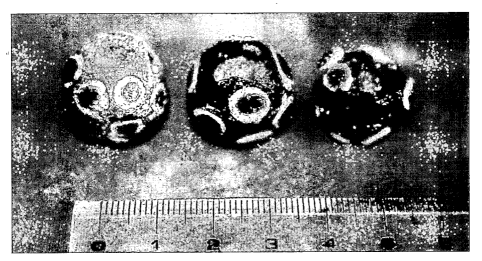

"Eye" beads, manufactured in the Middle East and found in the Intan shipwreck off the Java Coast. Such beads have been highly valued in Southeast Asia for more than two thousand years and were routinely traded for incense, spices, and medicines. (Photo by Michael Flecker.)

Printed cotton from Gujarat on the west coast of India that was excavated near the Cairo Geniza. Similar patterns have been found in Indonesia, suggesting a sophisticated production and trade in these textiles that spanned Asia. The earliest examples date from the twelfth century, the time of Abraham bin Yiju. (Kelsey Museum, University of Michigan. Gujarat Floral, Chevron and Vine, Acc#000.09.4139. Ann Arbor.)

As in the time of Abraham bin Yiju, freshly picked pepper berries must dry in the sun for three days before packing and shipping. (Photo by the author.)

Solomon Schechter working on the Cairo Geniza documents, shortly after the opening of the repository in the 1890s. Of the more than 140,000 documents found, some 40,000 concern everyday life and trade. (Cambridge University Library T-S 10 J10.15 Recto.)

Chess was played throughout the Asian world, by the famous, such as Ghenghis Khan, and the ordinary, such as Abraham bin Yiju, the pepper trader. (*The Vizier Buzurghmihr Showing the Game of Chess to King Khusraw Anushirwan, Page from a Manuscript of the Shahnama [Book of Kings]* Turkey, 1525–1575. Los Angeles County Museum M.73.5.586)

In this letter, Abraham bin Yiju desperately inquired about the circumstances of his brothers and sisters who had been kidnapped from Tunisia to Christian Sicily. Against all odds, the letter did reach them and Abraham eventually rescued them all. (Taylor-Schechter Collection, Cambridge University Library)

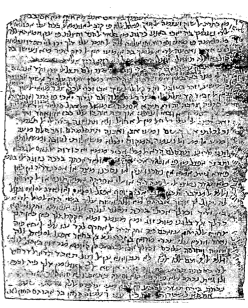

Blue and white Chinese floor tiles of the Jewish Synagogue, Cochin, India. (Photo by the author.)

Teaching institutions like this were found in cities from Spain to China. Ibn Sina studied in a similar school in Bukhara and Ibn Battuta stayed in such schools during his early travels in the Middle East.

(A School Scene, Painting from a Manuscript of Yusuf and Zulaykh Jami. Iran, Bukhara, 1564–1565/A.H. 972. Los Angeles County Museum M.73.5.440)

Among the millions upon millions of Muslims who have made the required pilgrimage to Mecca were Ibn Battuta in the fourteenth century and Ma Huan in the seventeenth century. ("The Mount of Mercy." *Aramco* Photo Archive, 3511 005.JPG)

The complex tiles of the Blue Mosque of Tabriz in northwest Iran. The mosque was built in 1455, about a century and a half after Ibn Battuta passed through the city. He was impressed with the trading wealth, some of which was channeled into this mosque. Subsequent earthquakes have destroyed much of the building. (Photograph by Sussan Babaie, University of Michigan.)

A pillared hall of public audience at Delhi, perhaps similar to the scene Ibn Battuta encountered. This image is from three centuries later. (Los Angeles County Museum AC 1992.94.1)

Cutaway drawing of a mid-twelfth century Chinese seagoing ship almost 100 feet long and 30 feet wide. Based on a wreck discovered in Houzhou, Fujian province. Note the bulkheads that divided the hold. Ibn Battuta saw larger versions of this type of ship on the Malabar Coast of India in the fourteenth century. (Sketch by the author of a model in the Overseas Communication Museum, Quanzhou, PRC)

A performance scroll, in the tradition seen by Ma Huan and Tomé Pires. This version is modern, from Rajasthan, India. At night, the performer holds up a lamp to illuminate a scene on the scroll and tells the corresponding portion of the story. (Collection of the author.)

Battle scene showing the use of the reverse-curve bow from horseback. Note that the rider controls his horse with his knees. *(Battle Scene and Text (recto), Text (verso), Folio from a Shahnama (Book of Kings),* Delhi, early seventeenth century. Los Angeles County Museum AC1993.187.1)

Babur returns at night from a drinking party. As Babur notes in his memoirs, some of his parties became so riotous that they had to be broken up and the comrades sent to their tents. *(Illustrated Version of the Baburnama commissioned by Akbar, 1589.* Sackler Gallery S 1986.231)

Babur attacks India in 1507. Note the horse armor and the bow and arrows, typical of steppe armies of the time. *(Folio from a Baburnama.* Delhi, circa 1589–1590. Los Angeles County Museum M.91.348.1)

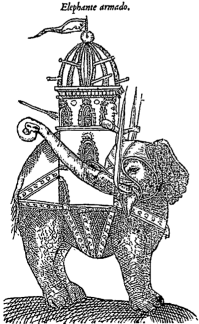

Elephante armado.

War elephants typical of armies Babur fought in India in the sixteenth century. A Portuguese artist who may not have actually seen such elephants drew this picture. (Christobal Acosta, Tractado de las drogas y medidinas de las Indias oreintalis [Venetia: F. Ziletti, 1585]. In the Rare Book Collection of the Museums Collection, University of Michigan.)

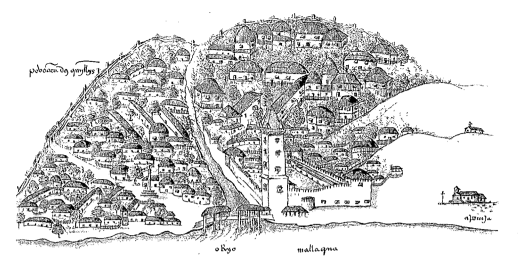

View of Malacca, three decades after Tomé Pires lived there. Note the new fort and watchtower and the movable wall across the river's mouth. (Gaspar Correa, *Lendes da India* [Lisboa: Da Academia real das sciencias, 1858–66])

View of a Malabar fort built soon after the arrival of the Portuguese. The gunports show that cannon was already in use by non-European powers. (Photograph by author.)

Ginger, as illustrated in the first Portuguese treatise on tropical medicines, 1530. (Gaspar Correa, *Lendes da India* [Lisboa: Da Academia real das sciencias, 1858–66] University of Michigan.)

Aden, as drawn by a Portuguese artist in the 1550s. Abraham bin Yiju apprenticed there as a trader in the thirteenth century and Ma Huan visited the port in the fifteenth century. The straight-masted vessels are Portuguese of the type Tomé Pires sailed into Guangzhou harbor. The lanteen-rigged craft are vessels from the region. (Christobal Acosta, Tractado de las drogas y medidinas de las Indias orientalis [Venetia: F. Ziletti, 1585]. In the Rare Book Collection of the Museums Collection, University of Michigan.)

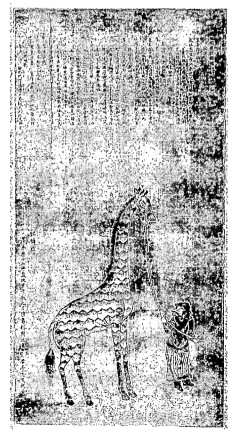

A giraffe brought by one of the Zeng He expeditions from Africa to Beijing in the early fifteenth century. (Yongle Period Scroll. c. 1414. Philadelphia Museum of Art. 1977-42-1.)

includes a delightfully accurate description of the cultivation of pepper.

> The pepper-trees resemble grape-vines; they are planted along-
> side coco-palms and climb up them in the same way that vines
> climb, except that they have no shoots, that is to say tendrils, like
> those of vines. . . . It produces fruit in small clusters, the grains of
> which resemble the grains of the date palm when they are green.
> In the autumn they gather the grains and spread them on mats in
> the sun, just as is done with grapes in order to obtain raisins; they
> keep turning them until they are thoroughly dried and become
> black, and then sell them to the merchants. . . . I have seen pepper
> grains in the city of Kalikut being poured out for measuring by
> the bushel, like millet in our country.[37]

Ibn Battuta continued his journeys in the Maldive Islands and Sri Lanka. He claims that he went east from Sri Lanka through Southeast Asia and to the imperial court of China. Modern schol-ars doubt this trip. The geography is garbled and there are suspi-ciously few stories of the personal encounters that make up much of the rest of the narrative. To enhance his prestige, Ibn Battuta may have fabricated the trip out of information he heard.

The Maldive Islands, however, had recently converted to Is-lam, and there is no question that Ibn Battuta visited. He served as chief Muslim judge, meting out stern justice to those who did not attend evening prayers. Continuing his pattern of short-term marriages, Ibn Battuta married locally, and within a few months, he had wed four different elite women. He had learned courtly intrigue at Delhi and was involved in an unsuccessful plot to con-quer the Maldive Islands.[38]

After an extended trip to Sri Lanka and the east coast of India, Ibn Battuta lost his wealth to pirates on the Malabar Coast, who attacked in twelve small ships. In terms of piracy, little had changed since the time of Abraham bin Yiju two centuries earlier.

> They took everything I had preserved for emergencies; they took the pearls and rubies that the king of [Sri Lanka] had given me, they took my clothes and the supplies given me by pious people and saints. They left me no covering except my trousers. They took everything everybody had and set us down on the shore.[39]

Nevertheless, Ibn Battuta survived. Local merchants and the head of the local mosque gave him clothes and he started off again. Within days, he was once again in the company of kings, telling stories and passing information.

In 1348 CE, when Ibn Battuta returned to the Middle East, he was in his early fifties. At Damascus, he paused to consider the costs of his choice of the traveling life. From the time he left Damascus twenty years earlier, he had cut himself off from his family in Morocco. He knew nothing of his parents or his siblings. Not until his return to Damascus did he learn that his father had died more than fifteen years earlier. The wife and son he left behind in Damascus were also dead. Ibn Battuta's pattern was short marriages and hasty departures; he left at least seven wives behind. He bought slave girls for sexual pleasure and apparently sold them along the way. He did seem genuinely sad about the death of a baby girl in Delhi, the daughter of his then concubine. He faced his old age without wife or children.

In 1348 CE, death was all around Ibn Battuta. He was one of the first to record the Black Plague that would also ravage Europe in the same year.

> [P]lague had broken out in Ghazza and the number of dead exceeded a thousand a day. . . . I went to Damascus and arrived on a Thursday: the people had been fasting for three days. . . .

The number of deaths among them had risen to two thousand four hundred a day. . . . Then I went to Cairo and was told that during the plague the number of deaths had risen to twenty-one thousand a day. I found that all the shaikhs I had known were dead. May God Most high have mercy upon them.[40]

From Cairo, Ibn Battuta traveled home to Morocco. "The memory of my homeland moved me, affection for my people and friends, and love for my country which is better than all others."[41] He reached Fez in November 1349 CE and found that his mother had died of the plague only six months earlier. As so many times before, Ibn Battuta turned to the court and the king. He approached the king of Morocco and told his stories of courts, cities, and monarchs. This time the king offered patronage if he would write his memoirs. Ibn Battuta wrote a book of 1,000 pages that mixed stories and homilies, trade possibilities and courtly ceremonies, relating what he had experienced and what he had heard in the towns and courts from China to Spain. It was his memoir that occupied the last years of his life.

Ibn Battuta's memoir is full of the stories of men rather like him. They had skills in Islamic law, or religious teaching, or administration. These men were the backbone of law, taxation, religious practice and scholarship across the Islamic world. From Spain, Tunisia, and Central Asia, they came and found employment in Baghdad or Delhi or kingdoms on the Malabar Coast. These men were more than mere functionaries. Like Ibn Battuta, they carried news, gossip, and descriptions of one court to another. They were the vital mechanism by which courts across the great Asian world came to be so similar in symbols, ceremony, and kingly culture. They were the agents by which a king, whether Muslim or not, might learn how much he would benefit by adopting this common culture.

7

TREASURE AND TREATY

Ma Huan, 1413–1431 CE

In 1413 CE, a Ming Chinese fleet of perhaps fifty-seven vessels—some more than 200 feet long—sailed majestically out of the shipyards associated with Nanjing, the imperial capital. The largest vessels were termed "treasure ships" for the vast quantities of Chinese goods they carried and the treasures they brought back in trade and tribute from faraway places. In the fleet were ships that carried an army of more than 20,000 fighting men, ships for horses, and ships that carried only water.[1] After more than a year of preparation, the fleet slowly made its way east 200 miles down the Yangtze River to the Yellow Sea.[2] It was commanded by Zeng He, a highly placed and powerful court eunuch and confidant of the emperor.

As the fleet sailed from Nanjing, among those aboard was Ma Huan, recruited "in a subordinate capacity as a translator of foreign documents."[3] He was thirty-two years old, Muslim, and spoke and read Arabic.[4]* Ma Huan was from a city a few miles south of Hangzhou, one of the major trading ports of the time and about 150 miles south of the Nanjing shipyard. He was no

---

*Ma Huan may have belonged to a village that was predominantly or completely Muslim, which seems to have been the common pattern. Muslim villages tended to locate along trade routes and center on a single local mosque.

noble or courtier, but rather a simple man, perhaps a low-level
official. He self-deprecatingly describes himself as a "mountain-
woodcutter."[5] Like the rest of the men aboard, he would be away
from his home and family for more than two years. Ma Huan's
memoir is particularly important because it is one of only two
surviving eyewitness accounts of these imperial fleets and their
voyages.

By the time of Ma Huan, Chinese goods had already circulated through Southeast Asia and the Indian Ocean for centuries.
Recall that Chinese goods formed much of the cargo of the tenth
century Intan shipwreck featured in Chapter 3. Chinese ships
did not, however, venture west of the Malay Peninsula. Even in
the thirteenth century, Abraham bin Yiju, the Jewish spice trader,
recorded no Chinese fleets during his twenty years of residence
on the Malabar Coast of India.

Something rather new happened in the late thirteenth century.
The Mongols, under a grandson of Genghis Khan, conquered all
of China in 1279 CE. Scholars still hotly debate how much the
Mongols adopted Chinese customs and how much they influenced China.* The Mongol invasions effectively closed any divide
between North and South China.** The Mongols sent expeditions of conquest into mainland Southeast Asia. They also sent a

---

*There was plenty to loot and conquer when the Mongols came into China.
China of the eleventh, twelfth, and thirteenth centuries had great cities, advanced industrial technology and agriculture, and a literacy-based bureaucratic
elite selected by examination.

**The older stereotype of China in the scholarly literature depicted a Confu-
cian anti-trade north and a trade-oriented south. This seems less and less sus-
tainable in the light of modern research. Rather, it now seems that even at the
time of Xuanzang (seventh century), trade heavily affected both regions. Trade
was especially important in the gradual amalgamation of cultures and languages that would become "China." By the time of the Ming (1368–1644),
trade was the active concern of regional officials and government policy.

mission against Java that dramatically failed and left large numbers of Chinese stranded on Java, resulting in a boost to both military and shipbuilding technology. Within China, Mongol
indifference to trade probably helped private traders avoid government control and taxation.[6]

By the early decades of the fourteenth century, large Chinese
trading fleets broke out of the boundaries of the Southeast Asia
trade and sailed west to India. Around 1330 CE, Ibn Battuta
(Chapter 6) personally saw such a fleet, entirely privately financed,
that consisted of thirteen ships. It docked at the Malabar port of
Kalikut. The fleet stayed for a few months and then departed together for China. The large traders aboard knew which spices
they wanted and carried specific goods to trade for them. Ibn Battuta was clearly impressed.

> The large ships have anything from twelve down to three sails,
> which are made of bamboo rods plaited like mats. They are never
> lowered, but they turn them according to the direction of the
> wind; at anchor they are left floating in the wind. A ship carries a
> complement of a thousand men, six hundred of whom are sailors
> and four hundred men-at-arms, including archers, men with
> shields and arbalests, that is men who throw naphtha. Each large
> vessel is accompanied by three smaller ones. . . .[7]

Ibn Battuta tried to book passage to China aboard one of the
large trading ships and discovered that, besides sails, they were
powered by large oars, each requiring fifteen oarsmen. The ships
had four decks and private cabins for the most important of the
traders, who brought along their wives and concubines. Also
aboard was the agent of the shipowner, and he traveled with a full
entourage, including African slaves.[8]

In the 1370s CE, half a century after Ibn Battuta, a new Ming
dynasty reconquered China, wresting it from the heirs of Genghis

Khan, and after two decades of isolationism, China developed an interest in the southern seaborne trade. By the early 1400s CE, the Ming dynasty was at the height of its wealth and power. The emperor commanded the building of the Forbidden City at Beijing, a new walled palace complex of 180 acres.[9] Using both diplomacy and warfare, the emperor extended Chinese power west along the caravan routes, fortifying the new territory with watchtowers and armed outposts. He attacked west into Xinjiang and south into current-day Vietnam. His administrators commandeered labor to repair and rebuild large sections of the Great Wall. He sent ambassadors to and received ambassadors from many of the powers of Central Asia and the Middle East.[10]

In this ambitious milieu, Chinese fleets grew in scale and scope of activities. The Ming emperor Yung-le was personally involved in the planning of the fleets and appointed one of his chief eunuchs as commander. The great fleets were intended to establish trade and diplomatic dominance across the whole of Southeast Asia, Sri Lanka, coastal India, the southern shore of the Middle East, and the east coast of Africa.

Ma Huan caught the spirit of the expeditions in a poem he wrote a few years after he returned to China:

The Emperor's glorious envoy received the divine commands
"proclaim abroad the silken sounds, and go to barbarous lands."[11]

Ma Huan was on the fourth imperial expedition (1413–1415 CE) to sail south and west from China and into the Indian Ocean. Like earlier imperial fleets, this expedition set out in the autumn months to exploit the prevailing monsoon winds. The fleet followed the coast of China southwest for ten days to the kingdom of Champa, in the central section of what is today Vietnam. From the outset of the voyage, Ma Huan carefully recorded dress,

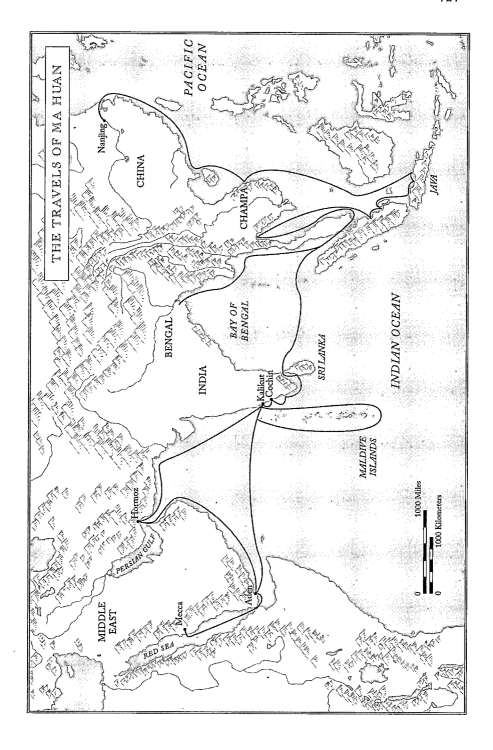

THE TRAVELS OF MA HUAN

PACIFIC OCEAN

Nanjing

CHINA

CHAMPA

JAVA

BENGAL

BAY OF BENGAL

INDIA

SRI LANKA

Kalikut
Cochin

INDIAN OCEAN

MALDIVE ISLANDS

Hormoz

PERSIAN GULF

Aden

MIDDLE EAST

Mecca

RED SEA

1000 Miles

1000 Kilometers

0

0

customs, and life as he saw it. He identified the king of Champa in central Vietnam as a "firm believer" in the Buddhist religion who wore a "three-tiered elegantly-decorated crown of gold filigree."* Both the king and his nobles wore long robes of indigenous manufacture over wrapped silk that covered the legs. The king forbade others to wear white or have doorways taller than a designated height. Ma Huan noticed that the headgear of the nobles had painted and gilded decoration that denoted rank. From his first contacts in Champa, he found that nobility lived well. "The house in which the king resides is tall and large. The four surrounding walls are ornately constructed of bricks and mortar, very neat."[12]

Ma Huan next noted the climate as "pleasantly hot, without frost or snow, always like the season in the fourth or fifth month. The plants and trees are always green." He then turned to the description of useful flora and fauna:

> The mountains produce ebony, ch'ieh-lan [a top grade of incense], Kuan yin bamboo, and laka-wood. The ebony is very glossy black, and decidedly superior to the produce of other countries. The ch'ieh-lan incense is produced only on one large mountain in this country, and comes from no other place in the world; it is very expensive, being exchanged for [its weight in silver].[13]

He also listed the possible trade items that the people of Champa liked: "dishes, bowls, and other kinds of blue porcelain

---

*Throughout his memoir, Ma Huan did not differentiate between Buddhist and Hindu states. Modern scholars have tried to trace the influence of each belief system in many Southeast Asian kingdoms but with little success. Ma Huan may have been closer to the truth that Hinduism and Buddhism were much mixed and, to an outsider, practices in Southeast Asia looked quite similar to Hindu practices in India.

articles, the hemp-silk, silk-gauze, beads, and other such things"
from China.[14]

Ma Huan tried to make the foreign places comprehensible to
his readers by comparing the food and domestic animals to what
prevailed back home:

> Their horses are short and small, like donkeys. Water buffaloes,
> yellow oxen, pigs and goats . . . all these they have. Geese and
> ducks are scarce. . . . The cock birds have red crowns and white
> ears, with small waists and high tails; they crow, too, when people
> take them up into their hands; [they are] very likeable.[15]

In Champa as in later ports, Ma Huan sought out ordinary folk
and described their customs. After marriage, "the man's father and
mother, with their relatives and friends, to the accompaniment of
drums and music escort husband and wife back to [the paternal]
home; they prepare wine and play music."[16] In Champa, he found
legal judgment harsh. "For light offences, they employ thrashing
on the back with a rattan stick; for serious offences, they cut off
the nose."[17] Ma Huan noted that there was no paper in Champa.
The people used pounded bark or goatskin for keeping accounts
and other writing. From Champa, the fleet sailed south to Java,
which remained deeply involved in maritime trade.

While in Java, Ma Huan also wrote about house types, the
dress of the king and his court, and trade possibilities. Ma Huan
had read earlier Chinese travel literature and knew what was expected. He even listed these topics in the introduction to his
memoir: "climates, topography . . . appearance of the people . . .
local customs . . . natural products, and . . . boundary limits."[18]

Ma Huan's sensitivity to detail and difference set his account
apart from run-of-the-mill travel accounts. His observations still
seem fresh and interesting even after the passage of five centuries.

The houses are constructed in storeyed form, each being . . . [about forty feet] in height; they lay a plank [flooring, over which] they spread matting [of] fine rattans, or patterned grass mats, on which the people sit cross-legged; on the top of the houses they use boards of hard wood as tiles, splitting [the wood into] roofing.[19]

Ma Huan noticed that unlike the king of Champa, the Javanese king and his nobles did not wear a robe but only wrapped silk from the waist down. Men, from the king on down, wore a dagger tucked into the waistband of this garment.[20]

It was on coastal Java that Ma Huan first located a resident community of overseas Chinese. "Tu-pan . . . is the name of a district; here there are something more than a thousand families, with two head men to rule them; many of the people are from [Guangdong] province."[21]

Trade ties between Fujian and Java were centuries old by the time of Ma Huan in the early 1400s. The province produced most of the Chinese goods found in the tenth-century Intan shipwreck of Chapter 4. Chinese emigration probably followed these long-standing close trade ties between Fujian and Java.

Ma Huan and the fleet soon arrived at a port on the coast of Java founded and run by overseas Chinese. Its prosperity was based on spices brought from the Molucca Islands to the east and sandalwood from the island of Timor.

Originally it was a region of sand banks; and because people from [China] came to this place and established themselves, they therefore called it New Village; right down to the present day the ruler of the village is a man from [Guandong Province]. There are something more than a thousand families [here]. Foreigners from every place in great numbers come here to trade. Gold, all kinds of precious stones, and all varieties of foreign goods are sold in great quantities. The people are very wealthy.[22]

In the early fifteenth century, Java consisted of a large kingdom, Majapahit, and a few smaller ports.* The Chinese fleet,
therefore, made several stops to deal with local powers along the
north coast of Java. Ma Huan generally found three categories of
people in the ports: Muslims (Arabs and local converts), Chinese, and local Hindus or Buddhists. As usual, he observed general patterns of life in these port towns:

> The people of the country have no beds or stools for sitting on or
> sleeping on; and for eating they have no spoons or chopsticks.
> Men and women take areca-nut and betel-leaf, and mix them
> with lime made from clam-shells; and their mouths are never
> without this mixture.[23]

In Java, Ma Huan watched performances by men who made
paintings on paper of "men, birds, beasts, eagles, or insects." These
paintings, he thought, "resembled scroll pictures." During the performance, the man unrolled a section, thrust it toward the audience,
and told the story. "The crowd sits round and listens to him, sometimes laughing, sometimes crying, exactly as if the narrator were
reciting one of our popular romances."[24] With this insight, Ma
Huan came incredibly close to recognition of the common pattern
of scroll-painting performance that stretched across much of Asia
at the time. It was common to Bengal, Rajasthan, Persia, Southeast
Asia, and China. Only in the last few decades have scholars realized
the common features of this form of popular entertainment.[25]

One story of the fleet in Sumatra suggests the complex relation
of imperial China to overseas Chinese communities and pirates.

---

*In the last decades of the thirteenth century, the key states in the region had
been Kediri and Singosari, but they were then superceded by the developing
empire of Majapahit. By the fifteenth century, the time of Ma Huan's memoir,
Majapahit was in decline and new successor states were emerging.

Sometime in the late fourteenth century, a group of Chinese fled
to a port on the north coast of Sumatra "with their whole households." One Ch'en Tsu-i from "Kuang-tung . . . set himself up as
their chief; he was very wealthy and tyrannical and whenever a
ship belonging to strangers passed by, he immediately robbed
them of their valuables." The first of the imperial expeditions in
1407 CE captured this Chinese pirate and took him to the capital,
where he was executed.[26]

Other Chinese communities, such as the one at Malacca,
seemed to retain close ties with the imperial court and sent tribute
missions. On some islands, Chinese traders settled, married local
women, and largely merged into the local society. Overall, there
was a general idea at court that some of the Chinese in Southeast
Asia were still connected to China, called the Central Country.[27]

After stops on Sumatra, where Ma Huan also found Chinese
trading communities, the fleet sailed north along the east cost of
the Malay Peninsula to current-day coastal Thailand. The capital,
Ayuthia, was close to the location of the modern city of Bangkok.
Along with the standard description of the climate, flora, fauna,
prevailing customs, and trade goods, Ma Huan noticed that Thai
Buddhist monks and nuns were vaguely similar to the Buddhist
monastic tradition in China.

> In this country the people who become [monks] or become nuns
> are exceedingly numerous; the habit of priests and nuns is some-
> what the same as the Central Country [China]; and they, too, live
> in nunneries and monasteries, fasting and doing penance.[28]

Ma Huan was, as a Muslim, probably unaware of old, deep
doctrinal splits within Buddhism, primarily between Hinayana
(the Little Vehicle) and Mahayana (the Larger Vehicle), which
were responsible for the differences in practice that he noted. Re-

call that Xuanzang, the Buddhist pilgrim of Chapter 1, debated these differences in interpretation 800 years earlier.[29]*

From Ayuthia, the fleet sailed back down the Malay Peninsula to the port of Malacca, close to current-day Singapore. Malacca, founded sometime between 1375 and 1400 (only a generation before Ma Huan's first voyage), was the rising star of ports in the western portion of Southeast Asia and the major transshipping point between the Indian Ocean and the water routes of Southeast Asia. Ma Huan recorded that Malacca had been formerly controlled by Thailand, but a local king had asserted independence and an earlier imperial fleet recognized his independence with "two silver seals, a hat, a girdle, and a robe."[30] The head of the expedition set up a stone tablet in Malacca, and the king subsequently visited the Ming emperor.

By the time of the fourth imperial fleet, the king of Malacca was chafing under Chinese dominance. He had just converted to Islam and dressed, as Ma Huan noted, as an Arab. He "uses a fine white foreign cloth to wind round his head; on his body he wears a long garment of fine-patterned blue cloth, fashioned like a robe; [and] on his feet he wears leather shoes."[31] It is interesting that adoption of this dress accompanied the king's conversion to Islam. These are the sorts of robes that would have been familiar to most of the travelers of previous chapters, such as Ibn Fadlan, the diplomat; Abraham bin Yiju, the Jewish pepper trader; Ibn Sina, the philosopher; and Ibn Battuta, the jurist. The Chinese imperial relationship with the king of Malacca was still close at the time of the fourth expedition. Ma Huan noted an extended stay in Malacca. The fleet's crew off-loaded tribute and trade goods they had

---

*Doctrinal differences had also resulted in warfare. A kingdom in Sri Lanka used its troops to shut and destroy Mahayana monasteries sometime in the fifth century. Sri Lanka remains Hinayana to this day.

collected into a secure compound to await their return from the Indian Ocean.

At Malacca, imperial fleets typically divided, some heading for Bengal, others for Africa or the west coast of India. In 1413 CE, Ma Huan's portion of the fleet sailed northwest between Sumatra and the Malay Peninsula, stopping at two ports. Lesser states were of minimal importance, and Ma Huan rather wrote them off. "The land has no products. It is a small place."[32]

Tin mining on the Malay Peninsula caught Ma Huan's attention. Tin was just as important a trade item in the fifteenth century as it had been in the tenth century, the time of the Intan shipwreck.

> As to "flower tin": there are two tin areas in the mountain valleys; and the king appoints a chief to control them. Men are sent to wash [for the ore] in a sieve and to cook it. [The tin] is cast into the shape of a tou-measure . . . to make small blocks which are handed to the officials.[33]

The blocks were of a standard weight and were bundled into units of forty. Salvage divers of the tenth-century Intan shipwreck found the tin in exactly this ingot form.

Once clear of the island of Sumatra, the fleet headed west via the Andaman Islands to Sri Lanka. Although the Chinese fleet had an army of more than 20,000 men and Ma Huan's portion might have had 6,000 troops, he recorded no battles. The fleet never attacked or sacked a port. In Sri Lanka, as in all other stops, the aim of the fleet was to awe local and regional states, not attack them. Still, the Chinese did occasionally use their military might. A decade prior to Ma Huan's expedition, an imperial fleet attacked both Sumatra and a Sri Lankan king who had refused to offer tribute. Ma Huan noted with satisfaction that subsequent to the attack, the Sri Lankan king remained firmly subordinate to China. He "constantly sends men with offerings of precious stones and other such things; they accompany the treasure-ships returning from the [Western] Ocean and bring tribute to the Central Country [China]."[34]

The assessment of tribute required conversion of local coinage, weights, and measures into standard Chinese ones. This subject is a constant theme throughout Ma Huan's memoir. In Sri Lanka, the king "uses gold of ninety per cent [purity] to cast coins of current use. Each weighs one *fen* and one *li* on our official steelyard."[35]

The fleet continued west from Sri Lanka around the southern tip of India to Malabar. Ma Huan was quite aware that this lush coast, dense with coconut palms, was pepper country.

> The land has no other product, [but] produces only pepper. The people mostly establish gardens to cultivate pepper for a living. Every year when the pepper is ripe, of course, big pepper-collectors of the locality make their purchases and establish warehouses to store it; [then] they wait until the foreign merchants from various places come to buy it.[36]

By the fourth expedition, Ma Huan's first, both the Chinese and regional kings of major ports seem to have worked out a relationship. Head diplomats of the fleet honored the king with robes and charters. Then representatives of both sides got down to business. The king's agent and the chief trader of the fleet first examined the Chinese silks and other goods and fixed a date for setting prices. On that date, "all joined hands" and agreed that "whether the price be dear or cheap, we will never repudiate it or change it." Next, the traders of the city brought "precious goods," such as pearls and coral. Determination of their prices "cannot be settled in a day; if done quickly, it takes one moon, [or more] slowly, two or three moons." All of the fleet's subsequent trading then took place at these fixed prices.[37] In spite of the strength of the Chinese fleet, a negotiation of several months meant that the Chinese were not simply dictating prices and terms.

This large-scale negotiated price-fixing was not the typical
pattern in Malabar ports of the time. Traders simply bought what
they could and the market set the price. Later in the memoir, Ma
Huan described this regular trade at Kalikut:

> Foreign ships from every place come there [to Kalikut] and the
> king of the country also sends a chief and a writer and others to
> watch the sales; thereupon they collect the duty and pay it to the
> authorities.[38]

The Chinese court had grand plans for long-term domination.
At several ports, Zeng He set up carved stone proclamations an-
nouncing their intentions that stated:

> Though the journey from this country to the Central Country
> [China] is more than a hundred thousand *li*, yet the people are
> very similar, happy, and prosperous, with identical customs. We
> have here engraved a stone, a perpetual declaration for ten thou-
> sand ages.[39]

What could a regional king like Zamorin of Kalikut gain from
the Chinese connection? With an army of several thousand Chinese soldiers in his port, perhaps he had little choice. Still, there
were some political benefits. The Chinese committed to support
him against family rivals and external enemies. Practically, this
promise meant relatively little, as a fleet arrived unpredictably only
once every few years. Ma Huan records only one case in which the
Chinese actually captured a local usurper in Southeast Asia and
restored the king to his throne.

From Kalikut, possibly during the extended negotiations, Ma
Huan got an opportunity to go to Mecca alone, possibly on a local
ship. The holy city moved him. He wrote about many of the expected subjects: architecture, local fruits and vegetables, and trade

products. "The customs of the people are pacific and admirable. They observe all the precepts of their religion; and law-breakers are few. It is in truth a happy country."[40]

After the lengthy stop in Kalikut, the fleet sailed west to the Maldive Islands. If Malabar was pepper country, the two important commodities in the Maldives were cowry shells, used as minor coinage, and coconuts.

> The fibre which covers the outside of the coconut is made into ropes both thick and fine; men come from every place on foreign ships to purchase these too. . . . In the construction of their foreign ships they never use nails, they merely bore holes, and always use these ropes to bind [the planks] together.[41]

Sewn boats were common all across the Indian Ocean, the Bay of Bengal, and Southeast Asia, and had been for a thousand years before the time of Ma Huan. Recall that this was exactly the construction of the Intan shipwreck explored in Chapter 4.[42]

A century before Ma Huan's voyage, Ibn Battuta visited the Maldives, islands off the west coast of India that were then newly converted to Islam. He railed against the women who were naked from the waist up. They laughed at him. By the time of Ma Huan, Islamic modesty prevailed. "The women wear a short garment on the upper [part of the body]; and on the lower [part] they, too, wear a broad kerchief round them. They also carry a broad, large, cotton kerchief which passes across the head and covers it, disclosing only the face."[43]

From the Maldives, the imperial fleet sailed northwest to Aden and Hormuz. In the twelfth century, Aden had been the home of Abraham bin Yiju's senior partner. It was still a rich sophisticated port when Ma Huan arrived there three centuries later. "They have seven or eight thousand well-drilled horsemen and foot soldiers; therefore the country is very powerful and neighbouring states fear it." Just as at Kalikut, diplomacy was in the foreground with exchange of costly presents, while trade filled the background. Ma Huan wrote paragraphs listing precious goods available, their prices, and local weights and measures.[44]

Hormuz was the westernmost point of the fourth imperial expedition of 1413–1414 CE. There, Ma Huan saw a street performance that charmed him.

> [The man] directs a bystander to take a kerchief, fold it several times, and tie it tightly around both eyes of the monkey; he directs a different person to give the monkey a surreptitious hit on the head and hide himself in the thick of the crowd; after this [the man] releases the kerchief and directs [the monkey] to seek out the person who struck him on the head; however vast the crowd, the monkey goes straight to the man who originally [struck him] and picks him out; it is most strange.[45]

From Hormuz the fleet quickly retraced its route around India to Malacca, picked up the goods left there for safekeeping, and returned by the shortest route to the south coast of China.

By the time the fourth fleet returned to China in 1415 CE, the costs of the emperor's grand plans were beginning to show. Taxes were high and there was unrest in the countryside.[46] There were rebellions on the periphery, both in what is now Vietnam and along the Silk Road, in addition to new threats from the Mongols. Ma Huan went on a second expedition in 1421, and by the time he returned, there were even more imperial problems. At court, a strong faction of the literati opposed the court eunuchs who favored the expeditions.

In the spring of 1422, a catastrophic fire burned many of the buildings in the newly finished Forbidden City and killed hundreds of people, including the emperor's favorite concubine. A

Persian ambassador, witness to the fire, described the emperor's self-doubt:

> The god of Heaven is angry with me, and hath therefore burned my palace; although I have done no evil act: I have neither offended my father, nor mother, nor have I acted tyrannically.[47*]

At court, the fire only strengthened the literati faction that opposed the eunuchs and the fleets.

After the old emperor died in 1424 CE, the literati faction controlled his young son, the new emperor. An edict reversed the policy of imperial fleets, declaring them a waste of money with no benefit for China. The edict did not wholly stop the fleets, however. There was one more expedition, in 1431 CE, and Ma Huan was aboard once again as a translator of Arabic.

By the 1440s CE, the expansionist policy was eradicated with imperial thoroughness. An edict ordered all records of the fleets burned. Only a handful of memoirs, a couple of charts, and one map survive. Another edict ordered an end to foreign trade and even ordered the seacoast population moved inland. This inward-turning policy was much the same as seventy years earlier in the first decades of the Ming dynasty and was a recurrent feature of Chinese history for the next 500 years. Trade, of course, did not stop. It was too important. Goods were smuggled out through the independent kingdom in what is today Vietnam.**

---

*Incidentally, the Persian ambassador was an avid chess player and found many worthy opponents in Beijing, though the players shared no common language.
**The withdrawal from foreign trade is a recurrent theme in Chinese history. The withdrawal in the 1440s corresponds to a similar policy seventy years earlier under the early Ming, and like that period, it took several decades to reverse.

What, then can be made of these fleets and their journeys to the Western Ocean? The imperial fleets followed the most well known trade routes in sailing patterns that private Chinese fleets had plied for more than a century. They stopped at only the largest ports and capitals, ignoring any out-of-the-way places where things might have been "discovered." Rather than being voyages of discovery, the imperial fleet journeys were a combination of trade and what, in modern parlance, is known as gunboat diplomacy. The whole operation undoubtedly seemed like a good policy choice in Beijing, or such effort would not have been expended on it. One potential benefit was that the emperor could extend his sphere of influence by forcing subordination treaties on a host of kings along the way. And the venture might well pay for itself with favorable trading and tribute gifts from the subordinated kings. As in modern times, however, gunboat diplomacy proved far more costly and had far more meager results than expected. It is perfectly understandable that a faction at court argued for attention to the immediate danger of rebellion on the eastern steppe that threatened the northern heartland of China rather than wasting money on great fleets.[48]

For Ma Huan however, the voyages were something else entirely. Like many travelers—Ibn Fadlan, Ibn Battuta, Xuanzang—Ma Huan searched for pattern and structure among unfamiliar beliefs and customs. He analyzed and sought to make comprehensible what he saw and experienced. There was a continuing need for such writers and interpreters across the Asian world. His memoir is, however, far more than just a report of diplomacy, products, and the wonders of faraway places.

Compared to other travel writers of the time, Ma Huan's writing was distinguished by his simple, unvarnished observations, his respect for those he encountered, and his awareness that at least some ways of doing things in foreign lands were not so different from back home. He compared games in Southeast Asia to those found in China. Many peoples were termed "neat and clean" and industrious in the development of local manufactures. Their foods were different but interesting. Ma Huan was moved by his acceptance as a Muslim in the ports of the Middle East and, more important, at Mecca. Unlike Ibn Battuta, Ma Huan never spoke either of factional conflict or opportunities within Islam. It was enough to be among fellow believers and be part of the far-flung community that stretched from Mecca to China.

Years later, a highly placed friend of Ma Huan's wrote a brief epilogue to the memoir. He hoped that it would help as Ma Huan struggled to find patronage at court to have his book printed.*

The epilogue speaks of Ma Huan returning to his native village and describes him as a man who "constantly went out to enlighten other people, to enable everybody to acquire knowledge about conditions in foreign regions."[49] Ma Huan's memoir is infused with how much he appreciated the opportunity to experience and interpret peoples outside of China—how they lived, married, and practiced their many beliefs. Ma Huan was profoundly changed and moved by what he experienced.

---

*It was difficult to get a book printed in China at this time. Books were scarce and expensive. The generally xenophobic attitude of the court could only have made the process more difficult. Still, the memoir survives.

8

BLOOD AND SALT

Babur, 1494–1526 CE

In June 1503 CE, a battle raged through the town of Akhsi, which at the time was the strongest fortified oasis town in the Fargana Valley. Nearby was the canyon of the Amudarya River. Side ravines formed natural moats that various defenders had deepened over the years. Inside the town walls, several thousand men on horseback in chain mail shot arrows where there was room but mainly struggled hand to hand with swords in the narrow streets and lanes. Late in the afternoon the outnumbered defenders, perhaps 400, defeated and desperate, fought their way out of the east gate and fled helter-skelter to the orchards and hills. Pursued by enemy cavalry, the troop split up; some escaped, some were captured, a few were killed.

Eight companions fled with their leader, Babur, and one finally gave him his horse because it could still run. Babur's memoir, written many years later, says, "It was a miserable position for me; he remained behind, I was alone."[1] Babur hid among the rocks but was found by two pursuers. Their general would reward them handsomely for capturing an enemy commander. Babur, however, convinced the two cavalrymen that if they helped him escape, his powerful relatives would employ the troopers and give them opportunities. The incident suggests the charisma of a born leader; Babur was twenty-one at the time.

Babur and his two new followers eluded patrols for the next three days, hiding among rocks and abandoned orchards, seizing food and fodder where they could. The remnants of his small army eventually found Babur. Together they escaped east to the heart of the Fargana Valley, home territory to Babur and many of his relatives.

Although Akhsi was a rather small place, the Fargana Valley (north of Afghanistan), only 200 miles across, was one of the most lush and fertile regions on the Silk Road caravan routes. Ambitious generals had fought over the valley for centuries. It was part of a network of supply and military recruitment whose western end was the Middle East and eastern end was China. Such a far-flung network had grown slowly from modest roots.

A thousand years before Babur, the armies of the steppe were small tribal bands. Success in yearly raids brought animals, slaves, and better pastures. Defeat meant slavery, submission to a more powerful tribe, or long, dangerous migration. The central technology to both hunting and raiding was the short, reverse-curve, compound bow. This masterpiece married the tension and compression of horn and wood into a short bow of extraordinary power. An arrow from this bow penetrated armor at more than fifty yards. Unlike any other bow, it could be shot at full gallop from horseback. The rider had to free both hands and guide his horse with his knees, but these were skills learned from childhood by steppe nomads.[2] The unequaled horsemanship of every soldier yielded a wide range of battle tactics, from the feigned retreat to the around-end sweep. Such armies could move quickly, choose their battle sites, and retreat in order. Unusually successful leaders forged bands into armies—the feared Huns, who attacked Europe, and the equally feared Hsiung-nu, who attacked China.[3]

More than anyone else, it was Genghis Khan (1162–1222 CE) who, three centuries before Babur, established the networks that

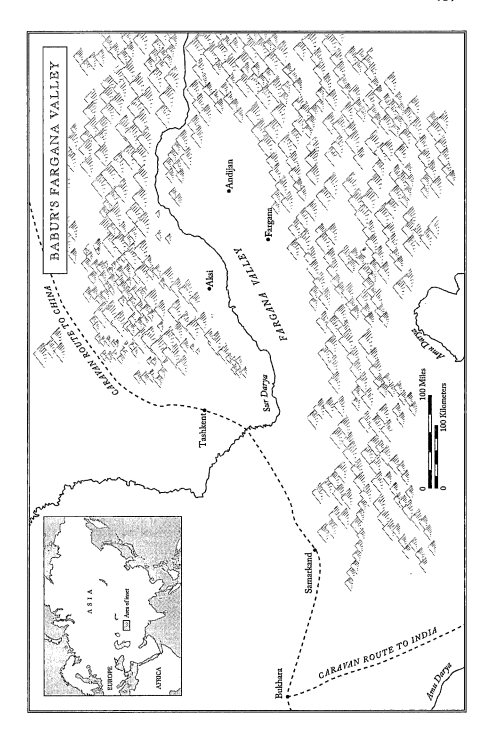

BABUR'S FARGANA VALLEY

CARAVAN ROUTE TO CHINA

•Andijan

•Fargana

•Aksi

FARGANA VALLEY

Sur Darya

Amu Darya

Tashkent

100 Miles

100 Kilometers

0

0

ASIA

Area of inset

EUROPE

AFRICA

Samarkand

Bukhara

CARAVAN ROUTE TO INDIA

Amu Darya

Babur both relied on and suffered from. Genghis Khan grew up in a minor Mongol clan in a poor region of Mongolia. In his teenage years, he learned from his mistakes and developed winning military tactics and a thorough ruthlessness toward his enemies, whether close relatives or nearby clans. He early established the policy of integrating conquered men and families into his army, rather than the common practice of selling them into slavery. Soon, his vision widened beyond clans and he demanded that his men serve in mixed units composed of many different clans.

Based on superb horsemanship, the same powerful reverse-curve bow that Babur and his men still used, and thorough training in large-scale cavalry tactics, his armies defeated virtually every opponent for the remainder of Genghis Khan's life. It is almost impossible for us to imagine the speed and success of these armies. They ranged across the 3,000 miles of steppe, conquered every kingdom in their path, defeated the Chinese army, and occupied the northern half of China. Genghis Khan's armies swept through southern Russia, Poland, and Hungary, defeating armies and looting cities. Europe, for centuries, viewed the Mongols as a scourge of God. He unsuccessfully attacked both India and Japan.[4]

On his death in 1222 CE, Genghis Khan's vast empire broke into large kingdoms, but the conquests continued for two generations and included the rest of China, Korea, Persia, and the remaining crusader states of the Middle East. Genghis Khan and his heirs produced several important long-term changes in the Asian world. Their ruthless tactics, especially toward cities that did not pay their taxes, resulted in the destruction of several caravan cities. Merv and Balkh were still in ruins when Ibn Battuta visited them a century later.[5] They never recovered. The Mongol conquest of Baghdad included the destruction of the royal library. It is said that the Tigris ran blue for weeks with dissolving ink from the books thrown in the river.

Some whole regions were permanently altered. The Mongols killed every man, woman, and child in the Bamian Valley of present-day Afghanistan. The Buddhist culture there abruptly ended. Genghis Khan's forces drove out much of the agricultural population of the northern plain of Persia, returned it to grazing land for their flocks, enslaved all the skilled artisans of several Persian cities, and took them to their camps on the steppe. They killed a substantial portion of the population of northern China and planned to turn the land to grazing, though the plan was not realized.[6]

Based on taxes of broad regions and the loot of many cities, the Mongol camps and capitals became demand areas for all sorts of high-end goods: glassware, gold drinking cups, cloth of gold for robes, and carpets. Visitors, such as Marco Polo, found them places of fairy-tale luxury.

Babur was a direct descendant of Genghis Khan, but so were hundreds and hundreds of his rival generals in the 1400s who seized what they could from northern Persia across 3,000 miles of steppe to the borders of China. All was, however, not chaos and anarchy. One enduring legacy of the empire was a set of unwritten and almost unspoken rules of military service by which a man might honorably serve a leader to whom he was not related. The general and the recruit did not even have to share a common language. These ceremonies of honor drew on the tradition of luxury at Genghis Khan's court and used the presentation of silk robes and horses in the commitment to serve. A second legacy of Genghis Khan was that all descendants were not equal. A handful of Great Khans held the best grazing area and, therefore, could support the largest armies. As a third legacy, Babur had to deal with ethnic groups such as the Uzbegs and certain Mongols who had never accepted Genghis Khan or any of his descendants as overlords.

Babur's father, ruler of the Fargana Valley, died in a fall in 1494, and the young boy, only twelve years old, inherited the throne. He

soon felt the weight of his legacy. First, his father's nobility demanded a demonstration that he could lead in battle, take part in
strategy discussions, and understand the system of honor under
which they served and were rewarded. If the nobles sensed vacilla-
tion or weakness, they would invite another member of the family,
a cousin or uncle, to rule. Second, neighboring enemies, such as
the Uzbegs, attacked to test the young king's leadership. Finally,
there were Babur's uncles, the Great Khans, the most powerful
descendants of Genghis Khan, who held lands and major trading
cities. Within months of his father's death, Babur had to face an
invasion by both uncles, but his father's army prevailed. For the
Great Khans, the yearly campaign season always included ambitious invasions, tenuous alliances, betrayals, family feuds, and calls
for support that Babur could not refuse. The result of these obligations and challenges was a decade of incessant warfare, barely
broken even by fierce winter weather.[7]

In the summer of 1500 (three years before the desperate flight
at the opening of the chapter), Babur attacked Samarkand, a major city along the Silk Road about 200 miles west of the Fargana
Valley. About 600 Uzbegs held the city. Babur says, "Our men,
good and bad, were 240."[8] Before he attacked the city, Babur discussed the situation with his leaders, who wore armor, and his
troops, who did not. He concluded that Samarkand had been
taken by the Uzbegs so recently that the people of the city owed
them no loyalty. "If we set ladders up and took the fort, the
Samarkandis would be for us; how would they not be?"[9] A few
days later, Babur's soldiers made a night attack on the city. They
"set up their ladders opposite the Lovers' cave, got in without
making anyone aware, went to the Gate, attacked Fazil Tarkhan,
chopped at him and his few retainers, killed them, broke the lock
with an axe and opened the Gate."[10] Most of the townspeople
welcomed Babur. "Some of the notables and traders, hearing what

was happening, came joyfully to me, bringing what food was ready and putting up prayers for me."[11] The townspeople finished the rout of the Uzbegs. "When, a little later, the news spread through the town, there was rare delight and satisfaction for our men and the townspeople. They killed the Auzbegs [Uzbegs] in the lanes and gullies with clubs and stones like mad dogs; four or five hundred were killed in this fashion."[12] As Babur says, "My affairs were in a very good way."[13]

In the months after the capture of Samarkand, various leaders, particularly Mongols from the Samarkand area, "bent the knee" in loyalty and service to Babur. It was a ceremony that both sides knew well. In July, however, the Uzbegs returned in force. Babur chose to face them with his new allies in the plains outside the city. "As we wished to fight, we marched from our camp at dawn, we in our mail, our horses in theirs."[14] Babur formed up his forces in an array of right and left, center and vanguard, exactly as his ancestor Genghis Khan had done three centuries before. The Uzbegs were similarly arrayed. The Uzbeg right wheeled around Babur's left side, so Babur moved his vanguard to the left to help. In minutes the Uzbeg center attacked the opening created when Babur's vanguard shifted. The enemy attacked front and rear, "raining arrows on us." Babur's fickle allies, the Mongols from Samarkand, attacked and plundered Babur's forces. Babur escaped the rout with fifteen men. They drove their horses across a nearby river, left their armor on the opposite side, and rode for their lives back to the city fort of Samarkand. Following a siege of several months, Babur surrendered the city on a makeshift negotiated truce and retreated at midnight with his wives, his mother, and the remaining troops.

Many years later, Babur coolly considered the Uzbegs' advantages in the plains battle. Besides being outnumbered, Babur had been outmaneuvered:

144

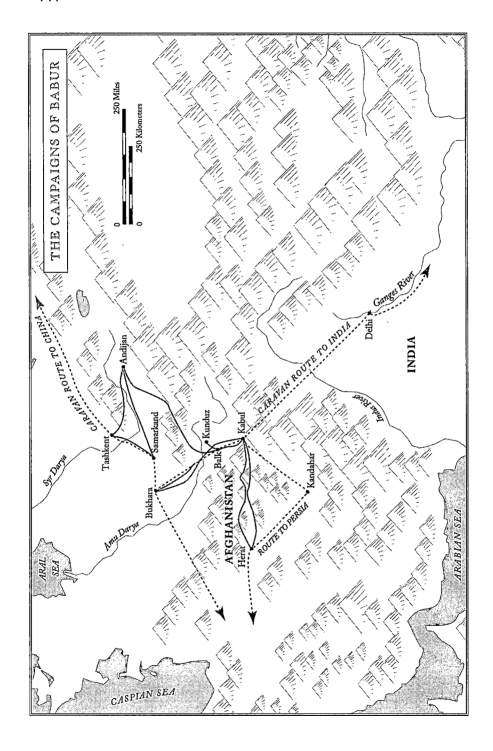

This same turning-movement is one of the great merits of Auzbeg fighting; no battle of theirs is ever without it. Another merit of theirs is that they all, begs [nobles] and retainers, from their front to their rear, ride, loose rein at a gallop, shouting as they come and, in retiring, do not scatter but ride off, at the gallop, in a body.[15]

What was this system that allowed unrelated Mongols to serve under Babur?* In his memoir, he himself describes the unwritten code as "salt." Much of Babur's 800-page memoir is concerned with men who were loyal or disloyal to their salt. What did he mean? Salt was costly and was served at the leader's table.[16] Salt symbolized both the sustenance and opportunities the leader provided and the service the soldier was honor bound to give in return. In this system, the soldier and the leader did not necessarily belong to the same tribe or even speak the same language. Their initial interaction was virtually nonverbal. The soldier merely stood in his armor before the leader and slightly bowed his head or bent his knee; the leader nodded agreement. Certainly, there were implicit expectations on both sides. The follower would fight and die for his leader. The leader would fight by his side, eat and drink with him, and share whatever fortune might bring. The salt system allowed Babur to receive soldiers and leaders of many ethnicities. He could also take into his army soldiers he defeated, with no loss of honor on either side.[17] Sometimes, the bonds between comrades-in-arms were close. "His death made me strangely sad; for few have I felt such grief; I wept unceasingly for a week or ten days."[18]

The salt system was more than loyalty between leader and soldier. It was a wider shared system of honor and included, in good

---

*The system of honorable service was so thoroughly ingrained across a vast region that the phrase "loyal to his salt" is current today in Central Asia, Turkey, and northern India.

times, lavish common dinners, gold and silver drinking vessels, silk furnishings, and elegant robes of gold brocade. There was an honorable way to treat prisoners, apportion conquered land, receive conquered leaders, share spoils, and take care of the destitute.[19]

Babur knew every nuance and regularly highlighted honorable and dishonorable behavior in the events he recounted.[20] For example, if a leader could no longer maintain his followers, they had the choice to stay and suffer or could, without shame, seek service with another leader. It pained Babur that late in the siege of Samarkand when there was no food, "trusted men of my close circle began to let themselves down from the ramparts and get away; begs of known name and old family servants were among them. . . ."[21] He did not, however, condemn them; their behavior was within the code of salt. For someone who violated the code, Babur had only harsh judgment. One of his nobles first betrayed Babur, deserted to his enemies, the Uzbegs, and later also betrayed them. When the Uzbegs subsequently captured and blinded the noble, Babur said with some satisfaction, "The salt took his eyes."[22]

By the time of Babur, three centuries after Genghis Khan, salt was a way of integrating non-kin into armies, but blood, that is, lineage, was still important. Babur was a king because he inherited the Fargana Valley. On his mother's side, his grandfather was a direct descendant of Chaghatai (1162–1227), a son of Genghis Khan. This maternal grandfather was, at the time, a Great Khan and held the traditional camping ground of Chaghatai and the large trading city of Tashkent. Babur's royal lineage was, at best, a mixed blessing. It meant that the more powerful relatives could, and did, call on Babur for troops and support for their campaigns. It also meant that Babur, at a young age, was embroiled in every diplomatic twist, power shift, and scheme for conquest across a 1,000-mile swath of Central Asia. Exactly whose salt he needed to honor was never entirely clear. He knew that mistakes and misjudgments could bring low even the powerful.

> This man, once master of 20 or 30,000 retainers [who] had made us march, had made us halt . . . so abased and so bereft of power that, with no blow struck, no sound made, he stood, without command over servants, goods, or life, in the presence of a band of 200 or 300 men, defeated and destitute as we were.[23]

Still, there were some advantages to having powerful kin. Their courts were places of refuge if all else failed. In 1502 CE, after the loss of Samarkand and Fargana, Babur spent the winter in the hills above Dhizak, about sixty miles northeast of Samarkand, merely surviving, with no "place." In his memoir, he wrote poignantly of this time. "It passed through my mind that to wander from mountain to mountain, homeless and houseless, without country or abiding place, had nothing to recommend it."[24] Babur decided that he would visit his "clan uncle," the powerful half brother of his father known as the Elder, even though this same uncle had attempted an invasion of the Fargana Valley early in Babur's reign. The best that a defeated relative like Babur might expect was service in the Great Khan's army, perhaps commanding 100 troops, and the chance to work his way up through battle and service. Babur found service in his uncle's army odious.

> During my stay [in Tashkent], I endured much poverty and humiliation. No country or hope of one! Most of my retainers dispersed, those left unable to move around because of their destitution![25]

At this low point Babur considered releasing his remaining men; he intended to seek service with another Great Khan in China. It is important to note how far-flung Babur's perspective and family ties were.

> From my childhood up I had wished to visit China but had not been able to manage it because of ruling and attachments. Now

sovereignty itself was gone! And my mother, for her part, was
re-united to her (step-)mother and her younger brother; the hin-
drances to my journey had been removed.[26]

The plan never materialized because the very khan he intended
to seek in China, known as the Younger Khan, appeared at Tashkent a few months later. Babur, by chance, met him several miles
outside the Younger Khan's camp. They exchanged courtesies, and
a few days later the Younger Khan honored Babur with robes, a
pan-Asian ceremony in the tradition of Xuanzang's receipt of robes
south of the Gobi Desert, 1,000 years earlier. The Younger Kahn
bestowed on Babur "arms of his own and one of his own special
horses, saddled and a Mughal head-to-foot dress—a Mughal cap,
a long coat of Chinese satin with embroidered stitching, and Chinese armor."[27]

The following year (1502 CE), the combined armies of the Elder
and Younger Khans attempted to reconquer the Fargana Valley.
Babur commanded only a few hundred troops in the expedition.
At a critical juncture, the khans retreated rather than support
Babur at Akhsi. This is the background to the flight from Akhsi
that opened the chapter.

The siege at Akhsi was, thus, only a skirmish in vast ongoing
conflicts and rivalries that stretched across much of southern
Central Asia. In 1503 CE, young Babur was, unfortunately, on the
losing side in a series of decisive battles. The Great Khans to
whom he owed family loyalty were captured, their armies defeated. Through the winter and spring of 1504 CE, Babur and his
small band wandered, homeless and fugitive, dependent on the
kindness of the tribes in the wild hills. By summer his inheritance,
his beloved Fargana Valley that his father had ruled and he had
ruled for nearly ten years, was lost.[28] He was barely twenty-two.

Babur left the Fargana Valley in the summer of 1504 CE and, with
a few hundred ragged followers, rode south into Afghanistan. Dur-

ing that fall and winter, the principal leaders of the area "bent the knee" and accepted Babur as ruler. The previous ruler, none other than the powerful noble who had stood destitute before Babur, had oppressed one and all, and these local leaders welcomed a change. At Kabul, Babur literally showed his much-enhanced army outside the city wall. The fort commander negotiated terms to surrender the city and left with his soldiers, wives, and goods. The only problem with this peaceful transfer was a riot by the townsfolk. "In the end I got to horse, had two or three persons shot, two or three cut to pieces, and stamped the rising down. Muqim [the fort commander] and his belongings then got out, safe and sound."[29]

Life was again good for Babur. For the first time in almost a decade, he had a secure "place," the tax revenues of the cities and districts of Kabul and Ghazni, and "shared out" portions to his nobles.[30] It was not pastureland that he gave to his nobles but productive agricultural land, taxable in donkey-loads of grain. The whole of the army shared the pastureland.

Kabul was a major trading city. Caravans came from much of Central Asia, from Fargana, Turkistan, Samarkand, Bukhara, Balkh, and Hissar. "Down to Kabul every year come 7, 8, or 10,000 horses and up to it from Hindustan come every year caravans . . . bringing slaves, white cloth, sugar-candy, refined and common sugar, and aromatic roots."[31] The city was one of the crossroads of the Asian world. "Eleven or twelve tongues are spoken in Kabul— Arabi, Persian, Turki, Mughuli, Hindi, Afghani, Pashai, Paraji, Biri, Birki, and Lamghani. If there be another country with so many differing tribes and such a diversity of tongues, it is not known."[32]

In his memoir Babur lingers over meadows of tulips in the spring, the view from the Kabul citadel, snow from nearby mountains to cool summer drinks, and the pleasures of local fruit.

> Amongst those of the cold climates, there are had in the town the grape, pomegranate, apricot, apple, quince, pear, peach, jujube,

almond, and walnut. . . . Of fruits of the hot climate people bring
into the town—orange, citron . . . and sugar-cane . . . the rhubarb
of the Kabul district is good, its quinces and plums very good . . .
Kabul wines are heady.[33]

In winter, he burned a particular oak that made "a hot fire with
plenty of hot ashes and a nice smell. It has the peculiarity of in
burning that when its leafy branches are set alight, they burn
with amazing sound, blazing and cracking from bottom to top. It
was good fun to burn it."[34]

Babur had the leisure to explore the pleasures of the noble life.
He laid out several gardens in and around Kabul and oversaw their
irrigation and construction.[35] This pattern continued throughout
his life; where Babur conquered, he built gardens, several of which
still exist.

In his love of gardens, Babur was part of an old and widespread Asian noble tradition. In the dry climates of the Middle
East and the steppe, water and pleasure were closely intertwined.
To create a place of pools, streams, and fountains was to create a
paradise. In the Quran, written almost 1,000 years earlier, Paradise was a garden.

About love and sex Babur was modest. He was first married at
sixteen.

Though I was not ill-disposed toward her, yet, this being my first
marriage, out of modesty and bashfulness, I used to see her once
in 10, 15, or 20 days. Later on when my first inclination did not
last, my bashfulness increased.[36]

His first feelings of love came at about the same time, but for a
boy from the camp bazaar. "In that frothing-up of desire and
passion, and under that stress of youthful folly, I used to wander,

bare-headed and bare-foot, through street and lane, orchard and vineyard."[37] In a few months, according to the much later perspective of the memoir, Babur got over what he termed this "youthful folly." Throughout the memoir he generally disapproved of homosexuality, but it was clearly common among nobles. Multiple wives were expected, but Babur spent little time writing about them, treating his wives collectively, rather like cumbersome baggage that had to be stored in a safe place. Concubines were also an expected part of the noble life, but Babur mentions only those belonging to others, never his own. Babur reserved his passionate writing for battles and conquest, not for sex.

Drugs and alcohol were common in the noble life. In his youth Babur abstained from alcohol, as the Quran required, but he began drinking in his thirties during the years in Kabul. He seems to have preferred hashish to alcohol, though parties generally kept to one or the other. In December 1519 CE, he and a group of nobles went on a boating excursion. One group drank alcohol, not realizing that at the other end of the boat, other nobles were eating hashish. Babur knew there would be trouble and tried unsuccessfully to keep the two groups apart.

> A hashish party never goes well with a wine party; the drinkers began to make wild talk and chatter from all sides, mostly in allusion to hashish and hashish eaters. . . . The drinkers made Tardi Khan mad drunk, by giving him one full bowl after another. Try as we did to keep things straight, nothing went well; there was much disgusting uproar; the party became intolerable and was broken up.[38]

At less riotous parties, the regular entertainments were poetry, music, and dance. Nobles were expected to try their hand at original poetry, though Babur found little merit in most of what was produced, including some of his own. In his estimation one of the

Great Khans of his father's generation produced mediocre poetry. "Many couplets in his *diwan* [collection] are not bad; it is however in one and the same meter throughout."[39] Babur, however, singled out one of this khan's nobles for his poetry. "For as long as verse has been written in the Turki tongue, no one has written so much or so well as he."[40] Another noble "danced wonderfully well, doing one dance quite unique and seeming to be his own invention."[41] As for the musical instruments at these frequent parties, Babur mentions the flute, the Jew's harp and the lute, played by both nobles and professionals.

Babur chided one noble as "a constant dicer and draught-player."[42] One official was "madly fond of chess so much so that if he met two players, he would hold one by the skirt while he played his game out with the other, as much as to say, 'Don't go!'"[43]

Another of the pleasures of the noble life was fine fabric. The amount of silk found among the nobility of a good-sized town astonished Babur. In 1508 CE, he conquered and sacked Kandahar in central Afghanistan. Two days later, outside of town, he reviewed the spoils.

> Excellent tipuchaqs [horses], strings and strings of he-camels, she-camels, and mules, bearing saddlebags of silken stuffs and cloth—tents of scarlet and velvet, all sorts of awnings . . . ass-load after ass-load of chests. . . . Out of each [treasury] had come chest upon chest, bale upon bale of stuffs and clothes. . . .[44]

Just possessing and wearing fine fabric was not enough. Fashion shifted frequently at court. Pleasures of the nobles included currently stylish shoes or a particular twist to the turban. Babur memorialized one of the Great Khans thusly: "Even when old and white-bearded, he wore silken garments of fine red and green."[45]

In the countryside around Kabul, Babur hunted, fished, and hawked. These leisure activities strengthened Babur's ties with his men. Many nobles stayed with him for years. In 1519 CE, Babur mourned the death of Dost Beg, one of the eight comrades who had fought their way out of Akhsi together sixteen years earlier.[46]

Embedded in Babur's memoir are patterns of honorable behavior and shared pleasure that were known and practiced from the Middle East to China. It was these commonalities of honor, decorum, and pleasure that made it possible for commanders like Babur to recruit soldiers from Central Asia, the Middle East, Persia, and Afghanistan in spite of varied traditions and languages. The Asian world of military opportunity was as broad as Ibn Battuta's world of law and administration or Abraham bin Yiju's world of trade.

The decades after the conquest of Kabul saw Babur on campaign in all the familiar places. He briefly again took Samarkand, fought over Hissar, campaigned in Badakshan. He captured and looted the Kandahar treasury; his men looted the town.

Babur consciously saw himself in the conquest tradition of Genghis Khan. "Ever since we came to Kabul it had been in my mind to move on Hindustan."[47] Babur's first raid into India began less than a year after the conquest of Kabul. "The sun being in Aquarius . . . we rode out of Kabul for Hindustan. Another world came into view—other grasses, other trees, other animals, other birds, and other manners and customs of clan and horde."[48] In 1519 CE, he asked the sultan of Delhi for the lands that had once been held by Timur the Lame (known today as Tamerlane). The sultan's representative in Lahore openly insulted Babur's ambassador by refusing him even an audience. He "came back to Kabul a few months later without bringing a reply."[49] Before 1525 CE, Babur made four raids onto the Punjab plains; each collected more cattle and loot and constituted a more serious threat to the Afghan sultan of Delhi.

Although there are few details because Babur did not finish these sections of his memoir before he died, the final massive battle in which Babur's forces defeated and routed the sultan of Delhi took place on the plains east of Delhi in April 1526 CE. Babur used the sweep tactics he so admired in the Uzbegs, the tactic that had defeated his forces outside Samarkand more than two decades earlier. Delhi fell only a month after this battle. Babur was forty-eight years old.

Although he held a spectacularly wealthy "place," Babur spent much of the remainder of his life on campaign. He fought rivals and launched campaigns against Afghan nobles in India who refused to pay tribute. It was for his son that Babur wrote his memoirs. After all his battles, Babur died in bed in 1530 CE. Although his son, Humayan, first lost and then reconquered the kingdom, Babur's dynasty would rule India for 200 years.

Most successful steppe conquerors, whether in India, Turkey, China, or Persia, changed dramatically in short periods from occupying armies to governments. Many found the lineage system too factionalized and salt too unstable for a dynasty and shifted the basis of their army to slaves, purchased as professional soldiers. It was the genius of Babur's son and grandson to craft a dynasty in India that fulfilled many of the expectations of their subjects, while keeping common traditions of honor that allowed them to recruit soldiers and administrators from Persia, the Middle East, Central Asia, and Afghanistan.

When he conquered Delhi, Babur found a treasury so rich that it staggered him. To his son, Humayan, he gave a treasure house, "just as it was, without ascertaining or writing down its contents."[50] The salt system mandated rewards to all the various ethnic groups that formed Babur's army.

> Suitable money-gifts were bestowed from the Treasury on the whole army, to every tribe there was, Afghan, Hazara, Arab, Biluch, etc. to each according to his position. Every trader and

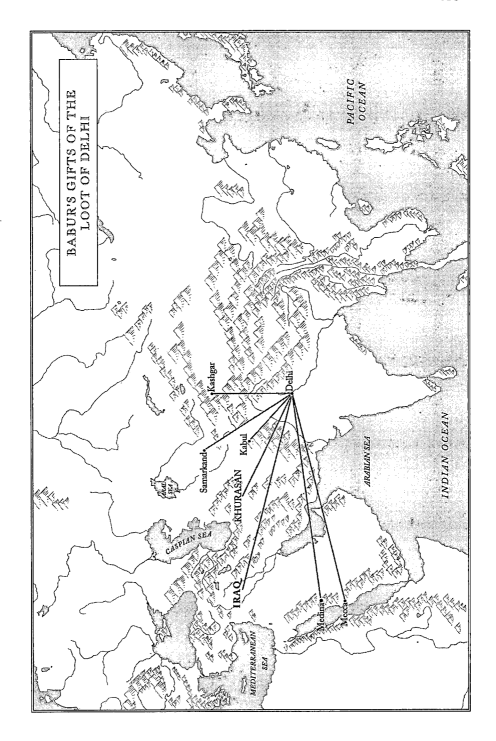

BABUR'S GIFTS OF THE
LOOT OF DELHI

student, indeed, every man who had come with the army, took
ample portion of bounteous gift and largesse.[51]

He sent gold and silver to his relatives in Kabul, Samarkand,
Khurasan, Kashgar, and Iraq. He sent gifts to holy men in
"Samarkand, Khurasan, Mecca, and Medina."[52] Babur's life, his
composite army, and his donations of loot well demonstrate the
far-flung military networks of the great Asian world—networks
of blood and salt.

9

MEDICINES AND MISUNDERSTANDINGS

Tomé Pires, 1511–1521 CE

In the port of Cochin in March 1516 CE, Tomé Pires, a Portuguese apothecary and government scribe, faced a choice. Like Abraham bin Yiju, who paced anxiously on the same coast 100 miles to the north four centuries earlier, Pires had a quandary related to drugs and spices. Whereas Abraham bin Yiju's problem was missing cardamom and financial loss, Pires had the enviable situation of a fortune made in just a few years dealing tropical plants. He wanted to go home with his money, presumably to retire, but the governor of the newly conquered Portuguese holdings in Asia, a friend of Pires, asked him to lead the first diplomatic mission to China. It was too tempting an offer to refuse—a chance to see Beijing and all that lay between the south coast and the capital, something no Portuguese had ever done. By summer Pires agreed to head east rather than west. In January of the following year, he departed with a fleet of four ships, carrying diplomatic letters, royal gifts, and goods to trade in China.[1] His life would be permanently and tragically altered by the expedition. His memoir, covering only his first five years in Asia, is rich in the assumptions and mistakes of the "first wave" of Portuguese conquest in Asia.

Tomé Pires was a small figure on the historical stage, not a great military leader or administrator. He was born a commoner, probably in Lisbon, around 1468 CE. Although not noble, his family had education and status and he wrote of a "luxurious" childhood. His father was apothecary to John II, king of Portugal, and the family probably owned a shop on a well-known street of apothecaries.[2]

These were exciting times for the Pires family and people like them, who were the educated elite associated with the court of Portugal. Beginning in the 1430s CE, the king sponsored attacks on Muslim North Africa, immediately opposite the Straits of Gibraltar, and exploration of the west coast of Africa. The goal was not the spices of India but the gold of central Africa. Muslims completely controlled the trans-Sahara trade, and Portugal hoped to gain a portion of this trade from the coast of West Africa.[3]

For sixty years, the Portuguese fleets conquered just enough valuable territory to justify continued royal patronage. Among the conquests were the Canary Islands, which grew wheat that Portugal needed, and the west coast of Africa, which yielded some gold, ivory, and slaves.[4] Important results of these decades-long explorations were steady advances in ship design, navigation, sail technology, and gun casting. As every schoolchild knows, the Portuguese finally hit pay dirt in the 1490s. Vasco da Gama's fleet rounded the Cape of Good Hope, hired a pilot on the east coast of Africa, and sailed to the Malabar Coast of India. In the same decade, Columbus sailed west to America.

Tomé Pires served as apothecary to Prince Alfonso until the prince's untimely death in 1491 CE. Exactly what he did after that or why Pires left Portugal for India in April 1511 CE is unknown, but he had letters of introduction from two important people: the chief physician of the king and the head of the overseas department in Lisbon. The fleet sailed down the west coast of Africa, around the Cape of Good Hope, and into the Asian world.[5]

In the decade after the first voyage of Vasco da Gama, the yearly
Portuguese forays had already had an impact on maritime Asia. As
trading competitors, the Portuguese had little to offer. Europe produced no goods that Asia needed and few that it wanted. Those few,
such as Venetian glass and olive oil, already arrived in Asia through
well-known sea routes from the Middle East to the west coast of
India and beyond. Spices, medicines, fabrics, and ceramics likewise
moved back along these same routes.[6] The new Portuguese route
around Africa was longer, more dangerous, and more costly than existing routes. Established traders were better organized and better
funded, and had much more knowledge of local conditions than the
Portuguese. For each Portuguese ship, there were dozens, if not
hundreds, of local ships.[7]* Portuguese navigational methods and instruments were in no way superior to Asian equivalents at the time.

The Portuguese, to their credit, realized all of this quite early on.
Their few advantages were military and organizational. Their cannons were of superior metal to those in Asia. During ceaseless wars
in the Mediterranean and the decades of exploration of the West
African coast, crews of ships had learned how to fire regularly, rapidly, and fairly accurately. When Vasco da Gama entered the Asian
maritime world, only Portuguese ships and crews were capable of
an effective cannonade of both ports and other ships.[8] Unlike any
other traders in the Asian maritime world, the Portuguese in Asia
had the backing of a king, self-confidence as Christians in a heathen world, and the beginnings of bureaucratic loyalty among
court appointees.

Using these advantages, the Portuguese quickly turned from
negotiating with local rulers to conquest, launching the most au-
dacious attempt to dominate maritime Asia since the Chinese

---

*Ships already plying the Indian Ocean were much larger than the early Por-
tuguese ships, which were in the 100-ton range. The larger dhows were in the
range of 500 tons, whereas Gujarati ships topped 800 tons.

expeditions a century earlier. The Portuguese approach was utterly unlike that of the Chinese. Instead of generalized dominance through diplomacy and recognition of local kings, their strategy was, in fact, much closer to that of Genghis Khan: Seize the trading cities and the important resources, destroy resistance, tax trade, and make conquest pay for itself.[9]* In the Indian Ocean in the first decade of the sixteenth century, the Portuguese took the unfortified ports of Goa, Cochin, and Cannore on the Malabar Coast and would soon unsuccessfully attack Aden at the base of the Red Sea. Farther east at the same time, the Portuguese negotiated rights to trade at Malacca and set up a trading station. Within a year, the Muslim sultan of Malacca closed the station and drove away the Portuguese. The following sailing season, a Portuguese fleet attacked and conquered Malacca and promptly drove out the Muslim and Indian traders. In both the Indian Ocean and Southeast Asia, Portuguese fleets burned or captured many local ships and attempted to extract taxes on trade.[10]

Pires arrived in Goa at a propitious time. A few months earlier, Albuquerque, the governor of the Portuguese conquests in Asia, wrote to his king that there was trouble in Malacca. The few Portuguese in Malacca were in serious conflict over the loot and spoils of the just-captured city. To restore order, the governor decided to send "Tomé Pires, apothecary of the Prince, because he seems to me to be a diligent man." At the time there were only a handful of literate members of the elite class suitable for this responsible job available at Goa. Pires sailed on the *Santo Christo*, which almost sank in monsoon storms off the Malabar Coast, but he reached

---

*Portuguese success was not a sure thing. Their main competitors for control of the Indian Ocean were the Ottomans, whose gun technology was equal to their own. For the Ottomans, the Indian Ocean was not critically important. For a poor, distant country like Portugal, conquests in the Indian Ocean seemed, literally, a god-sent opportunity.

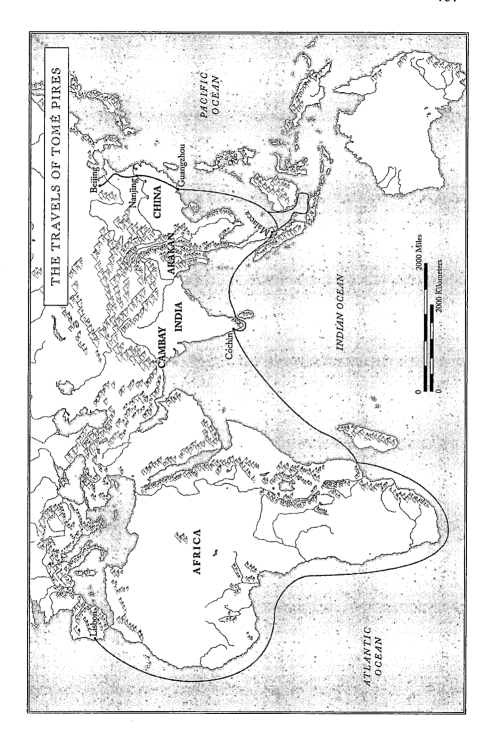

THE TRAVELS OF TOMÉ PIRES

Lisbon

AFRICA

ATLANTIC
OCEAN

CAMBAY

INDIA

Cochin

ARAKAN

CHINA

Nanjing

Beijing

Guangzhou

Malacca

INDIAN OCEAN

PACIFIC
OCEAN

2000 Miles

2000 Kilometers

0

0

Malacca in June or July of 1512 CE. A few months later, he wrote to his brother, "I am in Malacca as scribe and accountant of the trading warehouse and controller of the drugs." He described himself as in good health and rich, "more than you can imagine."[11] Tomé Pires listened to the local traders, occasionally traveled in charge of Portuguese goods, and wrote the *Suma Oriental*, his description of plants, markets, and politics in maritime Asia.

What sort of place was the Southeast Asia of Tomé Pires? In some ways it had changed little from Ma Huan's description eighty years earlier. Medicinal plants were still crucially important trade items. Pires, as an apothecary, knew them well. He noted that Sumatra and Java had pepper, cardamom, edible camphor, benzoin, "cassia fistula," and "apothecary's lignaoes." The islands to the east had black benzoin, two kinds of camphor, cloves, nutmeg, mace, and white sandalwood.

The spices and medicines moved from tropical sources both east and west. The trade from India and Southeast Asia to China was already 1,000 years old. A fifth-century Chinese botanical treatise discusses the banana, Indian myrobalan, and hibiscus.[12] Xuanzang, the Buddhist pilgrim of the seventh century, tried to bring Indian plants back along with his Buddhist sacred books. In the subsequent two centuries, several Chinese Buddhist monks ventured to India and Southeast Asia specifically to bring back useful plants.[13] Many tropical plants, such as the banana, banyan tree, and hibiscus flower, appear in an early Chinese book, *Nan Fang Cao Mu Zhuang*.[14] By the eleventh century, Chinese medical treatises routinely prescribed more than 100 tropical plants.

Tropical plants and extracts also moved west along the water routes of Asia. The caliphs of Baghdad actively sought useful plants and had them brought to the Middle East. By the ninth century, Arab books of remedies routinely recommended a wide range of tropical ingredients.[15] Ibn Sina's *Canon* mentions cinnamon, cardamom, nutmeg, cubeb, camphor, dragon's blood from a lily resin, tabasheer from bamboo, and cloves, all from Southeast Asia. From India came colyrium, turmeric, pepper, cumin, areca nut, saffron, various sandalwoods, jasmine oil, aloes wood, asafetida, tamarind, caltrop, and myrobolan. From China came jujube, rhubarb, Chinese ginger, and galanga.[16]

The long-term spice trade produced changes in Southeast Asia in the centuries before the Portuguese incursion. Entrepreneurs tried to grow various profitable plants in new locations. Pepper cultivation moved from India to Sumatra and the Malay Peninsula.[17] Mango cultivation began in Java with seeds from India. Many attempts to grow useful plants in new places failed because the microclimate required for the spice was confined to a single small group of islands or even a single island. Some islands were, however, so successful at growing steadily traded cash crops that the inhabitants stopped growing food. On these spice islands, such as Banda, food, particularly rice and fish paste, were imported.

> These islands have villages; they have no king but are ruled by [headmen] and by the elders. . . . In all there must be between two thousand five hundred and three thousand persons on these islands. Those along the sea-coast are Moorish merchants. . . . There are a few heathen inside the country. . . . About five hundred bahars of mace must be produced in every year in the islands . . . and six or seven thousand bahars of nutmeg. . . . The islands of Banda have hardly any foodstuffs. The surrounding islands bring foodstuffs.[18]

Pires only heard stories of the inland kingdom of Arakan, in present-day Myanmar, but he got the essentials right.[19] Arakan was typical of large inland states located on the mainland of Southeast Asia in today's Myanmar, Thailand, and Cambodia. The economies of these states were based less on trade than on rice production and taxation in labor.

> The king is a heathen and very powerful in the hinterland. It has
> a good port on the sea . . . but not much trade. . . . There are
> many horsemen in the land of Arakan and many elephants. There
> is some silver . . . [and] three or four kinds of cotton cloths . . .
> The kingdom abounds in meat, rice, and things that they eat.[20]

Pires's description is equally accurate about another type of
Southeast Asian kingdom, which was based on irrigated rice and
located either along a river or on a delta. Pegu, in current-day
Myanmar, was this kind of state.

> Pegu is a kingdom of heathens. It is the most fertile land of all we
> have seen and known. It is more plenteous than Siam and almost
> as much as Java. . . . The principal [merchandise] is rice. There
> comes every year . . . fifteen to sixteen junks, twenty to thirty . . .
> cargo ships. They bring a great deal of lac, and benzoin, musk,
> precious stones, rubies, silver, butter, oil, salt, onions . . . and
> things to eat like that. The king is always in residence in the city
> of Pegu which is inland . . . a day and night's journey. . . .[21]

Pires knew the port city best of all, the Southeast Asian entrepôt, based on a favorable harbor and location for transshipping
between regions. In the sixteenth century, Malacca was the prime
example. Pires described its far-flung connections prior to Portuguese conquest in the *Suma Oriental.*

> The said king Xaquem Darxa was very pleased with the . . .
> Moorish merchants; he did them honour; he gave them places to
> live in, and a place for their mosques; . . . they built beautiful
> houses. And people came from other places, from Sumatra, came
> to work and earn their living. . . . [The king] wanted to go to
> China in person . . . and he went where the king [of China] was
> and talked to him and made himself his tributary vassal . . .

[Xaquem Darxa's] name became so famous that he had messages and presents from the kings of Aden and Ormuz and Cambay and Bengal, and they sent many merchants from their region to live in Malacca.[22]

Tomé well understood the direct connections between various entrepôts in the Asian maritime system. Cambay, in present-day Gujarat, was one. "The Cambay merchants make Malacca their chief trading centre. . . . Malacca cannot live without Cambay, nor Cambay without Malacca if they are to be very rich and prosperous."[23] A port like Malacca grew virtually none of its own food and was dependent on imports.[24]

Like Ma Huan's memoir a century earlier, Pires's book is much more than a recitation of products and markets. It reveals two core attitudes and assumptions that are so different that they label Pires as an outsider to the great Asian world.

Throughout the narrative, Pires divided the world into Moors, that is, Sunni Muslims, who were anywhere and everywhere the "enemy," and Christians, anywhere and everywhere the "ally." Heathens were potential allies against the Moors and possible converts. In common with other early Portuguese in Asia, Pires brought the Crusades with him and imposed the centuries-old conflict, belonging to the Mediterranean, on Asia. The Portuguese never recognized that local history, regional loyalty, and family rivalry might be far more important than whether people were Christian or heathen. This shortsightedness dogged the whole Portuguese venture and, as we shall see, had tragic results for Tomé Pires.

Early in his memoir, for example, Pires described a Persian Shia Muslim king as great and noble because he was opposed to the Sunni Muslim powers to the west, the hated Moors.

And the ambassadors sent by this Sheikh are attended by many mounted men, well dressed people of good appearance, very sumptuous, with vessels of gold and silver, which show forth the greatness of the Sheikh. He says that he will not rest until all the Moors [are] made followers of Ali in his time.[25]

He saw the Hindu traders of western India as heathens, possibly lapsed Christians and potential converts.

The heathens of Cambay are great idolaters and soft, weak people. Some of them are men who in their religion lead good lives, they are chaste, true men, and very abstemious. They believe in Our lady and in the Trinity, and there is no doubt that they were once Christians and that they gradually lost faith because of Mohammedans.[26]

In fairness to Tomé Pires, he sometimes appreciated the heathen peoples he observed. His description of the shadow plays of Java reads surprisingly like Ma Huan's.

The land of Java is [a land of] mummers and masks of various kinds, and both men and women do thus. They have entertainments of dancing and stories. They are certainly graceful; they have the music of bells—the sound of all of them playing together is like an organ. At night they make shadows of various shapes like *beneditos* in Portugal.[27]

What Tomé did not understand is that although the Asian world had had its share of religious war, it remained a place of many religions and many loyalties. Abraham bin Yiju, for example, made his business alliances with Gujarati Hindus and Muslims from Mangalore. Almish refused caliphate Islam not out of conviction but because Ibn Fadlan had not brought the silver for the fort. Ma Huan respected the Buddhist and Hindu courts he visited.

Pires's narrative over and over connects strength with the white race. In previous memoirs, there were, no doubt, many biases. Xuanzang liked neither rival Hinayana Buddhists nor non-Buddhist kings. Ibn Battuta had no use for small towns in which he could not get tasty food and a clean bed. Ibn Fadlan found steppe nomads generally unclean and longed for the courtly pleasures of Baghdad. Ma Huan was happy enough to stay away from islands that were uncivilized. Still, none of this was couched in racial terms. Pires called the Persians strong, because they were white.[28] In describing the warring kingdoms of peninsular India, Pires said, "The man who has the most white men in his kingdom is the most powerful."[29] In this simple scheme, the Chinese were white and therefore should have had a natural affinity for the Portuguese. The Chinese, however, saw things quite differently.

When Tomé Pires and his small diplomatic fleet approached the coast of China in August 1517 CE, they unknowingly carried more than diplomatic letters, presents for the emperor, and trade goods. They also carried attitudes toward religion and race that would hamper them, a style of dealing with heathens that would get them in trouble, and the unforeseen consequences of a decade of burning fleets and seizing ports. To Tomé Pires, the Chinese were natural allies. The *Suma Oriental*, finished before he left Cochin, praises them highly:

> The King of China is a heathen with much land and many people. The people of China are white, as white as we are. . . . They wear round silk net caps like the black sieves we have in Portugal. They are rather like Germans. They have thirty or forty hairs in their beards. They wear very well-made French [-style] shoes with square toes. . . . The women look like Spanish women . . . and they are so made up that Seville has no advantage over them.[30]

He was equally sure that China would be an easy conquest.

Not to rob any country of its glory, it certainly seems that China is an important, good, and very wealthy country, and the Governor of Malacca would not need as much force as they say in order to bring it under our rule, because the people are very weak and easy to overcome. And the principal people who have often been there affirm that with ten ships the Governor of India who took Malacca could take the whole of China along the sea-coast.[31]

The first contact with the Chinese navy at the mouth of the bay formed by the Pearl River Delta was not promising. The Chinese harbor fleet fired on the Portuguese, thinking that they were pirates. The Portuguese did not return fire. Eventually, the commander of the Portuguese fleet, with much difficulty, convinced the Chinese that they were diplomats, not pirates.[32] To proceed up the delta to Guangzhou, the fleet needed permission from the Guangzhou authorities. Bureaucratic delays began almost immediately. When the Portuguese ships were damaged in a storm, the Chinese offered no assistance. Months passed. Initial optimism gave way to the Portuguese realization that they were of minimal importance and interest to the Chinese. The Portuguese were apparently unaware that ambassadorial missions had been arriving in China for more than 1,000 years. Their reception always depended on the politics of the imperial court.[33]* Finally, the Portuguese

---

*The delays and indifference of the Chinese officials were directed specifically at the Portuguese. Imperial policy was pro-trade and the port was extremely busy the entire time that the Portuguese waited. The imperial court was also not anti-foreign. Some two decades before the Pirés expedition, fifty-six Koreans were shipwrecked on the coast of Zhejiang Province, south of the current day city of Hangzhou. The captain's memoir recounts their discovery by a military patrol. Captain and crew were speedily and efficiently conducted by canal and land to the imperial capital and in due course repatriated to Korea.

commander forced local Chinese officials to allow the fleet to sail to Guangzhou without official permission.[34]

Nineteen months after his departure from Cochin, Tomé Pires arrived at Guangzhou. The fleet fired salutes and flew flags, both of which offended the local officials. Finally, negotiations by Pires convinced the officials of the city that firing the guns was a form of respect and that the mission had come to establish friendly ambassadorial relations with the Chinese court. The Portuguese disembarked "with a great thunder of artillery, and trumpets, and the men in gala dress, the Ambassador being accompanied by seven Portuguese, who remained with him to go on this embassy. They were taken to their lodgings, which were some of the noblest houses in the city." The Portuguese observed none of the local customs of diplomacy or honor. They presented no robes, gave no suitable presents, hosted no banquets, and perceived themselves superior to such practices.

For a while, things went well in spite of this. The Portuguese traded in Guangzhou and sent letters back to Malacca praising their treatment and conditions. The fleet left after fourteen months in China and arrived at Malacca "very prosperous in honour and wealth, things rarely secured together."[35]

Fifteen months after the fleet had departed for Malacca, Pires and his entourage were still awaiting permission to proceed to Beijing, the Chinese capital, when the Portuguese fleet returned to escort them back to Malacca. By this time, Pires had realized that keeping an ambassadorial mission waiting, especially one the court had not requested, was typical Chinese imperial practice. The commander of the Portuguese fleet was a short-tempered, rough man, and he confronted the Chinese, demanding that Pires and his seven attendants be allowed to depart for Beijing. He apparently offended the local Chinese officials in many ways, for example, by building a stone fort at the mouth of the Canton River and hanging one of his crew on Chinese soil.[36]

The Portuguese seemed unaware of the particular attention paid to control of seaports by the Chinese and of the centuries of tension between traders and the imperial bureaucracy. In Chinese ports, there had been rebellions by traders and complicity among Chinese officials, with subsequent massacres of foreign traders by local Chinese. As there was no special jurisdiction that protected foreign traders in China, many had been tried before Chinese courts and found guilty of violating Chinese law.

In response to the Portuguese commander's harsh threats and aggressive behavior, local officials in Guangzhou allowed Pires and his men to depart for the capital. The Pires expedition headed north, going upriver in Chinese boats, then overland to Nanjing, a journey of almost 1,000 miles. The emperor declined to see the Portuguese in Nanjing and sent them on to Beijing, another 1,000 miles north. In February 1521 CE, the emperor, who had been traveling, returned to Beijing. Pires had already arrived and awaited his reception.

Within days, events turned disastrous. An ambassador from the deposed king of Malacca arrived with a letter detailing the Portuguese assault and conquest of the city. The letter reminded the imperial court that Malacca was a vassal of China, and the king of Malacca was asking for help against the foreign foe. At the same time, letters arrived from local officials of both Beijing and Guangzhou detailing complaints against the Portuguese, including the charge that the Portuguese kidnapped Chinese children and ate them. When Pires's ambassadorial letter was opened and translated in Beijing, it showed that the Portuguese rejected vassal status and subordination to the imperial court. The letter, thus, refused a centuries-old pattern of China's relations with powers beyond its borders. (Recall that these sorts of vassalage treaties were the type that Ma Huan, as Arabic translator, helped negotiate.) The letter infuriated the court and made the situation even more precarious for Pires and his men.[37]

At this critical juncture, the emperor died. The new emperor was a boy of fourteen, controlled by court advisers. This court faction returned Pires's diplomatic presents and revoked his ambassadorial status. Many at court called Pires and his men impostors or sea pirates. The imperial court sent the Pires mission back to Guangzhou with instructions that they were to remain in prison until the Portuguese returned Malacca to its rightful king. The local officials rounded up and imprisoned any Portuguese traders found in the city. The Chinese coastal fleet killed or captured any Portuguese on trading ships that arrived and fought a pitched battle with a group of Portuguese warships from Malacca.

The authorities in Guangzhou insisted that Pires write a letter to the Portuguese in Malacca demanding the return of the city to its rightful king. Pires refused, and the whole party was put in heavy iron fetters. One man died. Pires was later released from fetters, but some months later, the situation worsened after another sea battle between the Chinese and a Portuguese fleet. One of the prisoners wrote to Malacca, "Before it was night, they put fetters once more on Tomé Pires and conducted him alone, barefoot, and without a cap, amid the hootings of boys to the prison." The officials seized all the cash, the trade goods, such as tortoise shells, cloth, and pepper, and the diplomatic presents of the expedition.[38]

Several prisoners died in the heavy iron fetters. On December 6, 1522 CE, sentence was pronounced on the remaining twenty-three Portuguese prisoners, including Pires's embassy and all Portuguese sailors and traders in the city of Guangzhou. The summation: "Petty sea robbers sent by the great robber falsely; they come to spy on our country; let them die in the pillory as robbers." In September of the following year, the prisoners were executed, dismembered, and their body parts displayed on stakes around the city. Each head had the respective man's penis in its mouth. Their bodies were later thrown on dunghills.

From the Chinese perspective, collective punishment of all of the Portuguese was predictable. In China, there had been, at various times, many official attacks on whole groups: Buddhists, Daoists, Khitan, and the elite class in Vietnam. Specifically, the Chinese officials and court found the Portuguese without a sense of honor and devoid of ambassadorial customs. They had seized a port that was a vassal of China and were thus strictly pirates. Particularly galling to the court was the claim that the Portuguese, including the traders, not only represented a king equal to the Chinese emperor, but that they were under his protection in China. No other trading group in the Asian world had ever claimed this close association between king and traders. Abraham bin Yiju, for example, while working on the Malabar Coast, would never have claimed protection of the emir of Egypt.

Within decades, the Portuguese grand plan for control of the Asian maritime world had failed. The scheme had been wrong in many of its assumptions. The Asian world had its own history, alliances, rivalries, and loyalties that had nothing to do either with the Moor-Christian-heathen view of the world or with the racial superiority so central to Portuguese thinking. The Asian world also proved much more resilient than the Portuguese expected. A wide variety of Muslims continued to trade throughout Southeast Asia and the Indian Ocean in spite of Portuguese hostility. The Portuguese were unable to stop or slow the conversion to Islam that proceeded through the islands of Sumatra and Java.[39] Atjeh, the Muslim rival to Malacca, fought the Portuguese to a stalemate.

Although grandiose schemes for the conquest of Southeast Asia continued to surface in Portugal for the next eighty years,[40] the reality was that kingdoms did not fall when ports were taken and control of ports was always tenuous if the center held. The Portuguese were forced to withdraw from Sri Lanka after protracted war.[41] The Portuguese learned that the big kingdoms of Asia were based on agricultural taxes. Trade, while important, was rarely critical to large empires. (This is something that Babur, for example, understood to his very bones in his conquest of India.)

The Portuguese were rather more successful in Gujarat on the west coast of India. They blockaded the narrow Gulf of Cambay and forced significant changes. Many Muslim merchants left. The remaining Hindu merchants often paid protection money to the Portuguese. Still, the Portuguese knew that they could not destroy Gujarati cotton production. They were dependent on Gujarati cotton as their major trade item, both in Southeast Asia and in Africa.[42]

Portuguese attempts to tax shipping through enforced monopoly also failed. Asian merchants built bigger, faster ships that evaded Portuguese fleets and retained the lion's share of the seaborne trade.[43] Right through the sixteenth century, more pepper and spices were transported to and sold in the Middle East and China than ever came to Europe. The Asian merchants developed new entrepôts to replace the ones seized by the Portuguese.

The Portuguese effort cannot, however, be dismissed as merely an overreaching failure. It had important and unexpected effects on the Asian world. In the short run, the Chinese reacted with a ban on foreign traders that lasted several decades, forcing such trade to offshore islands.[44] More important for the long run, the Portuguese incursion initiated a widespread arms race across the whole of the Asian maritime world. Within a few decades, local kings had fortified their ports from Aden to Southeast Asia.

The trade itself also had profound effects. Although the route was long and dangerous, the Portuguese trade tied the spice islands of Southeast Asia directly to Europe for the first time. New linkages connected the Molucca Islands, Malacca, Portuguese ports on the Malabar Coast, trading stations in Africa, and Portugal. In Southeast Asia, the spice trade involved captains and officials deeply in the politics of many small kingdoms. Some large kingdoms, such as Ayuthia, lost trade to Malacca and shrank in power.[45] Yearly fleets arrived from Portugal with news and orders. Although the spice trade to Europe was less than one-fourth of the trade to Asia, the Portuguese were, by the 1530s, shipping nearly one-half of the spices bound for Europe.[46] Tropical spices appeared in Europe in larger quantities than previously and consequently appeared in European cookbooks of the sixteenth century. The wealth this trade created was, however, concentrated in a few hands. Profits went only to the Portuguese ship captain, the owner, and the king.[47]

Some local officials made fortunes by evading the monopolies established by the Portuguese king. For ordinary Portuguese soldiers, however, service in Asia was not lucrative. Within a decade of the conquest of Malacca, many Portuguese soldiers and sailors drifted off to become mercenaries in the ensuing Asian arms race and became the source for new military ideas in many regional courts. Some Portuguese left official service and became private traders in the Asian maritime world.[48]

Worldview and race continued to bedevil the Portuguese in Asia. They never successfully recruited local educated elites unless they converted to Christianity and always preferred Portuguese blood, even if it was mixed with local.

And what of Tomé Pires? Was he executed and dismembered with the rest of his expedition? Possibly not. During the two years of his incarceration, two letters from prisoners arrived at Malacca. Neither original exists, and the surviving copies are garbled. It appears, however, that Tomé Pires was held in a separate prison. One of the letters assumes that he was executed. No one, however, was able to put a place or a date on Pires's death. The other letter, a somewhat later account, says that it was the emperor's order that "he should be taken to another town, where he lived for a long time, til it should be the King's pleasure to speak to him; but he never more let him come back, and there he died."

There is one piece of corroborating evidence. Two decades after Pires's imprisonment, a Portuguese cleric named Fernao Mendes Pinto arrived at a town he called Sampitay, on the northern border of current-day Jiangsu Province. A young woman approached him and said that her name was Ines de Leiria and that she was the daughter of Tomé Pires. She told a story of his banishment from Guangzhou, his arrival and marriage to her mother, who had some property, and his death only a few years previously. She said a bit of the Paternoster in Portuguese and had a cross tattooed on her arm. Some modern scholars have called Pinto a blatant liar, but others find the story plausible. Perhaps Tomé Pires escaped death and lived out his life with a wealthy wife in a Chinese provincial town.[49]

10

THE ASIAN WORLD

500–1500 CE

The Asian world, 500–1500 CE, was a place of great empires and large capital cities. In Southeast Asia were the kingdoms of Srivajaya, Pagan, Angkor, Champa, and Dai Viet. China went through dynastic changes but was strongly linked to the rest of Asia. India had empires as well—the Kushans, the sultanates, and the Mughals based at Delhi; the Cholas and Vijayanagara in the south. The Middle East had the Abbasid caliphate. Central Asia had Genghis Khan's empire, the largest the world has ever known, and it had the empire of Timur. The populations of these realms were in many cases larger than the whole of Western Europe.

Asia was a vast world of contrast, from deserts to mountains, from monsoon rain forest to dry plains. It held a bewildering variety of cultures and languages, many local religions and varieties of Buddhism, Islam, and Hinduism that spread across wide regions.

But it was its networks that made the great Asian world unique. Bureaucrats, scholars, slaves, ideas, religions, and plants moved along its intersecting routes. Family ties stretched across thousands of miles. Traders found markets for products ranging from heavy recycled bronze to the most diaphanous silks.*

---

*This volume explores only some of the networks found in Asia in the millennium from 500 to 1500 ce. There were many more. One could consider the

178

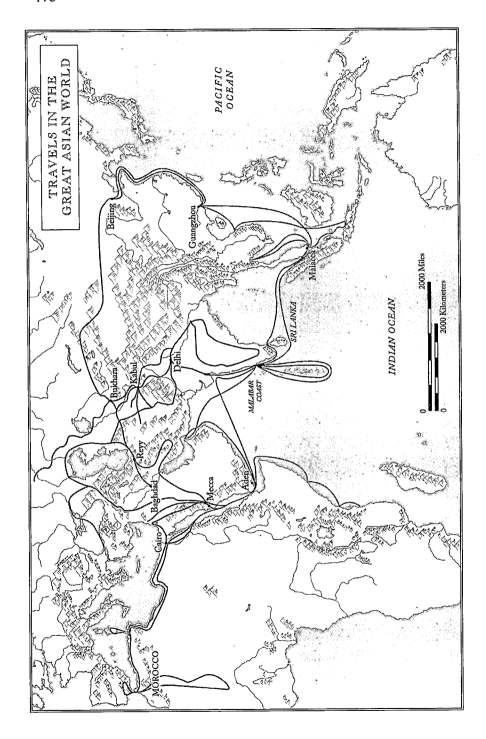

TRAVELS IN THE
GREAT ASIAN WORLD

PACIFIC
OCEAN

Beijing

Guangzhou

Malacca

SRI LANKA

INDIAN OCEAN

MALABAR
COAST

Bukhara

Kabul

Delhi

Reyy

Baghdad

Mecca

Aden

Cairo

MOROCCO

2000 Miles

2000 Kilometers

To clarify this world, here is drawn on a single map the routes of the travelers featured in the various chapters. "Crossing Points" are cities that two or more travelers visited. The routes and networks connected a world that went from China across Central Asia, into India and the Middle East, North Africa, Spain, and portions of sub-Saharan Africa.

EMPIRES AND CITIES

Asian empires tended to promote linkages and connections to other kingdoms in several ways. Often their own territories crossed "natural" ecological boundaries and brought together regions and societies in unexpected ways. The Kushans, the Afghans, and the Mughals established empires that successfully ruled both sides of the formidable Himalayas. The South Indian Chola kingdom built a navy and conquered the islands of Sri Lanka, Java, and Sumatra, politically tying together India and Southeast Asia. Genghis Khan ruled both the steppe and large areas of agricultural China. Administrative continuities generally promoted trade between ecologically different regions: the trade in horses from the steppe to the plains of India, in rice from south to north China, in steel from Damascus to Afghanistan. The big states also produced widely used currencies, such as Chinese cash[1] and silver dirhams, and established standards for normalizing local weights and measures.

---

many pilgrimage routes from the viewpoint of networks or bring the same kind of analysis to patterns of marriage that spread family or clan influence. Court painters corresponded, viewed each other's work, and moved to find patronage across a network that stretched from Spain to southern India. Systems of predicting the future, such as astrology and numerology, were broadly similar across much of Asia. Many of the practitioners formed networks of knowledge. Analysis of both slavery and piracy in Asia could benefit from this approach.

They also frequently organized postal systems for reliable communication. Abraham bin Yiju could send a letter from Mangalore and have it arrive in Cairo in slightly over a month. Ibn Battuta found that his letter of introduction went from the far western border of India to Delhi and back in less than two months.

Although the big capital cities—Delhi, Beijing, Baghdad, Vijayanagara—were impressive (and often many times the size of any European city of the time), the importance of medium-sized cities cannot be overemphasized. These empires, by and large, rose by the expansion of power of a regional family based in a medium-sized city, their regional capital. When empires fell, they generally devolved into regional successor states. The regional capitals usually not only survived, they thrived. Medium-sized cities thus remained long-term sources of demand, learning, and patronage, and in addition, they produced the bureaucrats necessary to run an empire.

Cities, large and small, needed basic food, fabric, fuel, and building materials. The elite of these cities attracted the more sophisticated trade goods of the Asian world. The Chinese urban elite generated an almost insatiable demand for ivory, both African and Southeast Asian, which found its way into religious statues, pens, fans, boxes, and the decoration of furniture. Their demand for the most aromatic incense in the world was filled by incense logs and bushes from Southeast Asia and India. The demand for elegant clothes and beautiful colors in population centers of the Middle East, India, and Southeast Asia pushed discovery of and trade in new plant dyes.

The urban centers were also places of specialized manufacture that created trade opportunities and employment for these skills. Cities produced books, artwork, fine fabrics, sophisticated musical instruments, jewelry, and scientific instruments, all of which were in demand throughout the Asian world. Damascus developed steelmaking to such a high art and in such quantity that traders brought its products to all parts of the Asian world. Damascus blades were just as ubiquitous in Indonesia as they were in Babur's Central Asia. China produced prodigious quantities of ceramics that were traded across the Asian world, from the Philippines and Japan to the west coast of Africa.

COURTLY AND POLITICAL CULTURE

As places of elite culture, these cities and courts had many similarities. Across the great Asian world, kings used broadly similar symbols, including the umbrella, sunshade, fly whisk, drums, horns, and jeweled weapons. Ceremonies, such as honorific robbing, were also similar. In the seventh century, a Buddhist king in Central Asia honored the pilgrim Xuanzang with ceremonial robes. Two hundred years later, Ibn Fadlan carried honorific robes from the Abbasid caliph of Baghdad and presented them to Almish on his ill-fated ambassadorial mission. Four centuries later, Ibn Battuta received honorific robes from kings across the Middle East, at Christian Constantinople, and in Muslim sub-Saharan Africa. A century later, Ma Huan recorded the diplomatic presentation of silk honorific robes to kings the Chinese fleet visited. In the sixteenth century in central Asia, Babur received robes from his powerful clan uncle. He later gave robes to his leaders after the victories at Kabul and Delhi. Similarly widespread was the presentation to honored guests of pan—betel nut wrapped in a special leaf, a pleasant substance to chew. The ceremony showed the largesse of the king, the honor demonstrated by the king's preparing it with his own hands, and the deference of public acceptance by the receiver. Kings from the Middle East to South China presented pan or robes, or both, to ambassadors, their own nobles, soldiers, guests, and their own family. The function of both ceremonies was to establish a relationship between the giver and the receiver in the presence of an approving audience.

The large empires also produced courtly cultures that became part of the practice of whole regions and local ethnicities. A Persianized culture, adopted by Afghan and Central Asian conquerors of India, merged with local practice to become a common elite culture across much of India. The culture of the Chinese court gradually spread to become elite culture throughout Vietnam. A Burman culture spread from the court at the expense of local ethnicities.

Across much of Asia, the political culture included common rewards and pleasures of courtly life. There was a common acceptance and understanding of the relationship between earthly pleasure and the pleasure of Paradise. One did not stand against the other. Among the travelers of this book, several were from the courtly class and indulged in the typical courtly pleasures. Babur had gardens built, named them, and enjoyed them immensely. He is quite open about his frequent use of alcohol and hashish, recounting their effects, and extolling the camaraderie of drinking parties. Both Ibn Battuta and Babur had slaves and concubines of both sexes. Fine fabrics were one of life's great pleasures in the Asian world. Both Babur and Ibn Battuta knew their fabrics and could name the origin of any particularly fine piece. Hunting with the king was another of the widely shared courtly pleasures. It was both a ceremony of noble solidarity and practice for war. Hunting figures prominently in Babur's memoir during periods of peace. The Central Asian notion of the king's table spread through the Middle East, Persia, and India. Nobles shared exotic foods and talk; some wrote books of recipes. Music and dance were the common entertainment. The pleasures of the noble life included patronage of intellectuals and artists, who produced books, poetry, painting, and calligraphy. Other common recreations were equally widely shared. Chess, for example, was played from Spain to China. The Persian ambassador to China at the time of Ma Huan was a great chess player and readily found opponents in Beijing.

BUDDHISM AND ISLAM

The great Asian world benefited from two major universalizing religions: Islam and Buddhism. Both addressed universal human needs and recruited on the basis of relatively simple personal commitment rather than ethnicity, region, language, or gender. Both required long-distance travel in pursuit of knowledge and training and built institutions that promoted and supported such travel. At the height of Buddhism, there was a chain of monasteries, rest houses, and sites of worship stretching across Central Asia, Afghanistan, India, Southeast Asia, China, Japan, and Korea. Islamic patronage eventually developed madrassas and rest houses that stretched from Spain across North Africa, through the Middle East, into both Central Asia and India, and certain cities of Southeast Asia and China. These institutions made it possible for believers to find shelter and worship with others thousands of miles from home. In both religions, building rest houses, establishing markets for traders, and planting trees for shade along roads were acts of religious merit.

Both religions offered legal systems that regulated relations within their communities. Both Sharia law and, to a lesser extent, Buddhist practice created far-flung communities that had the means to accommodate foreigners and settle disputes.

Both Islam and Buddhism provided the institutional framework for extraordinarily wide circulation and discussion of ideas. In the seventh century, Xuanzang debated much the same topics all along his journey from China across Central Asia and into South India. He would have found similar debates and the texts to support them all across Southeast Asia. Seven centuries later, Ibn Sina's books were discussed and criticized from Afghanistan to Spain.

It was important that neither Islam nor Buddhism held the dominant position that Christianity did in Europe. More than

Christianity ever did, Islam and Buddhism jostled for converts and competed with more local beliefs, large and small. For example, these two big religions vied with various sects of Brahmanic Hinduism in India, Zoroastrianism in Persia, local fertility and ancestral beliefs in Southeast Asia and Central Asia, and Confucianism and Daoism in China. This rich intellectual mix produced its share of factional wars, religious persecution, periodic calls for orthodoxy, and the occasional local suppression of one belief system or another. Nevertheless, the competition produced profound and widespread questioning and discussion of the place of man in society and the cosmos. Many of the most innovative answers came at the intersections of various faiths.

TRAVEL AND TRADE

Supporting institutions and similarities of courts and administrative practice made it relatively easy for men to move long distances in pursuit of position and employment. Ibn Battuta met jurists and religious teachers from Spain, Central Asia, and India, and even a friend of his father's from Morocco when he visited Mecca. Soldiers had equally widespread opportunities for employment. Babur considered disbanding his troops in Central Asia and migrating to find service with relatives in China, part of his complex web of family and friendship ties that stretched across much of the northern half of the Asian world. After the conquest of Delhi, Babur sent money to relatives in Central Asia, Afghanistan, and Iraq.

Traders moved most of all. Far-flung trading communities spread all across Asia: Gujaratis in Sri Lanka and Southeast Asia, Armenians through Central Asia, Chinese residents in Bengal, Arabs in Guangzhou. Most day-to-day activities, such as marriage, divorce, property ownership, and inheritance, were regulated within communities. Everywhere they settled, Jews operated within Jewish law and

practice. Transgression meant ostracism and serious financial consequences. Abraham bin Yiju certainly learned the consequences of
marrying a slave prostitute in Mangalore. Islamic traders, from Aden
to Canton, operated under Sharia law, which had its own courts,
judges, and rules of evidence.

Traders operated for the most part with little interference from
their host state, which often set only taxes and terms of trade.
These were rarely onerous restrictions, for two reasons. Most kings
needed taxes from trade, especially if much of the agricultural land
was taken up by nobility. Also, every port and capital had competitors. Aden competed with Hormuz for the trade from India. Kalikut competed with Cochin, Mangalore, Cannore, and half a
dozen other ports for the spice trade of the Malabar Coast. If
traders were dissatisfied, they moved individually or as a community to another port. Even the Portuguese could not stop this
process. This limited state involvement meant that piracy was a
continuing problem along the maritime routes, just as banditry was
on the land routes. Certain areas, such as the northern half of the
western coast of India, anywhere near Japan, and the Malacca
Straits, were pirate havens for centuries.

Overall, there was an extraordinary openness to traders and
whatever new goods and ideas they brought. Official Chinese ideology often disapproved of trade and made a virtue of tightly controlled ports and internal traders.[2] This attitude did not stop the
demand for ivory and incense, or the export of iron, silk, and
ceramics, or an insatiable curiosity about foreign plants, ideas, and
medicines. Advice manuals to kings, a common genre across the
Asian world, suggested that the ruler take joy in the novel and in
news from elsewhere. This advice is from an eleventh-century
Persian manual:

> In the same measure that you are informed of affairs in the world
> generally and the doings of its princes, it is your duty to be

acquainted with your own country and the conditions prevailing amongst your people and bodyguard.

These books of advice to kings celebrated travel. They lauded the role of traders and made it an obligation of kings to welcome and protect them.*

Trade mattered. The volume and variety of trade affected much of the population of the great Asian world. Tropical spices and medicines moved north to the plains of India, west into the Middle East, and east into China. These medicinal plants were not "discovered" by doctors in cities, much less by the traders who brought them. These spices and medicines were first discovered by the forest dwellers who experimented with their local profusion of plants. The great Asian world included not just traders and courts but reached deep into the forests of Southeast Asia, the hills above the Malabar Coast, and the pearl beds of Sri Lanka.

Trade served the spread of the universalizing religions. Ritual objects and books of both Buddhism and Islam came from specialized centers and moved along both water routes and caravan routes to Tibet, Central Asia, Southeast Asia, and China.

Trade in the great Asian world included the exotic, the prosaic, and everything in between. At one extreme, a giraffe was somehow transported from Africa to the imperial court of China. At the other extreme, fish paste produced on the coast of Thailand and ordinary Chinese iron cooking pots were regular, profitable items traded to the islands of Southeast Asia. Rice, the most prosaic of foods in India, China, and Southeast Asia, became a high-status food across the steppe world. Every ship and every caravan carried a range of goods from the precious to the mundane.

---

*The most famous book in this tradition is Italian, Machiavelli's *The Prince*. The author knew of Asian manuals when he wrote advice for his king.

Perhaps the most telling point in considering the importance and regularity of trade is that all across the Asian world, various peoples defined who they were with objects of trade as much as products of indigenous manufacture. The steppe was the perfect environment to raise horses, sheep, and cattle. As Babur observed, this natural advantage resulted in a trade of tens of thousands of horses each year to India, where horses did not breed well. For the nobility of India, the horse was a crucial symbol defining status. With the proceeds from the sale of horses, steppe people bought iron for horse trappings, elegant cloth for courtly robes, and steel for weapons, which in turn became defining features of their culture.

INNOVATION

There was a restless, even relentless, spirit of innovation common throughout the great Asian world. In politics, states experimented with bureaucracies and taxes. They developed currencies and defined new legal status for conquered peoples. From the Middle East to China, they produced advice manuals for kings. Kings eagerly awaited the return of ambassadorial missions so they could consider the latest ceremonies of loyalty or innovations in military organization. States undertook major economic development projects, such as the irrigation of land for growing rice and road building that connected regions.

In warfare, kings from Egypt to China well understood the limits of armies based on ethnic or regional loyalty. They successfully experimented with slave armies, armies based on religion, and prisoners as soldiers. Genghis Khan broke up clan-based service and formed new mixed units with men from a variety of clans.

In science, until at least 1300 CE, the Middle East, India, and China were the major centers of innovation. Hundreds of new tropical plants arrived at courts. Some entered pharmacopoeias, where they were described and often drawn by medical writers such as Ibn Sina. Other new plants graced the royal table. Kings and nobles would often attempt to grow new varieties in their gardens. Babur boasted in his memoirs that he was the first to grow the Indian orange in Kabul. Whole new medical techniques were discovered, such as the development of inoculation in China.

In mathematics and astronomy, developments were extraordinary. Out of India came a commonly used numeric system. From India and the Middle East came algebra, a variety of geometries, including solutions to conic sections, and even a primitive form of calculus. Astronomical observatories were features of many courts.

In trade, the millennium was equally innovative. Traders not only brought promising plants to new environments but financed attempts at cultivation. Jewish traders brought sugarcane from India and began plantations along the Nile. Mango and pepper cultivation spread from India to Indonesia, where these plants became cash crops. Entrepreneurs first opened new markets, then made cheap local copies of expensive import items, such as Gujarati printed cotton cloth, Baghdad tiles, caliphate silver currency, Chinese ceramics, Damascus blades, and Chinese silk.

SELF-REFLECTION

The Asian world noticed and commented on itself—a self-consciousness not yet typical of Europe. Especially in China and the Middle East, there was a flowering of biography and autobiography. In India, there were literally thousands of books written on how life was lived and how it should morally be lived. Poets reflected on the sorrows of love and the fleeting nature of beauty. Artists pictured their world and paid particular attention to the exotic. The giraffe brought to China is known both from descriptions and a painting. Histories and geographies abounded.

The great Asian world was robust enough to survive most day-to-day or even century-to-century changes and disruptions. When Baghdad declined as a great city, trade shifted to the successor capitals: Reyy, Balk, Bukhara, and Ghazni. When Arab traders became Muslim, they built mosques along the trade routes and practiced their new religion. Different groups rose and fell as the dominant traders: Jews, Armenians, Gujaratis, Malays, Yemenis, Tamils, Arabs, and Chinese. Considering the millennium as a whole, there was more integration, more movement of knowledge and talented men, and more innovation at the end of the period than at the beginning.

EUROPEAN COLONIAL CONQUEST

Many within the Asian world recognized that the Europeans, "hat-wearers" as they were labeled, were a different breed and brought different assumptions with them. For centuries Europe had been on the fringes of the Asian world. There were, of course, trading ties to Asia through Venice, Genoa, and Prague, as well as the long-standing trade down the Russian rivers that Ibn Fadlan observed. The more intimate networks of intellectual discussion, religious debate, family ties, trade partnerships, ambassadorial missions, bureaucratic service at courts, codes of honor, poetry, music, fashion, and art were, by and large, not exchanged between Europe and Asia.

When the Europeans arrived in Asia, they proclaimed themselves traders as well as representatives of kings, directly responsible to their sovereign. This was new and unexpected. No trader in the Asian world represented a king. Abraham bin Yiju, though he was from Cairo, would never have conceived of himself as somehow loyal to or a representative of the sovereign of Egypt. The European traders were also heavily armed. Although Asian traders regularly hired troops to protect caravans or ships, they were rarely involved in wars. The Europeans brought the notion of intertwining trade and warfare to Asia from centuries of practice on the European continent and in the Mediterranean. Royal involvement in trade and cannon casting, for example, was seen as a direct practice of profitable politics.[3] Finally, Europeans brought with them a sense that they were "Portuguese" or "English" and Christian. Indeed, there had been wars over sectarian interpretation of Islam and attacks on Buddhist institutions by expanding Islam, but there was nothing like the European definition of *Christian* and *heathen.* Recall that Abraham bin Yiju's business group included local Hindus, Gujaratis, and Muslims. The Europeans were truly outsiders to the Asian world. Europeans did not often recruit local men of talent who came from different racial and ethnic groups into significant positions. High posts always went to men from the home country or the white race. Europeans used their own ceremonies of reward and honor, and did not adopt such ceremonies as robing, found in Asia.

In practical terms, these European attitudes meant that conquests went to the European king, not the local commander. No European (with the exception of Raja Brooke in Borneo) founded an independent kingdom in Asia. How different this was from Babur, who knew that he had to "share out" portions of his conquests to commanders and family to keep his army and kingdom going. Babur's was the typical pattern across Asia. Even in the bureaucratized caliphate, imperial China, and the Mughal Empire, it was military commanders who carved out successor states based on their conquests. Europeans successfully merged the ideas of a corporate trading company, loyalty to a throne, and a professional officer corps and thereby prevented losing their conquests to military commanders. None of this happened overnight, but Asian observers noticed that European armies tended to stay intact as they approached battle, unlike Asian armies, in which portions of the army led by bribed individual leaders often changed sides on the eve of battle. Nor did European armies shatter when the leader was killed. Asian observers also noticed that treaties were always in the name of the European king or trading company, never in the name of the commander.

In spite of these advantages in military structure and the beginning of "national" loyalty, it is important to emphasize how slow the process of European conquest and colonization of Asia was. England became the largest power in India only in the nineteenth century. Holland had early success in the Southeast Asian islands and Sri Lanka, but did not expand its empire beyond the islands. Russia only conquered the eastern steppe in the seventeenth century. Except for the crusader states, European intervention in the Middle East is mainly a twentieth-century phenomenon, and China was never colonized to the extent that India was.

In spite of the European conquests, much of this vast, highly interconnected, and interdependent Asian world continued under colonial rule. Even under European domination, Arab ships still sailed every year to Africa carrying Gujarati cloth and returning with gold. Chinese traders moved into the new British port of Calcutta. Horses by the thousands still came down from Central Asia to India. It was only slowly that colonial powers undercut local political processes and reoriented Asian economies to serve the home country.

Notes

~~~

INTRODUCTION

1. This book generally uses social network theory, including older work such as Everett M. Rogers and D. Lawrence Kincaid, *Communication Networks: Toward a New Paradigm for Research* (New York: Free Press, 1981) and Mark Granovetter's work on strong and weak ties, in addition to more recent research on networks of trust, degrees of separation, and dense connections. I balance social network theory's focus on linkages with a focus on real people, connecting them with larger scale trends and developments. I also look to the analysis of the Scandinavian philosopher Per Otnes in *Other-wise: Alterity, Materiality, Mediation* (Oslo: Scandinavian University Press, 1998). He finds that the primary human unit is not the individual alone but a relationship between two people connected by a material object. This seems an astute way to describe many of the networks and relationships of the Asian world.

CHAPTER 1

1. Shaman Hwui Li, *The Life of Hiuen-Tsiang*, trans. Samuel Beal (London: Kegan Paul, Trench, Trübner and Co., 1911), 4–5. There have been several recent books on Xuanzang, all useful. Sally Hovey Wriggins, *Xuanzang: A Buddhist Pilgrim on the Silk Road* (Boulder: Westview Press, 1996), stays quite close to the memoir but adds useful maps and illustrations. The same author's *The Silk Road Journey with Xuanzang* (Boulder: Westview, 2004) is a revised version that adds more material on Xuanzang's visit to southern and western India. Richard Bernstein's *Ultimate Journey: Retracing the Path of an Ancient Buddhist Monk Who Crossed Asia in Search of Enlightenment* (New York: Alfred A. Knopf, 2001) is precisely what the title suggests. Bernstein went to China when the western regions

opened in the mid-1990s and followed Xuanzang's route. The people he met and the conversations add a layer to Xuanzang's trip.

2. Li, *Life of Hiuen-Tsiang*, 6.

3. Ibid., 2.

4. Ibid., 6–7.

5. These core ideas and a variety of practices can be found in Donald S. Lopez, ed., *Buddhism in Practice* (Princeton: Princeton University Press, 1995).

6. Li, *Life of Hiuen-Tsiang*, 8–9.

7. Helmut Brinker, "Early Buddhist Art in China," in Lukas Nickel, ed., *Return of the Buddha: The Qingzhou Discoveries* (London: Royal Academy of Arts, 2002), 24.

8. Lucas Nickel, "Longxing Temple in Qingzhou and the Discovery of the Sculpture Hoard," in Lukas, *Return of the Buddha*, 34–43.

9. Su Bai, "Sculpture of the Northern Qi Dynasty and Its Stylistic Models," in Lukas, *Return of the Buddha*, 54–59.

10. Li, *Life of Hiuen-Tsiang*, 10.

11. Ibid., 15. For a reinterpretation of frontier zones at this period, see Jonathan K. Skaff, "Survival in the Frontier Zone: Comparative Perspectives on Identity and Political Alliance in China's Inner Asian Borderlands During the Sui-Tang Dynastic Transition," *Journal of World History* 15 (2) (March 2004): 117–153.

12. Li, *Life of Hiuen-Tsiang*, 19–20.

13. Ibid., 25.

14. Ibid., 29.

15. See Roderick Whitfield and Susan Neville Whitfield, *Cave Temples of Mogao* (Los Angeles: Getty Conservation Institute and J. Paul Getty Museum, 2000). Also, Roderick Whitfield, *Dunhuang, Caves of the Singing Sands: Buddhist Art from the Silk Road* (London: Textile and Art Publishers, 1995).

16. Li, *Life of Hiuen-Tsiang*, 30.

17. Patricia E. Karetzky, "Imperial Splendor in the Service of the Sacred: The Famen Tea Treasures," *T'ang Studies* 18 (19) (2000–2001): 68–69.

18. Li, *Life of Hiuen-Tsiang*, 41.

19. Xinru Liu, *Silk and Religion: An Exploration of Material Life and the Thought of People, AD 600–1200* (Delhi: Oxford University Press, 1996). See also Xinru Liu, "Silk, Robes, and Relations Between Early Chinese Dynasties and Nomads Beyond the Great Wall," in Stewart Gordon, ed., *Robes and Honor: The Medieval World of Investiture* (New York: Palgrave, 2001).

20. Najmieh Batmanglij, *Silk Road Cooking: A Vegetarian Journey* (Washington, DC: Mage Publishers, 2004), 18, 46, 153–168.

21. Li, *Life of Hiuen-Tsiang*, 44.

22. Ibid., 49.

23. Ibid., 53.

24. Ibid., 57.

25. At the time, in portions of Asia, there were competing belief systems that claimed universality, such as Zoroastrianism, Jainism, and Nestorian Christianity. None achieved the widespread patronage and institutional development of Buddhism.

26. Li, *Life of Hiuen-Tsiang*, 90.

27. Ibid., 93.

28. Ibid., 94.

29. Ibid., 104.

30. The ruins of Nalanda monastery are in present-day Bihar state, India.

31. Li, *Life of Hiuen-Tsiang*, 169.

32. Ibid., 209.

33. See O. W. Wolters, *Early Indonesian Commerce: A Study of the Origins of Srivajaya* (Ithaca: Cornell University Press, 1967).

34. Li, *Life of Hiuen-Tsiang*, 174.

35. Tansen Sen, *Buddhism, Diplomacy, and Trade: The Realignment of Sino-Indian Relations, 600–1400* (Honolulu: Association for Asian Studies and University of Hawaii Press, 2003), 10–30.

36. In the three centuries after Xuanzang, hundreds of monks and students from Japan traveled to China to study Buddhism. In the first century of Tang influence, Chinese fashions, language, and literature were all the rage at Japanese courts, and the incipient Japanese monarchy attempted a Confucian model of government. Thereafter, Japan retuned to a more inward-looking phase. Locally powerful families used Buddhist monasteries as tax shelters, and Buddhist beliefs coalesced into local sects. A good general introduction to this period is Donald M. Shively and William H. McCulloch, eds., *The Cambridge History of Japan,* vol. 2, *Heinan Japan* (Cambridge: Cambridge University Press, 1999), chaps. 5–8.

37. For stories of individuals on the Silk Road in the three centuries after Xuanzang, see Susan Neville Whitfield, *Life Along the Silk Road* (London: John Murray, 1999).

38. For Xuanzang's later life, see the extensive documents in Li Rongxi, *A Biography of the Tripitika Master of the Great Ci'en Monastery of the Great Tang Dynasty,* trans. Sramana Huli and Shi Yancong (Berkeley: Numata Center of Buddhist Translation and Research, 1995).

CHAPTER 2

1. James E. McKeithen, "The Risalah of Ibn Fadlan: An Annotated Translation with Introduction" (Dissertation Abstracts International (40 [10A], 5437, 1979), 25 (UMI No. AAG8008223). A recent translation of Ibn Fadlan's memoir is Richard N. Frye, *Ibn Fadlan's Journey to Russia: A Tenth-Century Traveler from Baghdad to the Volga River* (Princeton: Marcus Weiner Publishers, 2005).

2. McKeithen, "Risalah of Ibn Fadlan," 26.

3. Robert G. Hoyland, *Seeing Islam as Others Saw It: A Survey and Evaluation of Christian, Jewish, and Zoroastrian Writings on Early Islam* (Princeton: Darwin Press, 1997), 555–556.

4. Marshall G. S. Hodgson, *The Venture of Islam: Conscience and History in World Civilization*, vol. 1 (Chicago: University of Chicago Press, 1974), 172–175, 185–186, 210–213.

5. Fred M. Donner, *The Early Islamic Conquests* (Princeton: Princeton University Press, 1981), 54–61. Donner disagrees with Hodgson on the basic tribal power structure of Arabia at the time of Muhammad and the importance of kinship. An interesting parallel anthropological discussion to Donner is found in Frank H. Stewart, *Honor* (Chicago: University of Chicago Press, 1994), 99–129. Hugh Kennedy argues that the tribal structure of early Islamic armies remained largely intact and was the basis for the brutal civil wars of the early period; see Hugh Kennedy, *The Armies of the Caliphs: Military and Society in the Early Islamic State* (London: Routledge, 2001), 60–70.

6. Donner, *Early Islamic Conquests*, 69–73.

7. Phillip K. Hitti, *Capital Cities of Arab Islam* (Minneapolis: University of Minnesota Press, 1973), 85–95.

8. Xinru Liu, *Silk and Religion: An Exploration of Material Life and the Thought of People, AD 600–1200* (Delhi: Oxford University Press, 1996), 138–140.

9. For example, two ninth-century Arab accounts of the maritime routes to China are now translated in S. Maqbul Ahmad, trans., *Arab Classical Accounts of India and China* (Rddhi, India: Indian Institute of Advanced Study, 1979).

10. Tarif Khaldi, *Classical Arab Islam: Culture and Heritage of the Golden Age* (Princeton: Darwin Press, 1985), 35–50. See also Hodgson, *Venture of Islam*, 197–198.

11. The rhythm of conquest followed by civil war is laid out in Khalid Y. Blankinship, *The End of the Jihad State* (Albany: State University of New York Press, 1994).

12. Hodgson, *Venture of Islam*, 18–21.

13. F. Daftary, "Sectarian and National Movements in Iran, Khurasan, and Transoxania," in M. S. Asimov and C. E. Bosworth, eds., *History of Civilizations of Central Asia*, vol. 4 (Delhi: Motilal Banarsidas, 1999), 57.

14. McKeithen, "Risalah of Ibn Fadlan," 2.

15. Some idea of these robes of honor is suggested by robes given to high military commanders of the caliph. See Muhammad M. Hassan, *Social Life Under the Abbasids* (London: Longman, 1979), 60.

16. McKeithen, "Risalah of Ibn Fadlan," 29.

17. Ibid., 32. See also Frye, *Ibn Fadlan's Journey*, 84–85.

18. McKeithen, "Risalah of Ibn Fadlan," 35.

19. Frye, *Ibn Fadlan's Journey*, 37.

20. McKeithen, "Risalah of Ibn Fadlan," 41.

21. The site of Jurjaniyah is currently the town of Kunya Urgench in northern Turkmenistan.

22. McKeithen, "Risalah of Ibn Fadlan," 46.

23. Ibid., 48.

24. Donner, *Early Islamic Conquests*, chaps. 3–5.

25. Dennis Sinor, ed., *Cambridge History of Inner Asia* (Cambridge: Cambridge University Press, 1990), 275–276.

26. Thomas Noonan, "The Khazar Qaghanate," in Anatoly M. Khazanov and André Wink, eds., *Nomads in a Sedentary World* (Richmond, United Kingdom: Curzon, 2001), 78–89.

27. McKeithen, "Risalah of Ibn Fadlan," 52.

28. Thomas Barfield, "Steppe Empires, China, and the Silk Route: Nomads as a Force in International Trade and Politics," in Khazanov and Wink, *Nomads in a Sedentary World*, 234–246.

29. McKeithen, "Risalah of Ibn Fadlan," 63–64.

30. McKeithen, "Risalah of Ibn Fadlan," 58–61.

31. Ibid., 69–70.

32. Ibid., 72–73.

33. Ibid., 90–91.

34. Ibid., 89–90.

35. Ibid., 110.

36. Sinor, *Cambridge History of Inner Asia*, 263–267.

37. McKeithen, "Risalah of Ibn Fadlan," 119.

38. Ibid., 120.

39. Ibid., 126.

CHAPTER 3

1. William E. Gohlman, *The Life of Ibn Sina: A Critical Edition and Annotated Translation* (Albany: State University of New York Press, 1974), 61.

2. Lenn E. Goodman, *Avicenna* (London: Routledge, 1992), 14. Also, George Sarton, *Introduction to the History of Science* (Baltimore: Williams and Wilkins Co., 1927), 537–543. See also Franz Rosenthal, *The Classical Heritage in Islam,* trans. Emile and Jenny Marmorstein (London: Routledge and Keegan Paul, 1975), 5–9.

3. Sarton, *History of Science,* 549–550. See also Donald R. Hill, "Mechanical Engineering in the Medieval Near East," *Scientific American* 264 (5) (May 1991): 100–105.

4. Sarton, *History of Science,* 598–604, 621–622.

5. Bernard Lewis, *Islam from the Prophet Muhammad to the Capture of Constantinople* (London: Macmillan Press, 1974), vol. 2, 70–71.

6. Jonathan M. Bloom, *Paper Before Print: The History and Impact of Paper on the Islamic World* (New Haven: Yale University Press, 2001), 47–50.

7. Fustat ("camp" in Arabic) was the armed camp built by the invading Muslim army in the seventh century. It developed into a large city and was the Egyptian capital until the Fatimid dynasty of the tenth century. Fustat was burned to avoid capture by a Crusader army in 1168 CE. Only the area along the river recovered, which included several Coptic churches and Jewish synagogues. Starting in the thirteenth century, most of old Fustat became a garbage dump for the developing city of Cairo to the north.

8. Quoted in Bloom, *Paper Before Print,* 49.

9. Gohlman, *Life of Ibn Sina,* 17–19.

10. Ibid., 19.

11. Yann Richard, *Shi'ite Islam: Polity, Ideology, and Creed* (Oxford: Blackwell, 1995), chaps. 1–3. See also Farhad Daftary, *The Ismalis: Their History and Doctrines* (Cambridge: Cambridge University Press, 1990), chaps. 2–3.

12. Heinz Hahn, *The Fatamids and Their Tradition of Learning* (London: I. B. Taurus, 1997), chaps. 2 and 5. See also Farhad Daftary, *A Short History of the Ismalis: Traditions of a Muslim Community* (Edinburgh: Edinburgh University Press, 1998), 41–43.

13. Gohlman, *Life of Ibn Sina,* 21–23.

14. Dimitri Guhas, *Avicenna and the Aristotelian Tradition: An Introduction to Reading Avicenna's Philosophical Works* (Leiden, Holland: E. J. Brill, 1998), 149–158.

15. Gohlman, *Life of Ibn Sina,* 33. The dirham (also spelled "dirhem") is a coin with a long history. The term derives from the Greek drachma coin, which was in common use in the Byzantine Empire in the fifth and sixth

centuries. By the eighth century CE, the coin was minted in Baghdad, the Muslim capital of the caliphate. By 1000 CE, dirhams were minted in various Islamic capitals. The production of such coins, with a sovereign's name on the reverse, was an important act of kingship. Dirhams are still a currency in Morocco, Qatar, Jordan, Libya, and the Arab Emirates.

16. Ibid., 25–26.

17. Ibid., 37.

18. Ibid., 25.

19. Goodman, *Avicenna,* 49–61. See also Robert Wisnovsky, "Towards a History of Avicenna's Distinction Between Immanent and Transcendent Causes," in David C. Reisman, ed., *Before and After Avicenna* (Leiden, Holland: Brill, 2003), 49–51.

20. Goodman, *Avicenna,* 91–93.

21. Gohlman, *Life of Ibn Sina,* 91–113.

22. Avicenna, *The Canon of Medicine,* adapted by Laleh Bakhtiar (Chicago: Great Books of the Islamic World, 1999), 9–44.

23. Ibid., 157.

24. Al-Kindi, *The Medical Formulary of Aqrabadhin of Al-Kindi,* trans. Martin Levey (Madison: University of Wisconsin Press, 1966).

25. Gohlman, *Life of Ibn Sina,* 41–43.

26. Goodman, *Avicenna,* 18–23.

27. Gohlman, *Life of Ibn Sina,* 43.

28. Ibid., 53.

29. Ibid., 51.

30. Charles Burnett, *The Introduction of Arabic Learning into England* (London: British Library, 1996), 59–80.

31. Quoted in ibid., 44–45.

32. Jules L. Janssens, *An Annotated Bibliography on Ibn Sina (1970–1989)* (Leuven, Belgium: Leuven University Press, 1991), and Jules L. Janssens, *An Annotated Bibliography on Ibn Sina: First Supplement (1990–1994)* (Louvain-la-Neuve, France: Fédération Internationale des Instituts d'Études Médiévales, 1999).

CHAPTER 4

1. "The Archaeological Excavation of the Tenth-Century Intan Shipwreck," *British Archaeological Reports International Series,* 1047 (Oxford: Archaoepress, 2002).

2. "Fund am schwarzen Felsen [The Discovery at the Black Rock]," *Der Spiegel* 13 (2004), 166–175.

3. Flecker, "Intan Shipwreck," 126–149. For a careful analysis of the archaeological data that comes to the same conclusions, see Pierre-Yves Manguin, "Trading Ships of the South China Sea: Shipping Techniques and Their Role in the History of the Development of Asian Trade Networks," *Journal of the Economic and Social History of the Orient* 36 (1993): 256–265. See also Anthony Reid, *Charting the Shape of Early Modern Southeast Asia* (Chiang Mai, Thailand: Silkworm Books, 1999), 65–59.

4. Flecker, "Intan Shipwreck," 18–26.

5. Gerald R. Tibbetts, *A Study of the Arabic Texts Containing Material on South-East Asia* (Leiden, Holland: Brill, 1979), 39.

6. It is quite possible that the copper in the Chinese mirrors came from Japan. Swords and copper were prominent Japanese exports to much of East Asia at the time. See Bennett Bronson, "Patterns in the Early Southeast Asian Metals Trade," in Ian Glover, Pornchai Suchitta, and John Villiers, eds., *Early Metallurgy, Trade, and Urban Centers in Thailand and Southeast Asia* (Bangkok: White Lotus, 1992), 71–72. In Arab accounts of the ninth century, copper was prominently mentioned as a desirable item to trade to China. S. Maqbul Ahmad, trans., *Arab Classical Accounts of India and China* (Rddhi, India: Indian Institute of Advanced Study, 1979).

7. The pattern of the rise and fall of these mainland kingdoms is explored in Victor Lieberman, *Strange Parallels: Southeast Asia in Global Context, c. 800–1830* (Cambridge: Cambridge University Press, 2003).

8. Kenneth R. Hall, "Eleventh-Century Commercial Developments in Angkor and Champa," *Journal of Southeast Asian Studies* 10 (2) (September 1979): 420–434.

9. Kenneth R. Hall, *Maritime Trade and State Development in Early Southeast Asia* (Honolulu: University of Hawaii Press, 1985), 108–110.

10. Flecker, "Intan Shipwreck," 54–60. See also Ranabir Chakravarti, "Seafarings, Ships, and Ship Owners: India and the Indian Ocean (AD 700–1500)," in Ruth Barnes and David Parkin, eds., *Ships and the Development of Maritime Technology on the Indian Ocean* (London: Routledge Curzon, 2002), 36–48.

11. Flecker, "Intan Shipwreck," 31.

12. R.A.L.H. Gunawardana, "Cosmopolitan Buddhism on the Move: South India and Sri Lanka in the Early Expansion of Theravada in Southeast Asia," in J. Klokke and Karel R. van Kooij, eds., *Fruits of Inspiration: Studies in Honour of Prof. J.G. de Marijke* (Groningen, Holland: Egbert Forsten, 2001), 135–155. The definitive new work on the interconnectedness of China, India, and Southeast Asia in this period is Tansen Sen, *Buddhism, Diplomacy, and Trade: The Realignment of Sino-Indian Relations, 600–1400*

(Honolulu: Association for Asian Studies and University of Hawaii Press, 2003).

13. Kenneth R. Hall, "State and Statecraft in Early Srivijaya," in Kenneth R. Hall and John K. Whitmore, eds., *Explorations in Early Southeast Asian History: The Origins of Southeast Asian Statecraft* (Ann Arbor, MI: Center for South and Southeast Asian Studies, 1976), 92–93.

14. Charles Higham, *The Archaeology of Mainland Southeast Asia from 10,000 BC to the Fall of Angkor* (Cambridge: Cambridge University Press, 1989), 320–350. See also Nidhi Aeusrivongse, "The Devaraja Cult and Khmer Kingship at Angkor," in Hall and Whitmore, *Explorations*, 107–148. A good interpretation of the mixing and merging of Hinduism, Buddhism, and local tradition in this period is Ann R. Kinney, *Worshiping Siva and Buddha: The Temple Art of East Java* (Honolulu: University of Hawaii Press, 2003).

15. See Keith Taylor, "The Rise of Dai Viet and the Establishment of Thang-Long," in Hall and Whitmore, *Explorations*, 171–181.

16. Flecker, "Intan Shipwreck," 36–41. Recent research suggests that Borobudur was primarily a Vajrayana monument. See Jeffery Roger Sundberg, "The Wilderness Monks of Abyayagirivihara and the Origins of Sino-Javanese Esoteric Buddhism," *Bijdragen tot de Taal-, Land-, en Volkenkunde* 160 (1) (2004): 95–123.

17. Flecker, "Intan Shipwreck," 53–54.

18. Bronson, "Patterns in the Early Southeast Asian Metals Trade," 65.

19. Flecker, "Intan Shipwreck," 83. For use of silver coinage in Java and Bali, see Jan W. Christie, "Asian Sea Trade Between the Tenth and Thirteenth Centuries and Its Impact on the States of Java and Bali," in Himansahu P. Ray, ed., *Archaeology of Seafaring: The Indian Ocean in the Ancient Period* (Delhi: Pragati Publications, 1999), 237–238. Substantial quantities of both silver and gold appear in the scattering of inscriptions from eastern Java that are roughly contemporary with the shipwreck. See Antoinette M. Barrett Jones, "Early Tenth Century Java from the Inscriptions," *Verhandelingen van het Koninklijk Instituut voor Taal-, Land-, en Volkenkunde* 107 (Dordrecht, Holland: Foris Publications, 1984): 32–34.

20. For the development of the Chinese process of cast iron, see Bronson, "Patterns in the Early Southeast Asian Metals Trade," 71.

21. Ibid., 89–90.

22. Flecker, "Intan Shipwreck," 78–79.

23. Alastair Lamb, "Takupa: The Probable Site of a Pre-Malaccan Entrepot in the Malay Peninsula," in John Bastin and Roelof Roolvink, eds., *Malayan and Indonesian Studies* (Oxford: Oxford University Press, 1964),

81–82. See also Peter Francis, Jr., *Beads and the Bead Trade in Southeast Asia: A Preliminary Report on Research into the Bead Trade of Southeast Asia as a Segment of the Indian Ocean Bead Trade* (Lake Placid, NY: Center for Bead Research, 1989). Also Peter Francis, Jr., *Asia's Maritime Bead Trade from ca. 300 BC to the Present* (Honolulu: University of Hawaii Press, 2002). In Southeast Asia, beads have long been used in healing, worn for ceremony, used as currency, and hoarded for personal power. See Heidi Munan, *Beads of Borneo* (Kuala Lumpur: Editions Didier Millet, 2004).

24. Himanshu P. Ray, *The Winds of Change: Buddhism and the Maritime Links of Early South Asia* (Delhi: Oxford University Press, 1994), 92–93, 118–119.

25. Flecker, "Intan Shipwreck," 101–103. See also Angela Schotenhammer, "The Maritime Trade of Quanzhou (Zaitun) from the Ninth Through the Thirteenth Century," in Ray, *Winds of Change*, 271–290. Also, John S. Guy, *Oriental Trade Ceramics in South-East Asia, Ninth to Sixteenth Centuries* (Singapore: Oxford University Press, 1986), 11–12.

26. Christie, "Asian Sea Trade," 225–226.

27. Ruth Barnes, *Indian Block-Printed Cotton Fabrics in the Kelsey Museum* (Ann Arbor: University of Michigan Press, 1993). See also Ruth Barnes, *Indian Block-Printed Textiles in Egypt: The Newberry Collection in the Ashmolean Museum* (Oxford: Oxford University Press, 1997).

28. Ruth Barnes, "Indian Trade Textiles: Sources and Transmission of Designs," paper presented at the conference Communities and Commodities: Western India and the Indian Ocean, 11th–15th Centuries, Kelsey Museum of Archaeology, Ann Arbor, Michigan, November 7–10, 2002.

29. Taylor, "Rise of Dai Viet," 169. More than five centuries before the *Intan* shipwreck, piracy was already a problem. In 414 CE, Fa Hien, the Chinese Buddhist pilgrim, described the area near Java thusly: "On the sea (hereabouts) there are many pirates, to meet whom is speedy death," Fa-Hien, *A Record of Buddhistic Kingdoms being an Account by the Chinese Monk of His Travels in India and Ceylon (A.D. 399–414) in Search of the Buddhist Books of Discipline*, trans. James Legge (New York: Paragon Reprint Corp., 1965), 112.

30. Tilman Frasch, "A Buddhist Network in the Bay of Bengal: Relations Between Bodhgaya, Burma, and Sri Lanka, c. 300–1300," in Claude Guillot, Denys Lombard, and Roderich Ptak, eds., *From the Mediterranean to the China Sea: Miscellaneous Notes* (Wiesbaden, Germany: Harrassowitz Verlag, 1998), 69–92.

31. Jones, "Early Tenth Century Java," 23–27. Evidence of South Indians trading in Southeast Asia comes from a few South Asian inscriptions.

See Meera Abraham, *Two Medieval Merchant Guilds of South India* (New Delhi: Manohar, 1988), 33–39.

32. Flecker, "Intan Shipwreck," 90.

33. Kenneth Hall, "Local and International Trade and Traders in the Strait of Melaka Regions: 600–1500," *Journal of the Economic and Social History of the Orient* 47 (2) (2004): 224. See p. 238 for discussion of perceived origin of traders rather than ethnicity or religion. See also Anthony Reid, *Southeast Asia in the Age of Commerce, 1450–1680* (New Haven: Yale University Press, 1993), 65–66.

34. Jan W. Christie, "Trade and Settlement in Early Java: Integrating the Epigraphic and Archaeological Data," in Villiers, *Early Metallurgy*, 181–195.

35. Flecker, "Intan Shipwreck," 101–103. Early Arab traders knew incense was an important trade item in China. See Ahmad, *Arab Classical Accounts*, 46.

36. Flecker, "Intan Shipwreck," 96.

37. See Sen, *Buddhism, Diplomacy, and Trade.*

CHAPTER 5

1. The opposite was also true. Spices in a ship that arrived early commanded high prices. See Shlomo Goitein, "Portrait of a Medieval Indian Trader: Three Letters from the Cairo Geniza," *Bulletin of the School of Oriental and African Studies* 50 (3) (1987): 461–462. For the general pattern of Indian Ocean mercantile monsoon trade, see Michael Pearson, *The Indian Ocean* (London: Routledge, 2003), 13–26.

2. Ibn Battuta, *The Travels of Ibn Battuta, AD 1325–1354*, trans. H. A. R. Gibb (New Delhi: Hakluyt Society, 1994), 808–809.

3. Anthony Reid, *Southeast Asia in the Age of Commerce* (New Haven: Yale University Press, 1993), vol. 1, 86–88.

4. Maxime Rodinson, A. J. Arberry, and Charles Perry, *Medieval Arab Cookery* (Devon, United Kingdom: Prospect Books, 2001). See also David Waines, *In a Caliph's Kitchen* (London: Riad El-Rayyes Books, 1989). Since 1995 or so, there has been steady publication of medieval European recipes, now including more than 2,000 of English provenance alone. Other than pepper, tropical spices such as ginger, cardamom, mace, cloves, cinnamon, and cubeb rarely seem to appear in England before the fourteenth century. See Constance B. Hieatt, "Making Sense of Medieval Culinary Records: Much Done, But Much to Do," in Martha Carlin and Joel T. Rosenthal, eds., *Food and Eating in Medieval Europe* (London: Hambledon Press, 1998), 101–116. See also *The forme of cury, a roll of*

ancient English cookery. Compiled, about A.D. 1390, by the Master-Cooks of King Richard II, presented afterwards to Queen Elizabeth by Edward Lord Stafford and now in the possession of Gustavus Brander, Esq. This text is available online at www.gutenberg.org.

5. Himansahu P. Ray, *Archaeology of Seafaring: The Indian Ocean in the Ancient Period* (Delhi: Pragati Publications, 1999), 55.

6. Shlomo Goitein, *Letters of Medieval Jewish Traders* (Princeton: Princeton University Press, 1973), 3–4.

7. Amitav Ghosh, *In an Antique Land* (New York: Vintage Books, 1994), 80–98.

8. Goitein, *Letters of Medieval Jewish Traders,* 192.

9. For Jewish traders, the route from Tunisia to Cairo in search of business opportunities was a common one. See Norman Stillman, "Eleventh Century Merchant House of Awkal (a Geniza Study)," *Journal of the Economic and Social History of the Orient* 16 (1) (1973): 17.

10. Goitein found no examples of Arabic-speaking Jews working in the European cities on the north shore of the Mediterranean in the twelfth century. Goitein, *Letters of Medieval Jewish Traders,* 8.

11. Shlomo Goitein, "Portrait of a Medieval Indian Trader," 449–450. See also Shlomo Goitein, *Studies in Islamic History and Institutions* (Leiden, Holland: E. J. Brill, 1966), 344.

12. See Stillman, "Eleventh Century Merchant House," 17.

13. See, for example, a letter of 1130 CE concerning an estate of a deceased trader from Tripoli. Goitein, *Letters of Medieval Jewish Traders,* 182–183.

14. Ibid., 183. At about the same time, Madmun proposed partnerships with three Indian Hindu merchants from Mangalore. See Shlomo Goitien, "From Aden to India: Specimens of the Correspondence of India Traders of the Twelfth Century," *Journal of the Economic and Social History of the Orient* 23 (1980): 53.

15. Goitein, *Letters of Medieval Jewish Traders,* 185.

16. See S. M. Stern, "Ramisht of Siraf, a Merchant Millionaire of the Twelfth Century," *Journal of the Royal Asiatic Society* 2 (1967): 10–14.

17. Shlomo Goitein, *A Mediterranean Society: The Jewish Community of the Arab World as Portrayed in the Documents of the Cairo Geniza,* 2 vols. (Berkeley: University of California Press, 1967), vol. 1, 203.

18. Ibid., vol. 1, 164–166, 182. See also Stillman, "Eleventh Century Merchant House," 23.

19. Goitein, *Letters of Medieval Jewish Traders,* 184. See Goitein, *Mediterranean Society,* vol. 1, 200–201.

20. Other traders occasionally brought silk to Malabar for sale rather than cash. Goitein, *Letters of Medieval Jewish Traders*, 190. See Yedida K. Stillman, "New Data on Islamic Textiles from the Cairo Geniza," in David Waines, ed., *Patterns of Everyday Life* (Aldershot, England: Ashgate, 2002), 199.

21. Ghosh, *Antique Land*, 178.

22. Goitein, *Letters of Medieval Jewish Traders*, 195–196.

23. Ibid., 185.

24. Ghosh, *Antique Land*, p. 267.

25. Goitein, *Letters of Medieval Jewish Traders*, 243.

26. Goitein, "From Aden to India," 52. See also Ghosh, *Antique Land*, 275–276.

27. Goitein, *Letters of Medieval Jewish Traders*, 193.

28. See Meera Abraham, *Two Medieval Merchant Guilds of South India* (New Delhi: Manohar, 1988), 33–39.

29. Goitein, *Letters of Medieval Jewish Traders*, 64–65.

30. Ghosh, *Antique Land*, 267–268. For the range of silks and other luxury fabrics in use in the Jewish community of Fustat, see Stillman, "New Data on Islamic Textiles," 195–206.

31. Goitein, "From Aden to India," 52.

32. Goitein, *Mediterranean Society*, vol. 2, 32–133.

33. Goitein, *Letters of Medieval Jewish Traders*, 194. Metalworking and reworking were common industries and crafts that Jews engaged in. See ibid., 17–18, 188–189. Madmun wrote to Abraham bin Yiju of the good market in Aden for Indian iron. Goitein, "From Aden to India," 52–53.

34. Goitein, *Mediterranean Society*, vol. 2, 20. See also Goitein, *Letters of Medieval Jewish Traders*, 202.

35. L. A. Krishna Iyer, *Social History of Kerala*, vol. 2 (Madras, India: Book Center Publications, 1970), 56–57. There is no documentary evidence of the beginnings of this matriarchal system, though indirect inscriptional evidence suggests that it was standard among Nairs in the ninth or early tenth centuries. See A. Sreedhara Menon, *Social and Cultural History of Kerala* (New Delhi: Sterling Publishers, 1979), 83–87. Poor Nairs are mentioned in Lieutenants Ward and Conner, *Memoir of the Survey of the Travencore and Cochin States* (Trivandarum, India: Government of Kerala, 1863), vol. 1, 130–131.

36. E. Kathleen Gough, "The Nayars and the Definition of Marriage," in Patricia Uberoi, ed., *Family, Kinship, and Marriage in India* (Delhi: Oxford University Press, 1993), 242–243. See Shlomo Goitein, "Slaves and Slavegirls in the Cairo Geniza Records," *Arabica* 9 (1) (1962): 13–18.

37. Sometimes the long periods away led to divorce. See Goitein, *Letters of Medieval Jewish Traders*, 224–225.

38. Aftab Husain Kola, "Navayaths of India—an Arabian Lake in an Indian Ocean," *Milli Gazette*, Oct. 17, 2002; retrieved Aug. 3, 2005, at www.milligazette.com/Archives/01072002/0107200296.htm. The taking of a temporary wife was a common pattern for traders in Southeast Asia. Often the wife was a partner in trade. See Anthony Reid, *Charting the Shape of Early Modern Southeast Asia* (Chiang Mai, Thailand: Silkworm Books, 1999), 159–160.

39. Other traders also suffered. See Goitein, *Letters of Medieval Jewish Traders*, 325–326.

40. Ibid., 206. Earlier Geniza documents discuss the disastrous conquest of Sicily by the Normans in the 1060s. See ibid., 167–168, 322–323.

41. Ibid., 204.

42. Ibid., 205.

43. Ghosh, *Antique Land*, 314.

44. Ibid., 317.

45. Shlomo Goitein, *From the Land of Sheba: Tales of the Jews of Yemen* (New York: Schocken Books, 1973, rev. ed.), 6–7, 25–26.

46. Ghosh, *Antique Land*, 348–349.

47. Goitein, *Mediterranean Society*, vol. 1, 59–61.

CHAPTER 6

1. The Hakluyt Society has published the only complete English translation of Ibn Battuta's long memoir: Ibn Battuta, *The Travels of Ibn Battuta, A.D. 1325–1354*, 5 vols., trans. H.A.R. Gibb (Cambridge: Hakluyt Society [new series, 110, 117, 141, 178, 190], 1958–2000). I have used a 1993 reprint of the first four volumes. The quote cited here is from Battuta, *Travels*, vol. 3, 660–661.

2. Ibid., 662.

3. Ibid., 595–596.

4. Ibid., vol. 1, 8.

5. Ibid., 12.

6. Ibid., 16.

7. Ibid., 15.

8. Ibid., 17–18.

9. Ibid., 42.

10. Ibid., 61.

11. Ibid., 60.

12. Ibid., 63–64.

13. Ibid., 98.

14. Marshall G.S. Hodgson, *The Venture of Islam: Conscience and History in World Civilization,* vol. 2 (Chicago: University of Chicago Press, 1974), 47. See also André Wink, *Al-Hind: The Making of the Indo-Islamic World,* vol. 1 (Leiden, Holland: E. J. Brill, 1990), 43.

15. See Shlomo Goitein, *A Mediterranean Society: The Jewish Community of the Arab World as Portrayed in the Documents of the Cairo Geniza,* vol. 1 (Berkeley: University of California Press, 1967), 53, 65.

16. Battuta, *Travels,* vol. 1, 85.

17. Ibid., 132.

18. Ibid., 64.

19. Ibid., 170–171.

20. Ibid., 188.

21. Ibid., 155, 182–183, 176, 204, 210–223, 355–357.

22. Ibid., vol. 2, 319–320.

23. Ibid., 282–283.

24. Ibid., 342.

25. Ibid., 345.

26. Ibid., 342.

27. Ibid., 376, 402–403, 446.

28. J. Spencer Trimingham, *The Sufi Orders in Islam* (Oxford: Oxford University Press, 1971), 1–30. For Indian Sufi orders at the time of Ibn Battuta, see Richard Maxwell Eaton, *Sufis of Bijapur, 1300–1700: Social Roles of Sufis in Medieval India* (Princeton: Princeton University Press, 1978), 13–45.

29. Battuta, *Travels,* vol. 2, 387. See also Anthony Reid, *Southeast Asia in the Age of Commerce, 1450–1680,* vol. 1 (New Haven: Yale University Press, 1988), 42.

30. Battuta, *Travels,* vol. 2, 370. See also 436, 441, 463, 487.

31. Ibid., 375–376.

32. Ibid., 461.

33. Ibid., vol. 3, 747.

34. Hodgson, *Venture of Islam,* 336–339, 349–351.

35. Battuta, *Travels,* vol. 3, 760.

36. Ibid., vol. 4, 808.

37. Ibid., 807.

38. Ibid., 822–846.

39. Ibid., 865.

40. Ibid., 920.

41. Ibid., 921.

CHAPTER 7

1. Ma Huan, *Ying-Yai Sheng-Lan: The Overall Survey of the Ocean's Shores*, trans. J. V. G. Mills (Cambridge: Cambridge University Press, 1970), 27–31.

2. Ibid., 31–32. These ships' appearance, number of sails, and tonnage have generated considerable scholarly debate. I generally follow Joseph Needham, *Science and Civilization in China, Civil Engineering, and Nautics*, vol. 4 (Cambridge: Cambridge University Press, 1971), pt. 3, 460–507. The current name of the Yellow Sea is Huang Hai.

3. Ma Huan, *Ying-Yai*, 69.

4. Dru C. Gladney, *Muslim Chinese: Ethnic Nationalism in the People's Republic* (Cambridge: Harvard University Press, 1991), 36–39.

5. Ma Huan, *Ying-Yai*, 178.

6. Anthony Reid, "Flows and Seepages in the Long-Term Chinese Interaction with Southeast Asia," in Anthony Reid, ed., *Sojourners and Settlers: Histories of Southeast Asia and the Chinese* (Honolulu: University of Hawaii Press, 1996), 17–20.

7. Ibn Battuta, *The Travels of Ibn Battuta, A.D. 1325–1354*, vol. 4, trans. H. A. R. Gibb (New Delhi: Hakluyt Society, 1993, reprint), 813–814.

8. Ibid., 15–26. See also the brief reference to large junks in Ibn Battuta's less accepted account of China, pp. 894–895.

9. Gilles Beguin and Dominique Morel, *The Forbidden City: Center of Imperial China* (New York: Harry Abrams, 1999), 18.

10. Geoff Wade, "The Zeng He Voyages: A Reassessment," *Journal of the Malaysian Branch of the Royal Asiatic Society* 78 (2005): 37–58.

11. Ma Huan, *Ying-Yai*, 73.

12. Ma Huan, *Ying-Yai*, 79–80.

13. Ibid., 81.

14. Ibid., 85.

15. Ibid., 81.

16. Ibid., 82.

17. Ibid., 83.

18. Ibid., 69–70.

19. Ibid., 87.

20. Ibid., 88.

21. Ibid., 89.

22. Ibid., 89–90.

23. Ma Huan, *Ying-Yai*, 92.

24. Ibid., 97.

25. Victor H. Maier, *Painting and Performance: Chinese Picture Recitation and Its Indian Genesis* (Honolulu: University of Hawaii Press, 1986).

26. Ma Huan, *Ying-Yai*, 99–100.

27. Kenneth R. Hall, "Multi-Dimensional Networking in the Fifteenth-Century Indian Ocean Realm: Communities of Exchange in Southeast Asian Perspective," paper presented at the conference of the Association for Asian Studies, Chicago, Illinois, April 2005.

28. Ma Huan, *Ying-Yai*, 103.

29. See Ronald Inden, Jonathan Walters, and Daud Ali, *Querying the Medieval: Texts and the History of Practices in South Asia* (Oxford: Oxford University Press, 2000), 99–165.

30. Ma Huan, *Ying-Yai*, 108.

31. Ibid., 110.

32. Ibid., 121.

33. Ibid., 111.

34. Ibid., 129.

35. Ibid.

36. Ibid., 135.

37. Ibid., 140–141.

38. Ibid., 143.

39. Ibid., 138.

40. Ibid., 174.

41. Ibid., 149.

42. See Rananbir Chakravarti, "Seafarings, Ships, and Ship Owners: India and the Indian Ocean (AD 700–1500)," in David Parkin and Ruth Barnes, eds., *Ships and the Development of Maritime Technology in the Indian Ocean* (London: Routledge Curzon, 2002), 46–47.

43. Ma Huan, *Ying-Yai*, 149.

44. Ibid., 154–156.

45. Ibid., 168–169.

46. Timothy Brook, *The Confusions of Pleasure: Commerce and Culture in Ming China* (Berkeley: University of California Press, 1998), 79–86.

47. Hafiz Abru, *A Persian embassy to China: being an extract from Zubdatu't Tawarikh of Hafiz Abru*, trans. K. M. Maitra (New York: Paragon Book Reprint Corp., 1970), 118.

48. See Wade, "Zeng He Voyages," 37–58.

49. Ma Huan, *Ying-Yai*, 180.

CHAPTER 8

1. Babur, *Babur-Nama* [Memoirs of Babur], trans. Annette Susannah Beveridge (New Delhi: Low Price Publications, 1989, reprint), 174–178.

2. Edward McEwen, Robert L. Miller, and Christopher A. Bergman, "Early Bow Design and Construction," *Scientific American* 264 (6) (June 1991): 79–82.

3. The cavalry tactics of the early steppe armies were quite different from the contemporaneous and also successful armies of early Islam. Muslim soldiers rode to battle but generally fought on foot. Archer infantry were an important part of these forces. See Hugh Kennedy, *The Armies of the Caliphs: Military and Society in the Early Islamic State* (London: Routledge, 2001), 8–11.

4. The story of Genghis Khan is told by a contemporaneous observer in Ata-Malik Juvaini, *Chengis Khan: The History of the World Conqueror,* trans. J. A. Boyle (Seattle: University of Washington Press, 1997).

5. Ibn Battuta, *The Travels of Ibn Battuta, A.D. 1325–1354,* vol. 3, trans. H. A. R. Gibb (New Delhi: Hakluyt Society, 1993, reprint), 574.

6. See Marshall G.S. Hodgson, *The Venture of Islam: Conscience and History in World Civilization,* vol. 2 (Chicago: University of Chicago Press, 1974), 287–291. See also, Svat Soucek, *A History of Inner Asia* (Cambridge: Cambridge University Press, 2000), 114–116.

7. Babur, *Babur-Nama,* 29–32, 40–44, 51–56.

8. Ibid., 131.

9. Ibid.

10. Ibid., 133.

11. Ibid.

12. Ibid.

13. Ibid., 135.

14. Ibid., 139.

15. Ibid., 140.

16. Babur described an old man whose station in life had much fallen with the description "His Table Lacked Salt," *Babur-Nama,* 277.

17. Babur, *Babur-Nama,* 58, 66.

18. Ibid., 152.

19. Ibid., 130, 248, 251, 321, 324, 383.

20. Ibid., 128.

21. Ibid., 146.

22. Ibid., 124–125. See also 397, 404, 417.

23. Ibid., 194.

24. Ibid., 153.

25. Ibid., 157.

26. Ibid.

27. Ibid., 159–160.

28. Ibid., 175–178.

29. Ibid., 199.

30. Ibid., 227.

31. Ibid., 202.

32. Ibid., 207.

33. Ibid., 202.

34. Ibid., 223.

35. Ibid., 208, 215–217. See Babur's description of one of his gardens several years later, p. 414.

36. Ibid., 120.

37. Ibid., 121.

38. Ibid., 386.

39. Ibid., 272.

40. Ibid., 271. See Babur's discussion of the various poets and musicians at the court of a great noble, pp. 286–292.

41. Ibid., 276.

42. Ibid., 278.

43. Ibid., 284.

44. Ibid., 338.

45. Ibid., 258.

46. Ibid., 395–396.

47. Ibid., 377.

48. Ibid., 229.

49. Ibid., 385.

50. Ibid., 522.

51. Ibid.

52. Ibid., 522–523.

CHAPTER 9

1. Tomé Pires, *The Suma Oriental of Tomé Pires*, trans. Armando Cortesao (London: Hakluyt Society, 1944), xxvii.

2. Ibid., xxi–xxii.

3. Michael Pearson, *The Portuguese in India* (Cambridge: Cambridge University Press, 1987), 6–9.

4. See Christopher Bell, *Portugal and the Quest for the Indies* (London: Constable, 1974).

5. Pires, *Suma Oriental*, xxiii–xxiv.

6. For a general description of the Indian Ocean trade in the early fifteenth century, see the description of Kalikut in Duarte Barbarosa, *Livro*, vol. 2 (London: Hakluyt Society, 1921), 76.

7. Michael Pearson, *The Indian Ocean* (London: Routledge, 2003), 68–69.

8. K. S. Mathews, "Navigation in the Arabian Sea During the Sixteenth Century: A Comparative Study of Indigenous and Portuguese Navigation," in *Ship-Building and Navigation in the Indian Ocean Region: AD 1400–1900* (New Delhi: Munshiram Manoharlal, 1997), 26–38.

9. Pearson, *Indian Ocean*, 33–34.

10. George W. Winius, "Early Portuguese Travel and Influence at the Corner of Asia," in *Studies on Portuguese Asia, 1495–1689* (Aldershot, England: Ashgate, 2001), 215–216.

11. Pires, *Suma Oriental*, xxv.

12. Joseph Needham, *Science and Civilization in China*, vol. 6 (Cambridge: Cambridge University Press, 1986), pt. 1, 451–459.

13. Ibid., 266.

14. Ibid., 452–456.

15. Aqrabadhin, *The Medical Formulary, or Aqrabadhin of Al-Kindi*, trans. Martin Levey (Madison: University of Wisconsin Press, 1966).

16. Avicenna, *The Canon of Medicine*, adapted by Laleh Bakhtiar (Chicago: Great Books of the Islamic World, 1999).

17. Pires, *Suma Oriental*, 138.

18. Ibid., 206.

19. There have been numerous theories that generalize about types of precolonial Southeast Asian states. See, for example, Jan Wisseman Christie, "Negara, Mandala, and Despotic State: Images of Early Java," in David G. Marr and A. C. Milner, eds., *Southeast Asia in the 9th to 14th Centuries* (Singapore: Institute of Southeast Asian Studies, 1986), 65–94. The typology of this chapter follows the survey of scholarly literature in Freek Colombijn, "The Volatile State in Southeast Asia: Evidence from Sumatra, 1600–1800," *Journal of Asian Studies* 62 (2) (May 2003): 499–500.

20. Pires, *Suma Oriental*, 95–96.

21. Ibid., 97–98. The typology of this chapter probably overstates the difference between rice-growing kingdoms and trade-based kingdoms. It is likely that kingdoms both plowed profits from trade into improvements in irrigation and traded surplus rice. See Denys Lombard, *Le Carrefour javanais: Essai d'histoire global* (Paris: Éditions de l'École des Hautes Études en Sciences Sociales, 1990), vols. 1–3.

22. Pires, *Suma Oriental,* 243–245. Even kingdoms based on an entrepôt needed to balance trade and agriculture. See Jorge M. dos Santos Alves, "The Foreign Traders' Management in the Sultanates of the Straits of Malacca," in Claude Guillot, Denys Lombard, and Roderich Ptak, eds., *From the Mediterranean to the China Sea: Miscellaneous Notes* (Wiesbaden, Germany: Harrassowitz Verlag, 1998), 131–142.

23. Pires, *Suma Oriental,* 45.

24. Pearson, *Indian Ocean,* 86.

25. Pires, *Suma Oriental,* 29.

26. Ibid., 39. Vijayanagara in South India was also portrayed as a heathen kingdom, but also as a potential ally. See Maria A. L. Cruz, "Notes on Portuguese Relations with Vijayanagara, 1500–1565," in Sanjay Subrahmanyam, ed., *Saints and Sinners: The Successors of Vasco Da Gama* (Oxford: Oxford University Press, 1995), 13–39.

27. Pires, *Suma Oriental,* 177.

28. Ibid., 23.

29. Ibid., 52.

30. Ibid., 116.

31. Ibid., 123.

32. The imperial government's strong anti-trade policies of the mid-fifteenth century changed within decades. By the time of the Pirés expedition, trade was not only restored but had considerable support among the official class. See "Zhang Han's Essay on Merchants," in Patricia B. Ebrey, ed., *Chinese Civilization: A Sourcebook* (New York: Free Press, 1981), 216–218.

33. See Timothy Brook, *The Confusions of Pleasure: Commerce and Culture in Ming China* (Berkeley: University of California Press, 1998), 38–51.

34. Pires, *Suma Oriental,* xxxi–xxxii.

35. Ibid., xxxiv.

36. Ibid., xxxvii.

37. Ibid., xxxviii–xxxix.

38. Ibid., xl–xli.

39. Anthony Reid, *Charting the Shape of Early Modern Southeast Asia* (Chiang Mai, Thailand: Silkworm Books, 1999), chap. 2.

40. C. R. Boxer, "Portuguese and Spanish Projects for the Conquest of Southeast Asia, 1580–1600," in *Portuguese Conquest and Commerce in Southeast Asia, 1500–1750* (London: Variourum Reprints, 1985), chap. 3.

41. See Jorge M. Flores, "The Straits of Ceylon, 1524–1539: The Portuguese-Mappilla Struggle over a Strategic Area," in Subrahmanyam, *Saints and Sinners,* 57–74.

42. Pearson, *Indian Ocean,* 131, 134–135.

43. See Michael N. Pearson, *Merchants and Rulers in Gujarat: The Response to the Portuguese in the Sixteenth Century* (Berkeley: University of California Press, 1976).

44. Brook, *Confusions of Pleasure,* 111–114.

45. Reid, *Charting the Shape,* 85–90.

46. Pearson, *Indian Ocean,* 82–83.

47. Pearson, *Portuguese in India,* 37.

48. Winius, "Portugal's 'Shadow Empire' in the Bay of Bengal," chap. 9 in *Studies on Portuguese Asia,* and "Private Trading in Portuguese Asia: A Substantial Will-O'-the-Wisp," chap. 19 in *Studies on Portuguese Asia.*

49. Pires, *Suma Oriental,* xlviii.

Chapter 10

1. Chinese cash consisted of coins—copper, brass, or iron—that had a hole in the center. Cash circulated tied on strings, a fixed number of coins on each string.

2. Sulayman Al-Tajir, "An Account of China and India," in *Arab Classical Accounts of India and China,* trans. S. Maqbul Ahmad (Rddhi, India: Indian Institute of Advanced Study, 1979), 46–47, 49–50.

3. The movement of gunpowder and firearms from their invention in China into Asia and Europe is complicated by fragmentary sources and shifting terminology. A good short introduction to the subject is Iqtidar Alam Khan, *Gunpowder and Firearms: Warfare in Medieval India* (Oxford: Oxford University Press, 2004), 3–11. The "guns" part of the thesis in Carlo M. Cipolla, *Guns and Sails in the Early Phase of European Expansion, 1400–1700* (London: Collins, 1965), has been supported by subsequent research. There seems to be general agreement among scholars that by the time the Portuguese arrived in Asia, their cannons were lighter, faster firing (because of breech loading), and more accurate than anything they encountered from their adversaries.

Suggested Reading

~~

CHAPTER 1:
MONASTERIES AND MONARCHS: XUANZANG

The standard English translation of the biography of Xuanzang is Samuel Beal, trans., *The Life of Hiuen-Tsiang* (London: Kegan Paul, Trench, Trübner and Co., 1911). There have been several reprints and retranslations since.

For Xuanzang's later life, see the extensive documents in Li Rongxi, *A Biography of the Tripitika Master of the Great Ci'en Monastery of the Great Tang Dynasty*, trans. Sramana Huli and Shi Yancong (Berkeley: Numata Center of Buddhist Translation and Research, 1995).

For a fuller treatment of Xuanzang's pilgrimage, see Sally H. Wriggins, *The Silk Road Journey with Xuanzang* (Boulder: Westview Press, 2004). Maps, illustrations, and bibliography are particularly useful.

Luce Boulnois, *Silk Road: Monks, Warriors, and Merchants on the Silk Road* (Odyssey Books: Hong Kong, 2004), is a series of short essays on various periods of Silk Road history from antiquity to the present. It also serves as a travel guide for those wanting to travel the Silk Road.

Richard C. Foltz, *Religions of the Silk Road: Overland Trade and Cultural Exchange from Antiquity to the Fifteenth Century* (New York: St. Martin's Press, 1999), explores the complex interchanges and influences that Xuanzang observed and that continued for the subsequent millennium.

Tansen Sen, *Buddhism, Diplomacy, and Trade: The Realignment of Sino-Indian Relations, 600–1400* (Honolulu: University of Hawaii Press, 2003), is an excellent new study of the connections of pilgrimage, trade, and diplomacy in the centuries after Xuanzang.

CHAPTER 2:
CALIPH AND CARAVAN: IBN FADLAN

A recent translation of Ibn Fadlan's memoir is Richard N. Frye, *Ibn Fadlan's Journey to Russia: A Tenth-Century Traveler from Baghdad to the Volga*

River (Princeton: Marcus Weiner Publishers, 2005). This volume has a useful introduction and notes.

The first few chapters of Michael Crichton's *Eaters of the Dead* (New York: Alfred A. Knopf, 1976) are based on the Ibn Fadlan memoir. The rest of the novel is more fanciful, based broadly on Beowulf.

For a sense of the luxurious cuisine in Baghdad in the time of the caliphs, there is a recent translation of a cookbook. See Charles Perry, *A Baghdad Cookery Book* (Devon, United Kingdom: Prospect Books, 2005).

Hugh Kennedy has produced excellent, readable studies of the caliphate. On the military side is *The Armies of the Caliphs: Military and Society in the Early Islamic State* (London: Routledge, 2001). Specifically on the court is *When Baghdad Ruled the Muslim World: The Rise and Fall of Islam's Greatest Dynasty* (Boulder: Da Capo Press, 2005).

The larger context of trade across Central Asia at the time of Ibn Fadlan is discussed in Xinru Liu, *Silk and Religion: An Exploration of Material Life and the Thought of People, AD 600–1200* (Delhi: Oxford University Press, 1996).

What is known about the Khazars is considered in Thomas Noonan's essay, "The Khazar Qaghanate," in Anatoly M. Khazanov and André Wink, eds., *Nomads in a Sedentary World* (Richmond, United Kingdom: Curzon, 2001).

CHAPTER 3:
PHILOSOPHER AND PHYSICIAN: IBN SINA

The standard English translation of Ibn Sina's autobiography is William E. Gohlman, *The Life of Ibn Sina: A Critical Edition and Annotated Translation* (Albany: State University of New York Press, 1974). The notes are particularly useful.

A portion of Ibn Sina's fascinating medical treatise is translated in Avicenna, *The Canon of Medicine*, adapted by Laleh Bakhtiar (Chicago: Great Books of the Islamic World, 1999).

On the influence of paper in the developing Muslim intellectual world, essential reading is Jonathan M. Bloom, *Paper Before Print: The History and Impact of Paper on the Islamic World* (New Haven: Yale University Press, 2001). The illustrations are stunning.

A well-written biography of Ibn Sina is Lenn E. Goodman, *Avicenna* (London: Routledge, 1992).

For those wanting to explore Ibn Sina's philosophy, a good introduction is Dimitri Guhas, *Avicenna and the Aristotelian Tradition: An Introduc-*

tion to Reading Avicenna's Philosophical Works (Leiden, Holland: E. J. Brill, 1998).

Mahmud of Ghazna, from whom Ibn Sina fled, was both patron of the arts and conqueror. To this day, his life and deeds are controversial, as discussed in Clifford E. Bosworth, *The Ghaznavids* (Edinburgh: University Press, 1963).

Recent research on all phases of Ibn Sina's writing and influence is covered in Jules L. Janssens, *An Annotated Bibliography on Ibn Sina (1970–1989)* (Leuven, Belgium: Leuven University Press, 1991), and Jules L. Janssens, *An Annotated Bibliography on Ibn Sina: First Supplement (1990– 1994)* (Louvain-la-Neuve, France: Fédération Internationale des Instituts d'Études Médiévales, 1999).

CHAPTER 4:
INGOTS AND ARTIFACTS: THE INTAN SHIPWRECK

The details of the undersea archaeology and the finds on the Intan wreck are thoroughly explored in Michael Flecker, "The Archaeological Excavation of the Tenth-Century Intan Shipwreck," *British Archaeological Reports International Series*, 1047 (Oxford: Archaoepress, 2002).

A recent introduction to the larger context of the Intan wreck is Lynda N. Shaffer, *Maritime Southeast Asia to 1500* (Armonk, New York: M. E. Sharpe, 1996).

The economic context of the wreck is found in Kenneth R. Hall's essay in Nicholas Tarling, ed., *The Cambridge History of Southeast Asia*, vol. 1 (Cambridge: Cambridge University Press, 1992).

Fiona Kerlogue, *Art of Southeast Asia* (London: Thames and Hudson, 2004), illustrates several types of Buddhist monuments that had elaborate doors—perhaps of the type that the Intan ship was carrying.

A marvelous history and illustrated anthropology on the trade and use of beads in Borneo is Heidi Munan, *Beads of Borneo* (Kuala Lumpur: Editions Didier Millet, 2005). The color photographs are superb. Many of the strings of old beads have "eye" beads of the type found on the wreck.

CHAPTER 5:
PEPPER AND PARTNERSHIPS: ABRAHAM BIN YIJU

Abraham bin Yiju and especially his slave-business partner are the subject of a readable and entertaining history and ethnography by Amitav Ghosh, *In an Antique Land* (New York: Vintage Books, 1994).

For the patterns of the Indian Ocean trade, there is a masterful synthesis. See K. N. Chaudhuri, *Trade and Civilization in the Indian Ocean: An Economic History from the Rise of Islam to 1750* (Cambridge: Cambridge University Press, 1985).

For information on Jewish communities and traders around the Mediterranean at the time of Abraham bin Yiju, see Shlomo Goitein, *A Mediterranean Society: The Jewish Community of the Arab World as Portrayed in the Documents of the Cairo Geniza* (Berkeley: University of California Press, 1967).

For more on Roger of Sicily, whose forces kidnapped Abraham's family, see John J. Norwich, *The Normans in Sicily* (London: Penguin Books, 1990).

A famous memoir of the twelfth-century Islamic world is that of Benjamin of Tudela, who traveled through Spain, North Africa, Egypt, and the Middle East. See *The Itinerary of Benjamin of Tudela: Travels in the Middle Ages*, introductions by Michael A. Signer, 1983, Marcus Nathan Adler, 1907, A. Asher, 1840 (Malibu, CA: C. Simon, 1983).

CHAPTER 6:
NOBLES AND NOTABLES: IBN BATTUTA

The Hakluyt Society has published the only complete English translation of Ibn Battuta's long memoir. See H. A. R. Gibb, trans., *The Travels of Ibn Battuta, A.D. 1325–1354*, 5 vols. (Cambridge: Hakluyt Society [new series, 110, 117, 141, 178, 190], 1958–2000). There have been several reprintings of this translation, though all omit Ibn Battuta's travels to China.

For an understanding of how Central Asia and the Middle East had changed because of the invasions of Genghis Khan and his heirs in the half century preceding Ibn Battuta's travels, see David Morgan, *The Mongols* (New York: Basil Blackwell, 1986).

On the Muslim trading culture of the East African coast, which Ibn Battuta visited, see Mark Horton and John Middleton, *The Swahili* (Malden, MA: Blackwell Publishers, 1988).

The Marco Polo journal is useful for comparison to Ibn Battuta's. Of the many editions, I like one that includes fourteenth-century illustrations. See *The Travels of Marco Polo* (New York: Orion Press, 1975).

For the political and architectural context of the court of Delhi, see Catherine B. Asher and Cynthia Talbot, *India Before Europe* (Cambridge: Cambridge University Press, 2006).

On the Black Death, which Ibn Battuta observed, most research is confined to its effects on Europe. A more interesting comparative perspective is found in Stuart J. Borsch, *The Black Death in Egypt and England: A Comparative Study* (Austin: University of Texas Press, 2005).

CHAPTER 7:
TREASURE AND TREATY: MA HUAN

The English translation of Ma Huan's memoir is Ma Huan, *Ying-Yai Sheng-Lan: The Overall Survey of the Ocean's Shores*, trans. J. V. G. Mills (Cambridge: Cambridge University Press, 1970).

For a simple introduction to China at the period of Ma Huan, see Patricia B. Ebrey, *The Cambridge Illustrated History of China* (Cambridge: Cambridge University Press, 1996).

More detailed and more thorough on Chinese culture at the time of Ma Huan is Timothy Brook, *The Confusions of Pleasure: Commerce and Culture in Ming China* (Berkeley: University of California Press, 1998).

Connecting the illustrated story performances of Java to a larger pan-Asian tradition is the work of Victor H. Maier, *Painting and Performance: Chinese Picture Recitation and Its Indian Genesis* (Honolulu: University of Hawaii Press, 1986).

The most sensible discussion of Chinese oceangoing boat building is Joseph Needham, *Science and Civilization in China, Civil Engineering and Nautics*, vol. 4, pt. 3 (Cambridge: Cambridge University Press, 1971).

The later history and urban form of Aden, which Ma Huan visited, is covered in Roxani Margariti, *Aden and the Indian Ocean Trade: 150 Years in the Life of a Medieval Arabian Port* (Chapel Hill: University of North Carolina Press, 2007).

For a fascinating study of ships and a culture along the western coast of India that connects back to the time of Ma Huan, see Edward Simpson, *Muslim Society and the Western Indian Ocean: The Seafarers of Kachchh* (London and New York: Routledge, 2006). This book is worth seeking out on interlibrary loan.

CHAPTER 8:
BLOOD AND SALT: BABUR

The standard translation of Babur's memoirs into English is by Annette Susannah Beveridge, under the title *Babur-Nama* [Memoirs of Babur].

There have been a number of reprints. I used the edition by New Delhi: Low Price Publications, 1989. Beveridge's notes are quite helpful.

On the physics of the reverse-curve bow, see Edward McEwen, Robert L. Miller, and Christopher A. Bergman, "Early Bow Design and Construction," *Scientific American* 264 (6) (June 1991): 79–82.

A well-illustrated article on the reverse-curve bow and the efforts of a modern craftsman to recreate it is Lee Lawrence, "History's Curve," *Aramco World*, September–October 2003, available online at www.Saudi aramcoworld.com/index.

For information on Genghis Khan and his descendants, see David Morgan, *The Mongols* (New York: Basil Blackwell, 1986).

For the situation in India when Babur invaded, see Catherine B. Asher and Cynthia Talbot, *India Before Europe* (Cambridge: Cambridge University Press, 2006).

For a thorough analysis of the empire that Babur's descendants built in India, see John Richards, *The Mughal Empire*, The New Cambridge History of India, vol. 1, pt. 5 (Cambridge: Cambridge University Press, 1993).

CHAPTER 9:
MEDICINES AND MISUNDERSTANDINGS: TOMÉ PIRES

The memoir of Tomé Pires is translated as Tomé Pires, *The Suma Oriental of Tomé Pires*, trans. Armando Cortesao (London: Hakluyt Society, 1944).

For understanding the Indian Ocean at the time of Tomé Pires, see two readable books by Michael Pearson, *Merchants and Rulers in Gujarat: The Response to the Portuguese in the Sixteenth Century* (Berkeley: University of California Press, 1976), and *The Indian Ocean* (London: Routledge, 2003).

For a general overview of Southeast Asia in the time of Tomé Pires, see Anthony Reid, *Charting the Shape of Early Modern Southeast Asia* (Chiang Mai, Thailand: Silkworm Books, 1999).

A few useful documents on the Chinese official attitude toward trade are found in Patricia B. Ebrey, ed., *Chinese Civilization: A Sourcebook* (New York: Free Press, 1981).

For tropical medicines imported into China, there is still no better discussion than Joseph Needham, *Science and Civilization in China*, vol. 6, pt. 1 (Cambridge: Cambridge University Press, 1986).

CHAPTER 10:
THE ASIAN WORLD, 500–1500 CE

For some "big system" approaches to the understanding of Asia, I suggest some of the following books:

Andre Gunder Frank, *ReOrient: Global Economy in the Asian Age* (Berkeley: University of California Press, 1998).
Christopher Chase-Dunn and Thomas D. Hall, *Rise and Demise: Comparing World Systems* (Boulder: Westview Press, 1997).
Thomas D. Hall, ed., *A World-Systems Reader: New Perspectives on Gender, Urbanism, Culture, Indigenous People, and Ecology* (London: Rowman and Littlefield, 2000).
Victor B. Lieberman, *Strange Parallels: Southeast Asia in Global Context, c. 800–1830* (Cambridge and New York: Cambridge University Press, 2003).

In contrast to these "world system" approaches, this book is generally based on social network theory, including older work such as Everett M. Rogers and D. Lawrence Kincaid, *Communication Networks: Toward a New Paradigm for Research* (New York: Free Press, 1981), and Mark Granovetter's research on strong and weak ties, along with recent work on networks of trust, degrees of separation, and dense connections.

Index